BOLDT

CASTLE

Boldt Castle by John A. Morrow
Original water color painting, 22" x 28"

Boldt Castle

In Search of the Lost Story

Paul Malo

The Laurentian Press

Copyright © 2001 by the Laurentian Press

2 Harris Hill Road

Fulton, New York 13069-4723

(315) 598-4387   phmalo@syr.edu

01 02 03 04 05   6 5 4 3 2

Includes Notes, Appendices, Bibliographic References and Index

ISBN 0-9669729-0-2

Library of Congress Control Number: 2001117257

PRINTED IN CANADA

The image on the covers was adapted from a photograph by Daniel A. Boyce,
http://www.northernphotography.com.

The frontispiece reproduces a watercolor painting by John A. Morrow,
http://www.jmorrow.com/northern.htm.
The painting shows Boldt Castle in 1985.

The medallion on the title page is a detail from a stained glass panel photographed by the author. This or a similar panel appears in the photograph of the saloon, La Duchesse, p. 96.

The author adapted the pair of portraits on the following pages from historic photographs.

Christine Wands contributed the pair of modern photographs on the following pages and other illustrations in the text.

Daniel Boyce provided the night view of Boldt Castle that faces the first page of text as well as the cover photograph and other illustrations in the text.

The Notes that follow the narrative mention photographers of subsequent text illustrations.

For Vincent J. Dee

1917 – 1995

Chairman, Thousand Islands Bridge Authority, 1977 - 1995

Co-founder, Thousand Islands Council, Inc., Chairman and President 1953 - 1995

President, Seaway Trail, Inc., 1984 - 1995

Faculty, Jefferson Community College, 1966 - 1995, and
Founder, School of Retailing, Hospitality and Tourism

He saved Boldt Castle for us and for future generations.

O you fables, spurning the known,
  eluding the hold of the known, mounting to heaven!

You lofty and dazzling towers, pinnacled, red as roses, burnish'd with gold!

Towers of fable immortal fashion'd from mortal dreams!

Walt Whitman [1]

Show me a hero and I will write you a tragedy.

F. Scott Fitzgerald [2]

---

[1] "Passage to India," from *Leaves of Grass*.

[2] F. Scott Fitzgerald, *Note-Books E*, quoted by Edmund Wilson, in *Crack-Up*, 1945.

Luisa Augusta Kehrer

b. Philadelphia, 1862

Georg Karl Boldt

b. Prussia, 1851

Boldt Castle is an international historic landmark, situated on Heart Island, among the Thousand Islands of the St. Lawrence River between the Province of Ontario and New York State. More than four million people have visited Boldt Castle since it first opened to the public more than eighty years ago. Accessible by arterial routes 401 in Canada and 81 in the United States, commercial boat lines operate from ports on each side of the border to bring an increasing number of visitors annually. Heart Island and the Boldt Yacht House on a nearby island now attract about a quarter-million visitors each summer. Boldt Castle is owned and operated by the not-for-profit Thousand Islands Bridge Authority, which has returned admission proceeds to an ambitious restoration campaign, investing some fourteen million dollars since it acquired the property in 1977.

Boldt Castle Traffic

Commercial tour boats arrive at this Heart Island pier.. Docks elsewhere on the island serve private craft. A shuttle boat is seen departing for the Boldt Yacht House.

Approaching Heart Island

Anticipation mounts as tour-boat passengers view the rising skyline,
the steep roofs and towers of Boldt Castle.

HEY, what's that?" Through the dark glass, beyond reflected chandeliers, loomed a luminous, faceted form. A jagged profile clawed scurrying, moonlit clouds.

His monologue interrupted, Courtney glanced up from the dinner plate to follow my gaze out across the water. "Oh, pretty sight, isn't it? Especially at night, with all those lights rippling across the water. We get used to the ships—call those ocean-going freighters 'salties.' But they still seem surreal sometimes, like big buildings—six or eight stories high, rising above the islands but slowly moving behind them."

"No, not the ship. Out there, beyond it, all lit up. What's that place?"

"Why, that's Boldt Castle. You've never seen it?"

"Never heard of it."

No one else in the restaurant dining room seemed so astonished by the apparition. Courtney focused again on his plate. "Oh, you New Yorkers," he sighed, cutting his steak. "Never heard of our great landmark, our biggest attraction." He chewed impatiently. "You don't know the mystery of Boldt Castle, eh? The controversy's been going on for a century about what happened over there on Heart Island."

"No, never heard that either."

"Never even heard of the Thousand Islands for that matter, had you? Would you believe that this place once was full of folks from the City? They built most of these big old summer homes. The yacht club even had its own train. Left Grand Central about six on Friday night—but some of the cottagers had their own railroad cars. Weekenders could take a sleeper, awaking in the morning at the water's edge. Steam yachts awaited them. Some things don't get better." Courtney's was the fourth generation—his children the fifth—to enjoy a barn of a "cottage" on one of the islands. With no private railroad cars anymore, or even any railroad, the Thousand Islands were now a full day's drive from Manhattan. Only an intimate clique of old families came so far from New York any more. Our business now brought me to Courtney's colony of "cottages."

"'Cottage?' That's no cottage. Is it as big as it looks, in the daylight?"

"It's big, all right. I suppose you'll have to go see it. Everyone does."

"It's not a private home?"

"Who could live there? No one ever did. That's part of the mystery—why is it so colossal?"

"No one used it? But it must have cost . . . millions. Who built it?"

 "It did cost millions, even then—George Boldt's millions. He founded the Waldorf-Astoria Hotel in New York."

"What a waste!"

Courtney shrugged as he raised his glass of Bordeaux. "But Heart Island is a money machine now. More than 230,000 visitors a year now—at $6.75 an adult head to see the whole works." He paused to sip. "Figure that out."

"That sounds like a gate of more than a million bucks a year."

"About a million and a half—in four or five summer months, actually."

"Boldt Castle, eh? It must be really something."

"An empty shell—a ruin, practically, before they began restoring it. They've put more than fourteen million into it in recent years. They're 'fixing it up,' alas. For tourists, you see. The tour boats all stop at Heart Island."

"I'll have to go. You've seen it, of course?"

"Not recently. Don't want to see it, anymore. Prefer to remember it—before they gussied it up. There'll be a scene in our play there—the second act opener." He flipped through his papers, then closed the folder, deciding that this wasn't a business venue. "On second thought, maybe you shouldn't visit Heart Island. You might have trouble visualizing it as it was. You're supposed to write about this place in nineteen-ought-five. T'was better then."

Courtney had been "retired" for years, he told me, but was (among other things, I supposed) a musician and composer. His current project, which brought us together, was a musical comedy, to be a period piece set in this resort region. We would be back in 1905—good year, Courtney figured, when Broadway star May Irwin cavorted here, along with her colleague, Fay Templeton. Both were to appear in the book that I was to write for his score. May and Fay were singers and comediennes. A lively pair. Great stuff. But an audience? Courtney was right. Who had heard of the Thousand Islands anymore?

The River was lively however, even if the resort was no longer a classy enclave of moneyed Manhattanites and Chicago barons. The Thousand Islands were still a tourist destination, the boat tours big business. There were more motels than hotels these days, and the hotels were less grand than they had been when steamboats plied the St. Lawrence. Where wasp-waisted ladies in organdy gowns had poured tea on the afterdecks of masted yachts, nowadays guys with beer bellies tipped cold cans on overpowered outboards. Our circular dining room was not unpretentious, however. Glass windows wrapping around us reflected a large crystal chandelier in the center. The centerpiece glittered above a fountain that played in a raised, circular pool. Not exactly the Four Seasons, perhaps, but a gesture in that direction.

"The second-act opener," Courtney continued, speaking up to be heard over band music drifting in from another cabaret room, "might be a party over there—not at Boldt Castle itself, of course, which was unfinished, but in the Shell Room at the Alster Tower, a smaller 'castle' on the island. That's the tall stone building you see to the left. It was one structure on the island that was completed, and actually used by the Boldts. Fascinating place. All different levels and crazy angles inside."

Approaching Heart Island:
the "Water Castle" (Power House) viewed from the upper deck of a tour boat

"I'll go tomorrow to see it."

"Don't be dismayed. Even the Alster Tower fell into ruin. I'm not sanguine about the purported restoration—although I must say it looks good from the water."

The rock music grew louder, and Courtney shook his head in dismay. He excused himself to rejoin a big house full of family and guests. Slightly envious, I went back to my generic hotel room, with its unnecessary second bed and equally unnecessary TV. If banal, it wasn't a bad place to work at my laptop, simply because it might have been anywhere. No distractions. It would have been a novel experience to be a houseguest at one of the big, old island summer homes, but Courtney and I were merely new professional colleagues. We weren't of the same economic strata or social culture. Our collaborative project was play for him, work for me.

2.   Approaching aboard a shuttle ferry in the hard sunlight of midday, Heart Island seemed less romantic but even more striking. Gleaming red-roofed towers appear and disappear above the treetops as one encircles the island while varied waterside stone structures passed in parade. The colossal central mass of granite looms on approach, contrasting in scale with miniature visitors moving about at its base.

At the pier, one is inundated with people. Huge, multi-deck tour boats line up

Boarding tour boats at Heart Island

where files of visitors wait to embark, while throngs of adults and children mill about, carrying cameras and souvenirs, eating ice cream cones. Conversations in French and Japanese mingle with Canadian and Long Island accents, with raucous laughter and crying children. The aroma of hamburgers and French fries blends with that of diesel fuel. Flags fly, balloons bob, loudspeakers blare. This is no romantic ruin; it's a carnival.

Passing through the ticket booth and turnstile, however, one leaves the sunny crowded dock and concession stands behind. Through dappled shade on a verdant lawn, a walk leads upwards to cliff-like granite walls. Immense size is the first impression. Suddenly people seem to shrink to insignificance. The hubbub recedes; there is less human communication. Everyone seems awed. Suspense and anticipation mount, as visitors walk around to another side of the immense pile. Rounding a bend on the crest of the island a vista opens down through a grove of tall trees, where beyond a lagoon a monumental stone Arch of Triumph rises from the water. Bizarre. Why was all this built, then never used? What does it all mean?

3. When I returned in my little rented boat to visit Courtney, the composer was out "catching the thermals," as he would say—sailing one of his antique skiffs. It was quite an athletic trick, even for a younger man. The little rowboat had lots of sail but no rudder—sailing was mostly hanging out over the whitecaps and ducking from side to side (somewhat like a wind surfer today). Seen at a distance

Small figures approaching the castle suggest its enormous scale. This view shows only the left quarter of the entire building seen in the following photograph.

only Courtney's white hair suggested his age. He was one of those lucky guys who could stow away the food and never put on a pound—or maybe he just worked it off. He spent much of his life outdoors. At close range, his deeply lined, weathered face revealed more of his years, but his manner was youthful. Like his small island, which struck me as still floating in waters of 1900, he hardly changed.

"What did you think of Heart Island?" he asked when we talked on the dock. "Isn't it Disnoid?"

"I was impressed, actually. It's really grand—grandiose, I suppose."

"Oh, the Castle is big, all right." He unbuckled his lifejacket. "Do they still have some outfit selling modern furniture in the Power House?"

"Yes, you can buy things everywhere. I did my share—booklets, video, CD, post cards, a hot dog. You're right about its being a commercial event—but the place is big enough to take it. All those people, even hundreds of camera-carrying tourists at a time, can't make a dent in it. Those colossal granite walls are overwhelming. The place has presence. Despite all of pretty flower beds, the stone mass is brooding, as if it has a life of its own."

"You got it."

　　Across the water, the steep red roofs of the Castle rose above the distant island treetops. Surely that landmark profile was intentional. The towering quality was artfully calculated. A jagged crown rose above the mound of folige to be visible for miles. That was why the building was seven-stories high, requiring an elevator. The monstrous pile presented an odd effect to viewers from constantly passing boats, the massive granite foundation disengaged by foliage from gables and spires, amid which a bronze stag reared his antlers. Why?

　　"What's that animal up on the roof?" I asked, "and why the hearts everywhere?"

"But it's Heart Island, you know. Surely you've heard the legendary love story?"

"Can't miss it—got it coming at you all ways. I took in the media show, and spent some time on the exhibition. Learned about that immigrant lad coming alone from Germany, the love story, and the rest. Saw it all. But then an attendant confided that I shouldn't believe it."

"An attendant told you that—a staff person?"

"An older woman. She was there, I suppose, to answer questions and keep an eye open for problems."

"Ah, a 'docent.' They're more or less volunteers, I understand—not really account-able to the management. So what did she tell you was the 'true story'?"

"She said that, actually, Mrs. Boldt didn't die when they said she did. She ran off with the chauffeur—or maybe it was the boatman. That's when her husband stopped work on the Castle." *

---

* Notes follow the text.

Boldt Castle, an early photograph by A.G. Marshall (c. 1912)
before trees concealed its full height of seven stories, from kitchen level to tower room

"Of course. Chauffeur, boatman, gardener—it's the same old tale. Local folks relish it."

"But the official presentations make so much of the tragedy of her sudden, unexpected death—and the grief of her husband, who never went back to the Castle but let it stand abandoned, as a monument."

"Yes, that's the approved line."

"It's not the real story?"

"Not exactly. They don't tell you how she died, do they?"

"No, not that I recall."

"And they don't show you Boldt Castle the way it's supposed to be—the way it was intended."

"But they're trying to do that, aren't they?—to make the place more like it would have been when completed?"

"No, you miss the point. When George Boldt stopped work over there he walked away from a ghost castle—unfinished. Even in his lifetime it become a ruin. That was the way he wanted it. That's why it left it unfinished for thirteen years, until he died. Check those booklets and videos."

"You mean that Boldt really *meant* to abandon the Castle after his wife died?"

"Did she?" Courtney glanced at me, eyebrows raised for theatrical effect. Then he went back to lowering the mast, placing it carefully atop the neatly folded sail, waiting for my reaction. I rose to the bait. "Did she what?"

"Die—but we all die, sooner or later, don't we?" He glanced upward again, smiling. Courtney was teasing me, but I had to play his game.

"The story isn't true?"

He hopped onto the dock. "There are lots of stories, you see. Variations have pro-liferated up here for generations. I don't know the truth, but I don't think that the Castle operators looked very hard for the truth. The legend of Heart Island is doing very well, thank you." He dropped his life vest on the dock.

"Tell me more. I smell the scent of a story."

"Not now. We've got work to do." Squatting, he deftly twisted a line around a cleat at the dock's edge. He coiled the spare rope artfully, just so, aligning it with the cleat. That's how things were done at Heron Island, like they'd always been done. Ship-shape.

I persisted. "What do you really think happened?"

"Let's stick to our own story." Courtney rose and started toward the cottage. "Bring your wand? We gotta send our Cinderalla fella off to an enchanted isle."

The book for our musical comedy was to be sort of a cross between the Pygma-lion tale of "My Fair Lady" and the comic odyssey of "The Wizard of Oz"—not exactly original, but tried and true. Courtney was of the opinion that musical com-edy was basically conventional anyway. As Willa Cather said, "There are only two or three human stories, and they go on repeating themselves . . . as if they had never happened before." And the Greeks, they tell us, all knew the old stories and how they turned out before they went to the theater. I wasn't expecting to create any-thing very original that summer, but I didn't suspect in June that I would end the season, not with the lightweight comedy that I came to write, but with a classical Greek tragedy.

Our projected musical comedy was to be the tale of a local boy, Bart, who hoses down railroad cars on the waterfront pier. Occasionally he watches, emerging from private cars, passing briefly on the dock, men in yachting caps and white trousers,

Approach to the main entrance, Boldt Castle

women in broad-brimmed hats and silk gowns, with youngsters and their pets, followed by a retinue of servants bearing trunks and hatboxes. They stroll up carpeted gangplanks to board great, masted steam yachts. Bart watches white-uniformed sailors untie the ropes and jump aboard, and he looks with envy from the village waterfront as they sail away regally to towered islands.

"How's that?" I thought I had it nailed. Courtney murmured reflectively.

"You've got the sense of it. Bart is bitten, and wants to follow, off to the inaccessible islands of fantasy. It works, as a word picture—but it's not theatrical. It's no way to open a musical comedy. How can I put that to music?"

"You need to open with a number?"

"Of, course. How else can you raise a curtain? It has to be rouser. Think 'Oklahoma!' Here's what I have in mind. The overture segues seamlessly into an upbeat period piece. We need movement, action. If not the whole company, at least some interaction. It's gotta move."

"Well, how about having Bart on the dock with his sidekick, a black waiter from one of the big hotels, so that there can be some business between them—and then May Irwin emerges from the railroad car—the famous Broadway star, who is on the way to her island?"

"Too early for the star's entrance, maybe. But the local guys in work clothes on the dock, Bart all wet from hosing cars, perhaps, contrasting with the spiffy Island-ers—that has possibilities."

Who was this May Irwin? The celebrity was no fictitious invention of Court-ney's. An autographed photo on his piano showed a jolly, robust woman sitting on the steps of this cottage verandah with young Courtney himself, back in the late 1930s. Then still a national celebrity on the vaudeville circuit, May had acquired wealth and fame during the four decades since she became a sudden sensation. This wholesome-looking woman had shocked polite, white Broadway audiences by belt-ing out ribald music from bordellos patronized by black men. One of the star's tro-phies was a fine island summer home, but she spent more time on the River at her working farm on the mainland shore. It was a short row from Round Island, where the grand Frontenac Hotel employed black waiters.

So much was factual, as was May's fondness for black music and her support for black musicians. Our tale supposed that May welcomes the waiters at her nearby farm, where they gather for "cakewalk parties," popular with the black community here at the time. One of the seasonal hotel waiters, Ben, is a buddy of Bart, a local handyman for May. Bart dreams of trying life in the fast lane of the New Rich at the resort. May, our fairy godmother, waves her wand and transports the yearning youth to the enchanted islands. I asked Courtney what he thought of this amalgam of fact and fiction.

"You got it. That works."

We were strolling up an intermittent path that linked expanses of exposed gran-ite. The route meandered through trees, amid banks of Juniper, sunny swales of blueberry and, shady hollows of fern. Heron Island was in a realm different from Heart Island. No metal-edged flowerbeds here, no mowed lawns, paved walks, in-formational signs, no plastic rubbish bins. The aroma of cedar and pine needles, baking on the warm rock, pervaded the wild scene. The big old house, clad with wood shingles now weathered dark, virtually disappeared into the shade of tall, wind-bent White Pines.

Generations had preceded Courtney at the family summer place, where nothing appeared to change—which was the way Courtney wanted it. On the interior walls of mellowed wood, amid dim photos of old steamboats, vintage Princeton tigers attested to familial bearings. Courtney moved his piano here every summer. He had studied music with Milton Babbitt at Princeton, but Courtney's own taste was hardly *avant-garde*. In fact, he was putting some period tunes into the score and composing others in a sort of ragtime mode. I was supposed to brush up on my period slang, as well as Thousand Islands lore—which would lead me back to Heart Island.

"If there's some mystery about Boldt Castle, can't we integrate it into our book?" I was trying to work my way back to the subject. "Intrigue would add another dimension. In 1905 everyone must have been curious about what was to become of the place."

"I've thought of that. That's why we'll introduce the Boldts' daughter, Clover, and her sister-in-law, Estelle. I have some dandy duets for them to sing at a party."

"Louise Boldt can't be there. She would be dead in 1905."

"Maybe." He smiled knowingly.

"Give me a lead."

"I'll say this: I've spoken with the present Clover—the granddaughter—who rarely talks about the past. She's quite a private person, anyway. But, suffice it to say, I've learned from her that there's more to the story than she's divulged publicly."

"But she wrote this little booklet telling the story. I bought a copy."

Courtney laughed. "Clover is content with the legend. Don't rely on her book as a source. And don't spend too much time on this research—but, if you must, the fellow to talk to is my neighbor, Professor Pete. He spends his summer on that island over there, the one with the green boathouse. Pete probably knows more than anyone about the Boldts—even more than Clover."

4. Surrounded by piles of CD-ROM disks in plastic cases, the professor sat in front of his luminous computer monitor, which seemed incongruous—high tech in a rickety old boathouse loft. Like Courtney and many of these Islanders, Peter's visage was weathered but indeterminate of age—but less sanguine, more intense. Thinning sandy hair receded above a freckled, furrowed brow. Tall and thin, he played the part of the professor as he peered over small, wire-framed glasses that slid down his long nose. An antique electric fan whirred in under the hot roof, rustling papers. The place smelled of musty books, blended with the subtle aroma of fuel from the boat slips below. Peter had pulled out several folders from files full of local lore in his study. He produced photos of the Boldts.

"Clover, here, their daughter, Clover One—that's the mother of the present Clover—refused to talk about it at all. She had been a teenager when they built the Castle. Hated the place. Thought it was an outrageous blunder, I suppose. Cost her a few million of her inheritance."

"She didn't want to finish it, to use it herself?"

Clover Boldt, 1917

"Lord, no. Kids don't want hand-me-down castles. Clover had a life of her own, a different kind of life. She was a very active sportswoman and times changed. In the very year that Louise Boldt died, *House Beautiful* published a devastating critique of pretentious show houses as being ". . . untrue to American life, to American thought, to American ideals." Clover didn't want to be pouring tea; she wanted to be on the golf course (they had their own, over on Wellesley Island, where the farm was) or on the tennis courts—they had those, of course, as well.

"She didn't like Heart Island but continued to come here?"

"All her life. Lived in one of their other places, Hopewell Hall. That big house is still standing on Wellesley Island, not far from Heart Island. The Boldts had multiple houses and dozens of other structures—scores of buildings, probably over a hundred. Never added them up. It's hard to imagine the wealth from the Great Bull Market at the opening of the twentieth century. Boldt got his initial capital from the hotel business, you know, but parlayed it by investing."

"Did George Boldt live with his daughter at Hopewell Hall, after his wife died and he gave up the Castle project?"

"Oh no. His place was another grand establishment, Wellesley House, also on Wellesley Island. That one is gone. His son had another house nearby, so George lived alone at Wellesley

Hopewell Hall, c. 1900

House, except for guests. He was a great host. Clover naturally wanted a place of her own, but couldn't be far from her father. Even after her marriage, while living at Hopewell Hall, she served as her father's hostess at Wellesley House, where he entertained 'enormous groups' of guests. Clover preferred her own Hopewell Hall as an escape from that regimen, and from Hopewell Hall she didn't have to look at Heart Island."

"Is Hopewell Hall still in the family?"

"Yes, Clover's daughter, Clover Two—that's the present Clover Boldt Baird—is at Hopewell Hall now. But don't get your hopes up. She doesn't care to be interviewed. There's been so much curiosity. She's a sweet and rather shy person, a poet who always says she really doesn't know much. I think she knows far more than she has told, however."

"There are skeletons in the family closet?"

"Ghosts, more likely."

"You write, too," I suggested. "Have you thought of doing something with this Boldt business?"

"Of course. I started various drafts but abandoned them."

"Why?"

"Because . . . I suppose, it all comes down to the Boldts' motivations. We can never know the personal reasons why, and that's what we want to know, isn't it?"

"I hesitate to ask, but could you . . . "

"You're not the first person to ask. I remember when a young woman called on me. She arrived with her mother. The daughter wanted to write about the *Golden Age of the Thousand Islands*—which as I recall she titled her little book. Laurie wanted me to open my files, turn over all my research, for her to use. Did I? What do you think?"

"She wrote the book?"

"Yes, printed privately, in a 1981 limited edition, before she died. Sad. The little book was Laurie Nulton's memorial—like the big Castle was Louise Boldt's. There's an odd parallel there—rushing to finish a life's dream. I wrote a commendatory review of Laurie's book for the *Thousand Island Sun*. But her dad remained miffed that I hadn't assisted her." Peter, seeing that I was wiping perspiration from my brow, got up and turned the fan more toward me. "Will I turn over my many years of research to you? Of course not. I'm still writing, and who knows what I may want to use myself."

"But can I continue to ask you questions?"

He laughed cordially. "Oh, I love to talk about my subject, but I can't guarantee an answer." He volunteered, so I decided to take the chance:

"Well, for starters, did Clover's mother die in 1904, as they say?"

"What?" Peter looked surprised, then frowned. "Oh, that story. There were many reports of her death in the press, but most importantly, there's a death certificate on file in New York City. I've seen it. So much for one myth—the one about her running off with the chauffeur, or whatever. But," he paused reflectively, "still there are odd accounts—one person said that he saw her, alive and well, at a German spa (she spoke fluent German) with another man, when she was supposed to be in the grave—and there are even reports of checks sent to Germany in Boldt's later years."

The Alster Tower

"Can certificates be faked?"

"George Boldt's physician, Graeme Hammond, was close to him—the only person ever known to call him by his first name. But I doubt that any professional would stake his career on any kind of fraud, even for a friend."

"What about the family now? They must know something." Peter didn't respond. I pressed forward: "Do you know how Louise Boldt died?"

Peter took off his spectacles, wiping them with a Kleenex from a box on his desk. He tossed the tissue into a wastebasket full of them. "I think so."

I was wary of pressing my luck, but the opportunity might pass. "Is it what they say?"

Again Peter collected his thoughts, now rolling a pen in his fingers. "Not Tuberculosis—that's the current misinformation being circulated. Our Clover Boldt—Mrs. Baird—no doubt inspired by *La Bohème*, started that one, in her little book, casting Louise as a frail Camille, expiring of consumption on her divan. Louise was more a robust Brunhilde type, in truth."

The Alster Tower
The "hart" or stag of Heart Island appears atop the central gable of the Castle beyond.

"The truth about her death is . . ?"

Peter set his pen carefully back on the desk. "The truth? The legend, and with it the mega-million dollar industry out there, might not survive the truth, I think it fair to say. Boldt Castle has taken on a life of its own. Sometimes silence is the wisest course. That may be why the family has never talked."

"But Clover Boldt Baird did write her book. I bought a copy."

Peter laughed again. "Oh, that. Clover was purported to be a co-author, but the tale was the work of a journalist friend of hers."

"Surely Clover approved it."

"The fairy tale was politically correct. It perpetuated, and confirmed (which was wanted) the official version, supplemented with some romantic clichés. Pure soap opera."

"Then there really is more to the story."

"Not merely more, but very different. Clover has told me that herself."

"What did she tell you?"

This time Peter rose, which suggested it might be time for me to leave. "That may be privileged information. You may try talking to Mrs. Baird herself, if you like."

Down on the dock, as I stepped down into my rented aluminum boat, the professor cordially invited me to return for more conversation. My rapport with Peter was encouraging, but not so was any approach to Clover Boldt Baird. For a long time, the closest I came was one midday when I saw her at a nearby table at the Thousand Islands Club. Mrs. Baird was a plump, pleasant-looking woman in a wheelchair, drawn up to a large, round table where she chatted with a group of matrons. Her secretary however returned my written requests to interview her with polite refusal. As predicted, the secretary said that Mrs. Baird had conveyed all that she cared to say in her little book, available for sale locally. Although drafted with elegant penmanship, I suspected that the secretary sent me number fifty or so of a form letter.

5. Musing on his verandah, Courtney waved his hand unconsciously, as if conducting music in his head. I hesitated to interrupt when I supposed he was pondering lyrics.

"Clover was fond of George M. Cohan," he suddenly commented. "In singing, she would naturally adopt his style, don't you think?"

"How do you know she liked Cohan?"

"She loved the theater, especially the musical theater. But she was especially fond of Cohan—personally, her daughter recalled."

"You mean romantically?"

"I'm not sure that it went so far. Cohan had an intimate fan club—'groupies,' we might call them today—who joined him at his regular table in the Oak Room of the Plaza. Clover may have had a crush, if not an affair. I think her daughter, the present Clover, thought it odd that her mother wanted to be buried next to Cohan, rather than with her parents. But Clover One wasn't sentimental about the past, of course."

"Isn't it a problem, only a year or so after her mother's death, for us to show her throwing a party in the Alster Tower? How do we make this seem plausible, when the story has it that the place was supposed to be abandoned in grief—or can we introduce the element of mystery about where her mother actually is, or at least why Clover is behaving this way?"

"Let's accept the fact that Louise Boldt died in 1904. If anything, we may leave it open *how* she died, or why Clover wasn't still in mourning. But we needn't go into that."

"Tell me, straight, Courtney."

"I don't have a straight answer to give you. I don't know that anyone has, even the present Clover."

"And she won't see me, at any rate."

Courtney wouldn't be pleased to see me going off on another tangent, but I was onto the scent. Millions of visitors had been told a story that might be wrong. My gut instinct was to pursue the enigma. Truth was a motivation, I suppose, but motives are never simple. I hadn't forgotten Courtney's tip that a quarter-million visitors a year were paying to see Boldt Castle. Big bucks. Courtney's play was his pastime, a hobby that he could afford—just as he could afford to put me up at a resort hotel for an expense-paid vacation in return for my summer's collaboration. I really didn't expect to see our play performed unless Courtney subsidized it or, if produced, to generate much income. I saw Courtney's book as a paid commission; my Boldt book, however, would be an entrepreneurial venture that might make some appreciable money.

I suspected that I could get to Mrs. Baird, barricaded at Hopewell Hall. If simple requests didn't work, I figured there was another sure way. I guessed that if I

The Hart of Heart Island

drafted the beginning of a major book, to be a biography of her grandfather, she couldn't resist reading and commenting. The door to Hopewell would open.

6. Professor Pete pulled from his file a Xerox copy. "Here it is. See for yourself." The death certificate confirmed that Louise Boldt had died in January of 1904. It seemed clear cut. She had died from a heart condition, it said. "Hmm. . . Heart Island—and all those hearts everywhere over there. Well, I guess that does it," I acknowledged reluctantly. "No question. . . ."

"No?" Pete smiled. "But that's not all."

 "What do you mean?"

"What caused the heart to stop?"

Of course! Pete had suspected what I had not. Out of consideration for the survivors, especially considering the prominence of the Boldts in New York City, the Boldts' physician might merely have recorded the immediate means of death, not the ultimate cause. "What do you think?"

"It's not just what I think, but what the family believes. I suspect that's why Clover One never wanted to talk about it. George Junior's secretary recalled the same version confirmed by Clover Two herself."

"What's that?"

Pete looked over the top of his glasses, staring beyond me.

"This is . . . important, to a lot of people. We're talking about an article of faith, accepted by the public for a century. A multi-million-dollar public facility has been—and continues to be—developed, on the basis of a legend. Do you think we ought to rock the boat?"

"You're a historian. What about the truth?"

"We don't need to volunteer it, do we?"

"Silence is consent, isn't it?"

"We're all complicit in a fraud, perhaps."

 "But you're still not going to tell me more specifically what you know?"

"As I said before, my most important source has been Clover Boldt Baird herself. I don't feel I can relate information that she shared with me in confidence."

"Let me do some digging, then, to see what I can find. Too bad I have to cover the same ground, when you have information right here, in those files."

"Sorry."

"Will you do this for me? Tell me, honestly, do you think it will be worth my time to pursue this?"

"I thought you were up here to work on Courtney's musical."

"Don't tell him. His work pace is pretty leisurely, and I can do some sleuthing on the sly. Should I?"

"There's more to be uncovered, I can tell you that."

"But enough more, you think, to justify a lot of effort on my part?"

"How far do you want to go? What's the information for? Simply to use in this play you're doing with Courtney?"

"No, I have in mind another book. A biography of Boldt, perhaps. I suspect Mrs. Baird would be interested in that."

"Not if it's to be uncomplimentary. Keep in mind the saccharine version she wrote herself, or allowed her name to endorse."

"We don't know how another work will turn out, do we, until we find out? I think an initial focus on her grandfather's early life and later achievements might engage her—prior to getting to the more difficult questions."

"Perhaps. But difficult questions may arise earlier than you suspect. Clover regards her grandfather as a saint—at least that's her public stance. The sort of Boldt hagiography published by Roger Lucas is more her preferred *métier*. But take that with a grain of salt. Was it Casey Stengel—or Yogi Berra—who said, 'Nice guys finish last'?"

"Leo Durocher, and that's not exactly how he said it."

"OK, so I'm not a sports historian. But Clover won't want to hear anything disrespectful of her grandfather. But your credentials are persuasive. She might cooperate."

"But tell me—just give me enough—to assure me that there will be something down the pike worth the journey. Will I come up with enough to warrant a new book about a familiar tale?"

"Yes. I'll encourage you, I suppose. In fact, I'll assure you. Don't quote me, of course, but I think you'll find that Louise Boldt did not die from natural causes."

7. I should have been contriving a jolly romp of singing characters, dancing their way through Courtney's improbable fairy tale of 1905. Louise Boldt wasn't even to appear in our musical comedy. But the missing character cast a long shadow over my enterprise. If her heart failure, as the death certificate indicated, had not been a "natural cause," what could have caused a heart failure? Some sort of substance? Why would she have taken it, or was it given to her—or do people really die of broken hearts?

   Hearts—hearts were everywhere on Heart Island. There were other symbols, curious icons, like the stag up on the roof, and the great, stone triumphal water arch to the lagoon. Peter, who had given much thought to all this, was cautious about giving away too much. I had allocated the entire summer to working with Courtney

Italian Garden and Power House

on our collaborative project, but he protested regularly that I shouldn't become distracted by this Boldt business. Suspicious about the hours I supposedly spent in my hotel room with laptop, Courtney wasn't particularly helpful in providing leads for my Boldt search. But I was drawn to Boldt Castle. What was the place really saying? I needed to know more.

Courtney did go so far as to call Meg, a local architect, to introduce me over the 'phone. After she said a meeting would be welcome, Courtney filled me in. Her family, like his, had been on the River for generations, and she had grown up with the local lore. Probably because of this influence Meg was drawn to history and now specialized professionally in historic restoration work. She had made quite a study of the Boldt project. "You have a treat in store," Courtney smiled, with a sigh.

"She's really well informed?"

"She's really something. You'll see."

I met, not at all what I expected—a severe matron with thick glasses and hair pulled back into a bun—but a charming, breezy young mother of toddlers (at home with a nanny). Meg's blond hair was worn simply, secured behind her pearled ears by a silk kerchief. In a tailored blouse and slacks, with penny loafers, sans socks, tanned Meg looked as if she should have been in the Caribbean, en route to Little Dix (where indeed they went in the winter) rather than in a walk-up architect's office over a tourist shop in Clayton. Her husband's profession, she explained, allowed them to settle anywhere, and she had become so attached to the River as a child that they bought a big, old Victorian house as a year-round home in Clayton.

A more conventional modern architect might have viewed Meg's office as a museum of architectural horrors. Framed drawings of Victorian villas surrounded us. It was curious to see a young woman amid so much that was old, but rediscovered as new. Oddly, the ornate houses on the wall contrasted with chromium Eames chairs. She laughed at my comment. "I went through my modern phase as an architectural student. When we bought the old house in town, we couldn't use this stuff, so here it is, in my office." Like Courtney, Meg seemed of uncertain age—not exactly girlish, far more poised, but difficult to imagine as the mother of several children.

"The curious thing about Boldt Castle," Meg observed, "is how it happened. You might think that the newly rich Boldts simply went to an architect and said, 'Give us a castle.' Life's not so conventional. The Hewitt brothers, of Philadelphia, were their architects—and it was William Hewitt, principally.

Terra cotta details, north side, Boldt Castle

The Boldt project was one of the major commissions of the firm. The buildings are landmark accomplishments, architecturally, but I suspect the architects were ambiguous about them." She spoke loudly, perhaps thinking my advanced years meant impaired hearing, or merely because she was aware of the racket made by a wheezing air-conditioning unit in the window. "You see, Boldt himself was a man mad-about-building, not one to give any architect free reign. When Heart Island was published in a national architectural journal, the article gave more credit to Boldt than to the architects." She went to a filing cabinet. "I've collected a bunch of stuff over the years. Here's the *Architectural Record* article. It says, 'While Heart Island is unusually interesting on account of its disposition and character of the buildings on it, it is notable also as being largely the idea of its owners.' You see, Heart Island was a sort of do-it-yourself project." She chuckled at the notion. "Boldt, more or less, was his own contractor. Here's another quote: 'Heart Island is a striking illustration of how a man can make use of his own facilities in creating a country seat even on such a scale.' It was indeed quite an operation. In terms of our modern dollars,

Belle Isle, built by the Boldts as a summer residence while the Castle was being constructed. To the left of the island is Wellesley House and to the right the Yacht House, both on Wellesley Island.

the payroll for Boldt employees at the Thousand Islands may have exceeded eight hundred thousand dollars annually at the turn of the century. He was doing his bit for the local economy."

"Hard to imagine."

"Yes, but even harder to imagine was Boldt's income. He was paying himself a salary of more than eight million, in terms of our dollars today. His payroll here on the River amounted to less than ten percent of his income—not insignificant, for sure, but the size of his income puts it in perspective. Remember that Boldt didn't have to pay modern income tax, which would have taken far more of his income than he spent annually on his River projects. And the projects! Wow, what a client!"

"Can you give me a general sequence of what they built?"

"How much time do you have? Get Roger Lucas's little booklets—they're fairly reliable. As a general outline, however, the Boldts had two campaigns on Heart Island, first expanding the wood-frame cottage that they bought, adding stone structures around it, then after only a few years deciding to remove the expanded frame house and build the Castle, the second campaign. Then there were projects on other islands: they built a grand, neo-classical house on Belle Island as temporary digs while the Castle was being built—which took years. And on Wellesley Island there were many projects—several other grand summer homes, the colossal Yacht House, the huge pier that served the golf course and other facilities, the big farm complex. . . . You see, it's too much to give you in short order. Just the story of the Castle campaign is difficult to reconstruct, but fascinating."

"Why did it grow to such proportions?"

"That's a long and complicated story. I can tell you how—the sequence of events—but probably not why."

"What about the symbolism? I'm interested in that."

Isle Imperial

"Me too. Boldt (I suppose he was responsible) was a clever man. He appreciated complicated puns and metaphors."

"All those hearts everywhere?"

"Well, on the face of it the heart represents romantic love, certainly. Methinks he protesteth too much." She smiled so knowingly. "Do husbands have to carve hearts in granite all over the place to make the point —and why did it have to be made so publicly?"

"I heard that Boldt Castle was to be a Valentine gift to his wife, whose birthday was on Valentine's Day."

"You'll hear lots of nonsense—but there may be some truth to that. 'Luisa' (they called her as a child) was indeed born on St. Valentine's Day, February 14. And so the recurring heart motif as the Boldt emblem, seen all over Heart Island. But the Boldts had acquired the island years before the Castle began, and development of the island, with its many structures, extended over a decade. In fact, Louise did own the island. The deed was in her name. George may have given it to her as a sentimental birthday present—who knows? And the

project, in many ways, was largely hers as well, I suspect—which is one major reason why it was discontinued when she died."

"The business about Boldt's telegram, stopping all work when she died. Is that true?"

"Oh, yes. There have been many workmen who recalled the very day—and the fellow who delivered the telegram, in fact, lived to an old age here. No doubt about that one."

"So Boldt abandoned the project because of his great grief."

"Well . . . again, who knows? We do know Boldt was keenly involved in building, but if the castle project had been Louise's costly whim, there may have been a practical reason to terminate it."

"But with so much invested!"

"You're right, of course. But talk to Pete about this. I've heard that there may have been financial reversals at the time. Boldt may have been in over his head."

The telephone rang and she rolled her eyes. "I need a secretary." I scanned her portfolio of restored summer homes until she concluded. "Sorry. The twins are quarreling. Where were we?"

"Do we know how much Boldt spent at Heart Island, and on the rest of his estate?"

"No way of knowing, since he was more-or-less his own general contractor, hiring large crews of workers, carried on his own payroll, and opening his own quarries and sand pits. He even acquired his own tug and barges, carrying granite from the Oak Island quarry ten miles away. Quite an operation. Furthermore, the castle campaign was concurrent with the building of his huge Bellevue-Stratford Hotel in Philadelphia. Same architects, and many of the same materials, like all the terra cotta detail on the exterior. Probably he siphoned off much stuff from the hotel project, shipping it up the River. Got it wholesale, as it were. Or as 'gifts' from contractors." She fingered quotation marks with her hands. "Who knows how much of its real cost was covered by, shall we say, 'favors'—or, less graciously, 'kickbacks' and ultimately by the Bellevue-Stratford mortgage? Of course, the Castle was so big that many folks expected it to be a Thousand Islands branch of his Waldorf-Astoria and Bellevue-Stratford hotels."

"Any truth to that?"

"I've seen speculation to that effect, at the time of construction and long after. Boldt, however, specifically

The Bellevue-Stratford Hotel, Philadelphia
Hewitt and Hewitt, architects, 1904.
The addition was built in 1911.

denied the rumors." She produced some clippings from her folder. "Listen to this: 'Just what George Boldt intends using the gigantic summer place for is unknown, but the fact that the building will contain twenty-seven suites of rooms gives credence to the report that Mr. Boldt will entertain multi-millionaires on Heart Island at their expense.' And then this: 'While here, one of his acquaintances hinted to [Boldt] that it was thought he intended to use his home in connection with his hotel in New York, for his more prominent guests.' And here's another: "'Ever since George C. Boldt began to make extensive improvements on Heart Island five years ago . . . it has been the opinion of the island population that Mr. Boldt would open to the smart set of New York one of the most modern hotels among the American summer resorts, where New York yacht men may come and enjoy service which will be unsurpassed, thus giving to the Islands a Newport aspect, which will mean a great boom.' Those comments appeared annually as the Castle rose, in three successive years. The notion was persistent. George Boldt specifically denied these rumors. Here are some of his responses: 'Mr. Boldt denied the report and said that it was simply his ambition to have one of the finest, if not the finest, place upon the St. Lawrence River.' And another: 'To his intimate friends Mr. Boldt always said that the magnificent mansion was for the occupation and enjoyment of his family, indignantly denying the report that it was to be used as an annex for the Waldorf-Astoria'

"Still the story wouldn't die. Much later, Judge Chester (who had known Boldt) was still of the opinion that the building was planned to serve, perhaps ultimately, as a hotel, for 'la crème de la crème.' Folklore tends to mix different events: the notion of a hotel on the island had been implanted in the popular imagination even before the Boldts acquired the island; fourteen years earlier there had been 'a report in circulation that the residence (on) Hart's Island . . . is going to be converted into a mammoth hotel.' It had been 'rumored that the Lelands of Albany are the ones who have purchased Hart Island for $23,000' and were 'to build a hotel immediately.'"

"Hart's Island—that's what Heart Island was called before the Boldts bought it?"

"Yes, Congressman Hart owned it. Everyone had called it "Hart Island" for years. Boldt, who was clever, changed the spelling and (as they say, decided to change the shape of this island in order to rationalize his new spelling). He also knew that 'hart' meant "stag" in German, hence that creature up on the roof. Clever fellow—but, you see, the simple love story gets complicated by complicated people."

"And did Boldt change the shape?"

"That accounts for the causeway project, enclosing the lagoon, with colonnades an all. Actually, the shape looks more like the real organ than the Valentine's heart."

"Amazing. But you were telling me about an earlier proposal to build a hotel on the island."

"It never came to pass, of course, although rumors persisted. Boldt did, in fact, begin construction of a hotel on Wellesley Island, a project that terminated with the outbreak of World War I. The old Hart House from Hart Island, relocated at the golf links, was indeed operated by him as a 'club,' affording lodgings for guests, mostly New Yorkers, many habitués of the Waldorf-Astoria. Whether they were paying guests is uncertain. Boldt hardly needed the income. The hotel rumor surfaced again immediately after abandonment of construction following the death of Louise Boldt. Three years later Boldt himself reportedly announced plans to finish the Castle, to be operated as a hotel. But of course, there was nothing to that story either. You see, folks were determined to have him make a hotel of the place."

"How much do you suppose he spent on the project?"

"The 'project'? Which ones?—there were so many. On Heart Island alone, in addition to the Castle, there were three other major projects: the Alster Tower, the 'Water Castle' or Power House, Arch of Triumph and Colonnades—to say nothing

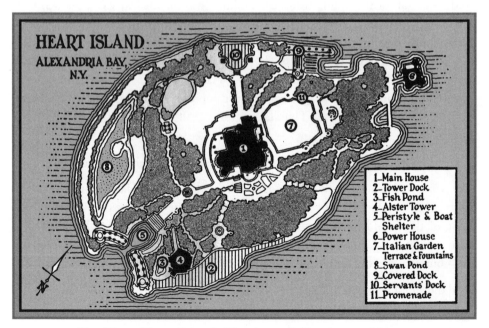

Site Plan, Heart Island, Hewitt and Hewitt, architects

of the great terrace that created the Italian Garden, plus smaller works, such as the Hennery, Conservatory, gazebos. . . . As you can imagine, there was always a lot of speculation about how much it all cost." She pulled out a clipping. "Here's an article of the time:

> Nobody but Mr. Boldt and his architects know exactly what his new home will cost. Ever since (he) bought Heart Island . . . he has been constantly improving the island. He has now enough work mapped out to last four years and there is a force of more than one hundred men working on the island nearly the entire year. When the work is completed, it is estimated that the outlay will be approximately three million dollars.

"Those were 1907 dollars. That appraisal may well have been realistic, but the architects' estimates were much lower. You know architects, however—or do you? We have a reputation for optimism about costs. But then we have to remember the economies of Boldt's do-it-yourself operations."

"So what do you think the Castle cost?"

"The *Architectural Record* in 1909 reported that even with Boldt's economical project management two million already had been spent on Heart Island—this without

The Boldt Yacht House

completing the house, gardens or colonnades flanking the Arch of Triumph, and without considering the Yacht House and projects on other islands.

"So what do you think the Castle would cost in today's dollars?"

"Oh, about fifty million dollars, give or take a few.

"Hard to believe."

"Well, they've put some fifteen million merely into repairs of the buildings in recent years, and they're far from finished. And when I say fifty million, that's just for the Castle. What would have been the outlay for the entire, three-thousand acre complex, including the Yacht House, Wellesley House, the Swiss Chalet, the Birches, the Tennis House, the Golf House, the golf course, its pier, tennis pavilion and polo field, the stables, the farm buildings (the farm was "one of the finest in the state")—to say nothing of Hopewell Hall, Belle Isle, Florence Island, Harbor Island, the great houseboat, yachts and fleet of racing, pleasure and utility craft? What would it have all cost?"

"Beyond comprehension."

"One writer at the time ventured that Boldt had spent on his River projects more than five million, today more like eighty million dollars, and another writer said that he had planned to expend ten million dollars, equivalent today to far more than one hundred and fifty million dollars."

"And this was just a summer home."

"He was up here only a few days a year. Oh well, easy come, easy go."

Meg's directness, her way of making immediate contact, her intelligent humor, were cheering, and she had suggested that I return, since she could only spare an hour or so at a time. I would be pleased to oblige. Courtney was right about Meg—being "really something."

8.   Professor Pete called down to the dock from a window above, telling me to come on up. He was seated at his computer again and swiveled around when I entered. I was pleased that he didn't feel required this time to rise to greet me. We seemed to be hitting it off. The loft floor appeared to sag under the weight of so many files. "Aren't you concerned about fire, with your life's work in this old building? Do you leave it all here during the winter?"

"Oh, everything important has been put on CD-ROMs. I can carry it all in a brief case. Modern technology still amazes me."

"Maybe you can tell me—Meg's been helpful about the buildings—but about the Boldts personally, as people. . . . Have you written anything I could read?"

"Oh, I've done scattered articles, but more about the Thousand Islands generally. I have several books in draft form. Some seem too specialized in focus to warrant trade publication. My more general history of the region has been completed, but on the shelf for years. A foundation proffered funds, but required that a not-for-profit organization write a grant proposal and serve as publisher. I found no local organizations willing to get into the publishing business. I don't want to be a publisher, either—driving around with books in my trunk, placing them on newsstand racks, like Roger Lucas with his Boldt booklets. So my history sits in the file."

"But what about the Boldts, as people? Was George Boldt your Alpha Male, a combative shark whose financial problems might have influenced his termination of the castle campaign?"

"Boldt? I've never pictured him that way. But Boldt was a big-time player at high finance—not in the same league as, say, Morgan, of course, but a pro. When asked about his vocation, for *Who's Who*, he said not what you would expect—that he was a *hôtelier*—but called himself a 'capitalist.'"

"Wonderful."

"And indeed he was a capitalist, involved in operating his own bank, as well as managing his personal investments."

"Boldt, a banker?"

"Yes. Boldt became a banker as part of his famous service to hotel patrons. Many wealthy guests didn't bother to carry much money, but spent prodigiously when visiting New York City. Some, like 'Bet-A-Million' Gates, lived at the Waldorf, where huge sums of cash were exchanged in his private gambling sessions. One of Boldt's innovative services was the lending of cash to guests. Boldt became private banker to many of his clients, who deposited huge sums with him for their use when in the City.

"Having depositors' money to invest, Boldt became interested in the stock and commodities markets. He was in the right place at the right time. His hotel was 'the only rendezvous, in the late afternoon and evening, of the nabobs of Wall Street and the whole financial community, as well as the local and visiting industrial magnates'—the 'Waldorf Crowd.' They said, 'Sometimes a man could learn more at the Waldorf bar than he could on the Street.' There had been no stand-up bar in the original Waldorf, only a sit-down café where J.P. Morgan was a regular patron.

Boldt yielded to male preference and created the four-sided men's' bar at the larger Waldorf-Astoria. It was popularly called 'Wall Street Uptown' at the time. There was a large bronze bull, and a large bronze bear atop the back bar, in the center of the bar, which was an island in the wood-paneled room. The nearby office of Benkhard & Co., stockbrokers, provided a ticker tape. The elite brokers dealt mostly in steel at the turn of the century, as well as Texas oil. The largest lot of steel stock ever bought changed hands in that small room, which was regarded as 'an exclusive club,' but made a profit of a million dollars a year. The Waldorf-Astoria bar 'was known all over the country—in mining camps from Mexico to Alaska . . . Its fame was world wide. . . . Anyone could look in, and most every man who entered [the hotel] did, at least once. . . . Ladies would pause in the corridor, look in, ask the headwaiter the identity' of famous men inside.' The New Rich felt privileged to be admitted into the company of power brokers and likewise to Boldt's excessively costly hostelry, especially when Boldt recognized them personally—and he made it his business to know who was who. Probably some insiders gratefully offered him stock market tips."

"Obviously, he did very well. But was there a financial crisis at the time he stopped work at the Heart Island?"

Pete fanned himself with a file folder. Forewarned by my previous visit, I had worn shorts myself this time, as he did, with sandals. "Depends on who you were and where you were. Boldt was a speculator. The major Heart Island campaign coincided with the Great Bull Market over the turn of the century. Consolidation of companies into large "trusts," as they called them, provided much of the wealth that built these showplace summer homes. A grand island edifice opposite Clayton, Calumet Castle, for instance, was enabled by formation of the American Tobacco Corporation. Morgan put together United States Steel after a dinner at the Waldorf where Charles Schwab planted the seed. If Boldt had plunged in United States Steel stock, he would have been a sorry man in a few years. The Great Bull Market was over, and much paper wealth vanished."

"The current presentations at the Castle don't mention these things."

"Of course not. They don't want to know."

"Were they aware that you had done research?"

"Of course. Vince Dee asked me to do the original visitors' orientation program at Heart Island, when the Bridge Authority acquired the property. My media

Boldt Castle roofscape

presentation ran for years at the Castle. Maybe it's still going. After Vince was gone, when a new, young fellow came on board to manage the operation, I learned that he planned new presentations, so I called him, suggesting that over many years I had assembled files full of material that might be useful. His response: 'Thanks, but we don't need any help'. Roger Lucas says he had the same experience."

"So you no longer contribute to the program?"

"Only indirectly. The Authority's architects have come to me from time to time, seeking specific information. Like Courtney, I don't care to visit the place. The last time I was over there I heard my own voice, amplified, resonating through the hard-walled chambers. The narrative and background music was familiar, but when I located the source in a darkened room, the images projected on the screen were different. So were the credits that appeared at the end of the presentation. The narrator—me, who wrote and read that script—no longer was mentioned. Other names appeared as authors of the presentation."

"Isn't that plagiarism?"

"Well, I was paid (modestly) for the original presentation package, so it was their property, I suppose. More important is what they say and do now."

"Who decides?"

"I expect that the manager of the operation does pretty much as he sees fit with interpretation. I wouldn't expect members of the Bridge Authority to be critical about scholarship or historical integrity of the project. The Authority has made some aw-ful booboos—like those big signs they erected around the island to tell visitors about various points of interest. I remember seeing one by the Arch of Triumph with la-dies in hoop skirts. The great arch was built in 1900, about a half-century after hoop skirts. That's the sort of thing one comes to expect over there. Those signs, at least, have come down, I understand. But other mistakes aren't reversible. When they put in a ramp to make the Castle wheelchair-accessible, they built it monu-mentally, of granite, to match the fabric. This sort of deception, suggesting that the Boldts needed a ramp, compromises the credibility of the landmark."

"You can understand their intent, to make the new addition seem inconspicuous."

Aboard a tour boat approaching Heart Island

"Good intentions aren't enough. There are lots of hor-ror stories of well-intended 'restorations' where old but honest buildings were gussied up to please modern tastes, but sometimes had to be redone right a few years later."

"But with so many visitors — some four million people since the Bridge Authority acquired the place—shouldn't Boldt Castle be regarded as a major public resource, with some sort of monitoring of what they do? Isn't it a matter of public education, when millions of visitors come away with mis-information?"

"Ha! They wouldn't even allow Heart Island to be listed on the National Register of Historic Places. Afraid someone might tell them what to do. The Authority has always been protective of its quasi-autonomous status, resisting public scrutiny. Heart Island should be, in fact, a National Historic Landmark. Surely it's more im-portant and more visited than, say, Camp Sagamore, the Vanderbilt place in the nearby Adirondacks, now a National Historic Landmark."

"But I noticed a plaque on the Yacht House, saying it had been listed on the Na-tional Register."

"Yes, June Larkin—Ed Noble's daughter—forced their hand on that one. She proposed a substantial gift for restoration, on condition that the Authority allow the property to be designated, to make it eligible for additional governmental funds, or so I heard."

"Who are the Nobles?"

"Of course you wouldn't know—you're new here. Edward John Noble spent his summers on the River when young, then became a multi-millionaire in his own right from LifeSavers—the candy with a hole. He invested shrewdly in Beechnut Food, then radio and motion pictures. When still amassing his fortune he formed a partnership with Clover Boldt's playboy husband —that's Clover One now (confusing I know)—and the two golfers built the Thousand Islands Club on the Boldts' Wellesley Island estate. This was after Boldt died. Noble wound up with all the Boldt's property on the River (except for Hopewell Hall, which Clover retained for her own use). June, Ed Noble's daughter, continued to summer here and she made a grant (from the Noble

The Arch of Triumph

Foundation, actually) for restoration of the Yacht House. June insisted that the Bridge Authority, which had taken title to the property, allow its designation on the National Register. But that was only the Yacht House. It's an anomaly that the Castle itself, and the other important structures on Heart Island, aren't listed."

"The Bridge Authority got the Castle from Noble?"

"Pretty much as a gift. The Foundation had let it deteriorate to the point where a massive infusion of money was required, even to make it safe for the public."

"What do you think of what they've done recently at Heart Island?"

"As I said, I don't go there anymore. I've seen some images on several of the web pages that feature Heart Island. Meg is more qualified than I as an architectural critic, but even this historian knows when period character is inappropriate. That massive new grand staircase, done in dark wood looks Victorian to me. It should be Edwardian."

"What's the difference?"

"Well, Heart Island's Triumphal Arch and Peristyle technically may be Victorian, since she reigned (although not here) until 1901. Boldt Castle, however, was built several years after the Chicago World's Fair, the neo-classical "Great White City," that changed taste in America. The fair provided the model for the arch and colonnades. They were seen in 1893, shortly after the Waldorf opened, when the Boldts were new owners of Heart Island. Turn-of-the-century taste favored simpler forms, lighter colors and more restrained décor. But judging by that staircase, with its gas-light sort of fixtures, the Authority seems to have the notion that to be old-timey the place ought to look like the final scenes of "Gone With the Wind." Amateurs always want to push history back, to make things seem older. The Bridge Authority has always been wary of anyone, including professional consultants—telling them what to do."

9.   If Pete always was at his computer when I visited, I never arrived to find Courtney at his piano. When do composers compose? I followed the sound of the axe to witness the master of Heron Island, clad solely in Lederhosen and running shoes, splitting chunks of the huge trunk of a felled White Pine. His wiry frame, glistening with perspiration, was covered with sawdust and bits of bark.

"Should have been here a bit earlier," Courtney complained. "We could have used another hand on one of the guy ropes. Had to bring down one of the big, old pines. Sad. But none of us last forever."

"I was working on *our* project—not Boldt research this time, but about May Irwin. Do you know they have a treasure at the Clayton Library—her scrapbooks and other personal papers?"

"Heard that, but never got into them. What did you find?"

"Loads—and through the 'Net. Did you know that she was a composer, too?"

"Guess I knew that, but never heard any of her tunes. Did you?"

"Not any that she wrote, but I heard a recording of one she made famous. In fact, it's still known as 'May Irwin's Frog Song,' even though she didn't write it. You've heard it?"

"Probably, but can't say I found it musically memorable."

"Oh, but it might make a great opening number." Courtney didn't need to respond. His scowl said it all. I persisted: "I know you've been thinking of something else, but listen to this: we open on the railroad dock at Clayton, Bart is pining to follow the gorgeous steam yachts and seductive power launches as they go off to island castles. May, his fairy godmother, appears and sings (I didn't make this up; it's an actual verse):

> Dere's some frogs I know is powerful fond
> Uf spendin' time in 'nother's pond,
> 'Cause day wasn't nuthin' else to do.
> An' all you frogs just list'n to me,
> Bettah stay at home wid yo' family
> When you havn't nothin' else to do.

Courtney didn't look thrilled.

"Of course, lyrics sound better when sung. I don't remember the tune. But here's the chorus:

> "An jus lots up folks is like dis foolish frog uv mine
> A runnin' into trouble jus' to pass de time
> An de devils allus loafin' roun' ' hea jus' to grab de kind
> Dat nevah hasn't nothin' else to do."

Courtney was speechless. Without changing his grimace he picked up the axe.

"No," I pleaded. "Spare me. It's really not so bad when sung—not when May does it, surely. You need to hear the music."

"I *have* the sheet music, along with a lot of May's period stuff. Fay Templeton's too. The tune's OK—but that dialect. Blackface is *out*. No way."

"But that's the way she sang it. Folks weren't politically correct back then."

"The audience is now, not then." He put the axe down. "But. . . you know, it *is* a rousing, rollicking number—could be a curtain raiser." It was in.

10. Her usual smile vanished when I asked Meg about architects' work at Heart Island. Meg hesitated, uneasy about discussing colleagues. "What can I say? About other architects, I mean? Professional courtesy's involved, you know." We sipped our cups of afternoon tea. The herbal aroma didn't mask the slightly moldy smell of a small room, closed and air-conditioned for a long period. Chic Meg was incongruous in her lair. She confided, "I hear that the Bridge Authority fired their first restoration architects. Or maybe the architects quit, finding it hopeless. That was while

I was away at school, so it's just scuttlebutt. But apparently at issue was the first major aspect of the campaign, which was to remove and replace the surfaces of the enormous roof. You can't imagine what a project that was!" Meg seemed relieved to get back to a less personal subject, and the usual laugh returned to her lilting voice. "They had to use photogrammetry—taking stereographic photographs from an airplane over head, then plotting a contour map as if it were a mountain range—in order to estimate the area of surface and quantity of material required. The architects at the time insisted on reusing the same sort of terra cotta tiles originally employed—not the Spanish sort of tile you see in Florida, of course, but rather a light orange rectangular shingle—not unlike what Boldt would have known in Germany. The Bridge Authority didn't want to spend the money, and found a cheaper, composition substitute. That was the bone of contention—authenticity. It has gone that way ever since over there. They spend a lot of money, but have different priorities than you or I might have. Vince Dee, Chairman of the Authority, once told me that historic restoration wasn't the primary objective, or even historical interpretation. Vince was a local businessman and great booster of the resort economy. He said candidly that the first order of business was to give the visiting public a good show.

"Of course, the place had been let go for many decades by the time the Authority got it, and really wasn't merely a disgrace, but a hazard to public safety. That was why the Authority accepted it, I gather, to prevent its closing and eventual loss as a regional attraction. Long before the restoration began, visitors complained about the big rip-off, finding that the castle was an empty ruin inside, vandalized and covered with graffiti. Much of it still is, of course, but the Authority has made remarkable—even astonishing—progress in attaining the objective: turning it around, into a genuine public attraction and crowd pleaser."

"How does the new roof compare with the original?"

"It's not bad. Maybe we're just used to it by now, but I can't say that's what offends me the most about what they've done."

"Such as?"

"Where to begin? One of the first things they did was to open the elegant reception room. That was the one room virtually complete and still intact. It was full of wooden barrels of plaster, moved in there to prevent vandals from throwing the material about, and the doorway and windows had been boarded over, securely nailed. You could only look in through the cracks. Well, the first year they took off the boards that secured the doors and windows. They discarded the barrels of

Main staircase, constructed in 1999. Only the steel framework existed.

plaster. When opened to the public, visitors tore the room to pieces, carrying off fragments of decorative plasterwork as souvenirs. Tragic."

"They've restored the room now, haven't they?"

"Yes, they've done an excellent job on the plaster, but more generally 'restoration' is a term to be applied loosely over there. Look at the adjoining Billiard Room. Some company as a favor 'restored' the room, as acknowledged by a plaque. But these rooms had never been finished, to restore. Even the reception room had no fireplace installed yet, although like so much material, it may have been crated in the lower level. For years crates of carved woodwork were brought up annually, opened as sacrifice for tourists to mutilate and devour, carrying away splinters as souvenirs. Well, the Billiard Room now has been newly 'finished,' even to a hanging lighting fixture over the billiard table. The fixture looks like it came from the current *Renovators' Catalog*: an itsy-bitsy, shiny brass item suitable for someone's basement game room. Totally out of scale with the big space, and totally wrong in character. They might have looked at some period billiard rooms, like those at Biltmore or Nemours, to see what would be more appropriate as a central feature of the room."

"They're fixing up the rotunda now."

Meg scowled. "The notion of 'finishing' the rotunda is a mistake. Look what they already have done. A clunky new wooden stair railing, atop new marble treads.

Wood and marble together? And, again, those lighting fixtures! Like the stair railing, they're mock Victorian, circa 1870. The fussy fixtures have too many little glass shades, too much bright brass. Wrong, wrong." She set down her cup of tea and sighed. "Oh, dear. I shouldn't have run on like that. Don't quote me!"

"I hear they've now commissioned restoration of the huge stained-glass dome over the central hall."

"Oh, lord, I hated to think of it, when I first heard of it. Only the main framework existed, you know, and there's no documentation of what the glass would have been. Probably it would come out Victorian, I thought, like a giant Tiffany lampshade—with all the flowers and fruit in living color. You know—the sort that were so trendy in fern bars not so long ago, and now have filtered down to the big-box discount retailers."

"Have you seen the actual design for the stained-glass dome?"

"Yes, and seeing what was being fabricated in Syracuse was a relief. If they had to invent something that never existed, they could have done far worse. The dome will be mostly plain cream-colored glass, in a simple rectangular pattern, with only a few decorative devices around the rim in color. I expect that their architect restrained them, pointing them away from more sensational alternatives."

"Wouldn't you think they would get more historical advice?"

"They might not even have needed a consultant for some things. Would you believe there are crates of woodwork stowed away in closed portions of the Castle? The original railing parts might have been found there, but they didn't look. That material has never been inventoried, while they're inventing new stuff instead. Imagine that! And advice from a historian? Probably our eminent historian hereabouts, Pete, told you about being rebuffed, when he volunteered to help them. Instead they just went about 'fixing it up.' I suppose the Bridge Authority's chief maintenance man was the designer of many things invented in the 'fixing up' process, like one of the first 'finishing' items to appear, a little wooden mantelpiece in the dining room, where the Boldts probably would have had a grand, monumental piece. A photograph of the dining room at Wellesley House shows a mantelpiece that appears to be white, carved stone—possibly originally acquired for the Castle, but used here when the Castle was abandoned. What we got instead was a carpenter's wood job, suited to a middle-class, suburban house. Ridiculous." She leaned forward as I jotted on my pad. "You're taking notes? Don't mention who told you this."

Wellesley House dining room

"I won't divulge the real name of real people, unless to compliment them." She didn't look placated, but I pressed on. "They have other architects now?"

"Yes. Two firms now. They're spending so much money so fast that they need help, preparing bid and contract documents. One firm has a young architect who is historically oriented and wants to do the right thing. He sometimes talks to Pete, who digs out old photographs for him. No architect would have an easy job of it, working with the Authority. They still have the do-it-yourself mentality, and still distrust consultants, I expect—or they suppose that staff can do much of the job without the nuisance of consultants telling them what to do. But with so much money to spend and so much to be done, they have to get help, even if they don't always take the advice they get."

11. Pete joined me for lunch at the Thousand Islands Club—the place that Ed Noble had built on the Boldts' Wellesley Island estate. We drove over, since the large island is now connected to the U.S. and Canadian mainlands by bridges. With Interstate Route 81 crossing the island, it has lost much of its sense of remote isolation.

Pete reminded me that Clover Boldt's first husband had been Noble's partner in this golf club venture (before Clover divorced her first husband). The 1920s' Mediterranean-style "T.I. Club" (as everyone called it) was near the golf course, tennis courts, and what had been the polo field.

"This place used to be something else," Pete recalled, as we entered the Club's classy, classical portal, passing under the stair landing, and into the lobby. I was self-conscious that we were an odd couple. I had taken the precaution of wearing a proper sport coat and slacks, but Pete arrived in his usual plaid shorts, sans coat, wearing a baseball cap, but incongruously carrying a professor's book satchel. Oblivious to appearance, he continued, "As a kid I regarded the T.I. Club with awe. Occasional visits here with my parents were indelibly imprinted. I remember when this lobby was lined with pictures of American Indians. I suppose, in retrospect, that they may have been Catlin's famous work—worth more today than the build-ing, perhaps. When Noble owned the place, it was a first class joint. He had a popular and suave manager—I forget his name—oh, yes: Lewis Beers, I think. The fellow moved seasonally to run a winter resort down south. Noble was concerned with the operating deficit, however, and hired an efficiency expert to look at Club operations. The consultant reported that every time the French chef turned around, he dumped a pound of butter into something. The food was marvelous." We moved out into a skylit area between the bar and dining room, which opening onto it through French doors. "Noble was funny about money. He'd spend it lavishly on some things, like the flower gardens here, which were gorgeous—but I remember him, when I was a kid, coming into the improvised bar in the basement of the Cha-let, where ice cubes had been dumped into a laundry tray. He was aghast to see ice melting, and returned with a burlap bag to keep it covered. Here was this multi-millionaire, worried about losing a few pennies on melting ice. Probably that's why he was the richest man on the River, we supposed, at the time."

"The Swiss Chalet was a small cottage?"

"Not exactly. It's still there, so you can see for yourself. Although the house has been remodeled, it originally had fourteen bedrooms and six baths. It was designed by the Hewitt firm that did the Castle and Yacht House."

We paused in the bright central space of the T.I. Club. It had little furniture but a terrazzo floor—for dancing, apparently. "This was originally an open court yard, with that arched loggia between it and the exterior terrace. Now they have loud rock music in here at night. No wonder they lost their resident guest trade,

The Chalet. The roof above the trees at left is The Birches, the summer home of George Boldt, Jr., on the bay where the large Boldt pier served the Boldt Golf Club. At the right between its boathouses and the white canal bridge is Wellesley House. The long line of the garden pergola extends from gazebo to the edge of the photograph.

and had to tear down the long bedroom wing." He chuckled. 'No, in truth, as I recall Meg telling me, they had code problems—to do with something unglamorous like sewage disposal. They got hardship variances for years, I hear. When the State finally compelled the new owners to correct the old systems, they decided to tear the bedroom wing down instead."

Through French doors we strolled onto a large flagstone terrace, cool under a huge awning. Lawns extended down to the water, where the shore was fringed with boat-lined docks, centered by a great pier—actually two piers, covered by a roof. At the end a glassy casino on its upper level seemed surrounded by a grove of masts and antennae. "Boldt built the pier decades before the construction of this 1920s' building" Pete told me. The pier served the golf course and original golf house, now known as Hart House. We'll take a look at that."

Small wooded islands sheltered the bay. "On the summit of that one," Pete advised with a wave of outstretched arm, "used to tower Castle Rest—the place belonged to Pullman, the Chicago railroad-car manufacturer. And over there used to be the Thousand Islands Yacht Club—a long, railroad-train sort of building, covered with weathered shingles. And, oh, the yachts that used to fill this bay! Here was the center of it all. All gone

Castle Rest, summer home of George M. Pullman

now." We settled into armchairs as Pete flagged a waiter. Nearby we heard the loud voices of children, splashing in the swimming pool.

"How did this Ed Noble come into the picture? Why did the Boldts need a partner to develop their property?"

"The Boldt kids weren't short of money to put into the place—they had inherited plenty of money. What they wanted was to get money *out* of all this stuff, not put more money into it. Their father had a notion of developing a colony of summer homes on the Wellesley Island property, oriented to the golf course. Boldt himself had started to construct a large hotel near the course—another project abandoned—so the idea of the T.I. Club was in the air. Noble was a golfer who summered here on Wellesley Island, and was interested in the courses. The Boldt kids wanted to sell the whole works—including the Castle. Noble was interested in the golf club notion and was minting money—lots of it—but he was too shrewd a businessman to tie up his resources in Boldt's crazy projects. Noble refused to bite unless Heart Island was left out of the deal. Astute though he was, Noble didn't foresee the potential of the place as a tourist attraction. Everyone thought it was a colossal white elephant, after it had been abandoned for many years."

"But Noble did get the Castle."

"He met his match in Clover Boldt—she, not her brother, had the smarts. Clover at first appeared inclined to sell everything to Noble except her own home, Hopewell Hall, leaving out Heart Island, which he didn't want. A seemingly casual negotiation between two golfers went on at the seventh hole, as recalled by their young caddy. When the price seemed agreeable, Clover sweetly insisted on throwing in the Castle for free, as it were—take it or leave it, Ed. Noble took it."

"How did Clover's husband become involved in Noble's T.I. Club project?"

"Well, Gus Miles didn't have much else to do, whereas Ed Noble was involved in all sorts of business ventures. I suspect that Noble wanted the Boldts to have a stake in the Club venture, to spare some of Noble's own working capital. The Boldts contributed the land and probably held a mortgage on the Club facility."

"Noble was about the same age as the Boldt children?"

"I suppose. Edward John Noble represented another generation of multi-millionaires at the Thousand Islands, a new generation that numbered far fewer of the very rich, and probably no longer any of the super-rich. The Noble fortune was popularly thought to be the largest at the River, after the passing of the halcyon days prior to World War I, when Noble himself had been a youngster. If not the

The Thousand Islands Club, c. 1930

largest, probably Noble's was the biggest *new* fortune at the Islands in the decades between the Wars. He hailed from nearby Governeur, N. Y., and spent boyhood summers on the River, but migrated to New York City after attending Yale. Noble derived his initial wealth by introducing a novel hard candy with a hole in it, Life-Savers.

"Noble came along as the resort was aging, in decline. He bought Belle Isle, with the splendid Peacock villa, built by Boldt and used while the Castle was being built. Boldt then rented the place to the Peacock family of Pittsburgh, who eventually bought it. Noble paid $100 for it in 1928—even before the stock market crash! Noble himself preferred Journey's End, a simple log cabin he built on the Lake of the Isles after buying the property of the Boldt estate. Life style had changed. His daughter, June Noble Smith Larkin of Greenwich, Connecticut, retained Journey's End. She's Chairman of the Noble Foundation, which conveyed most of the Noble property, including the Thousand Islands Club, to the Thousand Islands Bridge Authority. They gave away Boldt Castle and its Yacht House."

"Why?"

"Well, to get rid of the properties, I suppose. The Nobles had sold the Club previously, but after the new company failed to make a go of it, the Nobles bought it back, in order to keep the place alive. They subsidized operations for many years. They (or the Noble Foundation, I should say) didn't subsidize Heart Island or the Yacht House to the extent that maintenance required, however. At the point where closure loomed as an ominous prospect, Vincent J. Dee, Chairman of the Bridge Authority and a real community leader for the region, stepped in. He recognized the value of Boldt Castle as a regional attraction and persuaded the members of the Authority to accept Heart Island and the Yacht House as a gift from the Noble Foundation. To sweeten the deal, the Authority accepted the T.I. Club and golf course property. You see it was the reverse this time: Dee wanted the Castle, but had to take the rest of the real estate to get it. The Foundation, most concerned with health care, wanted to get out of the property management business."

"The Bridge Authority doesn't own the Club now?"

"No. Vince found another buyer—but the place has always been a marginal business operation and has changed hands several times. It's off the beaten path, and too small to be efficient as a self-sufficient resort facility. It's primarily a restaurant now—excellent fare."

"Noble's daughter—Mrs. Larkin—ought to be pleased to see the Club still going and the Castle and Yacht House so successful now."

"Yes, but not so happy with the subdivision of the Boldt estate, however. She had supposed, when selling the Club to the Authority, that the property would remain intact. She was displeased—'horrified' may not be too strong a word—to see the bulldozers move in and begin development of suburban-lot subdivision and condominium construction. On a happier note, however, the Hart House is doing well. We'll take a look at it."

Over lunch, Pete refreshed my memory, recalling that when bought by the Boldts, Heart Island had been called 'Hart Island," because it was owned by Congressman Hart. The original Hart cottage was dismantled and reassembled here on Wellesley Island. I asked him what he thought of the story that Boldt changed the shape of the island to substantiate the name change.

"Oh, that's one of those stories. I don't know how it got started, but I suspect that the creation of the embankment to enclose the lagoon was its genesis.' One might imagine that project made the island more heart-like in shape, but had that been the primary intent, I suspect the embankment would have had a different configuration."

"What was its purpose?"

"With those eccentric Boldts, who knows? It's on the windward side, so one might suppose it created a sheltered basin for small craft, which entered through the water gate, the Arch of Triumph. But with all the islands in this area, rough water isn't so much a concern as it is in some other situations, more exposed to wind off Lake Ontario. The Boldts probably anticipated inviting throngs of people to events at Heart Island, a large boat basin, with ample dockage provided by the causeway, may have seemed useful. In recent years the authority, in fact, has developed the embankment to provide dockage for many visiting boats." The waiter brought our gin-and-tonics.

"But the huge stone arch?"

Pete paused to savor his tonic. Fueled, he resumed the lecture with new gusto. "Ah, that's clearly an icon. The Boldts loved mystic symbols. The triumphal arch, merely a monument, was the most gratuitous of the Boldts' many projects at this time. It was totally without redeeming utility—beyond its 'significance,' in the literal sense of that word, that is: as a sign to convey meaning. It was symbolic, a very public statement, serving as the frontispiece and entry portal to the Boldt domain. Visualize it surrounded by great, masted yachts, with smaller tenders, operated by sailors in spotless whites, carrying guests throught the portal."

"You're saying the Boldts wanted to impress everyone."

"Oh, that's an aspect of it, surely, but there are more layers. The Boldts weren't simple-minded. Like a cornerstone laid ceremonially, the Arch of Triumph was built at the outset of the Castle campaign. A derrick raised the granite keystone with its carved heart and date, 1900. The advent of the new century no doubt was an aspect but, closer to the Boldts' hearts, the monument initiated a four-year construction project. Thereafter it would serve as entry portal to the island and its castle." Pete reached for his briefcase. "I brought along a few things that you might like to see." Adjusting his glasses, he drew a folder from his briefcase. He was shifting into his professorial gear.

"It seems evident that the immediate model for the idea of the arch, flanked by colonnades, derived from the World's Colombian Exposition." He produced a photograph. "The fair was held in Chicago in 1893, the year that Boldt's Waldorf opened in New York. Clearly the coincidence of events meant something to the Boldts. To this day, the remarkable freestanding clock that they acquired from the fair stands in the center of the Waldorf-Astoria Lobby. The world's fair celebrated the anniversary of the supposed discovery of America, and Boldts' own Waldorf was inaugurated on the same anniversary.

"And why a triumphal arch as a symbol? America had surpassed England as the industrial giant of the world. We were rich, and getting richer. As a contemporary observed, 'The age in which we live is beyond question the most marvelous that has yet been known to man. The whole world is being born again.' This was the 'Age of Confidence.' Sanguine seasons in the sun, those 'long golden summers of the Edwardians,' were whiled away by newly affluent families at many a comfortable cottage colony and splendid, sybaritic spa. These years at the Thousand Islands were an idyllic 'garden of a golden afternoon.' The Arch of Triumph represented self-reliance, self-achievement and self-satisfaction."

"You're very eloquent about the triumphal motif. You don't make so much of the heart motif, as a significant symbol, do you?"

"You mean in its conventional, Valentine sense, of romantic love? There may have been that aspect of it, but Boldt was not so simple minded as to leave it at that. He was quite a sophisticate, really. Very bright fellow, if not formally well educated. I find more characteristic and intriguing his pun on the "Heart-Hart" business. You know the Boldt crest? He invented it, probably, after acquiring Hart Island. It has the Valentine heart surmounted by the stag. That's why you see the bronze statue with the antlers, standing up on the central gable of the channel façade. Below it, set into the masonry wall, is a large heart carved of granite. In German, the word for 'stag' is 'hart,' which had been the name of the island's previous owner, and everyone called it 'Hart Island.' Boldt probably figured they would continue to do so, hence he decided merely to change the spelling.

"There were to have been more bronze stags atop the triumphal arch, above the carved granite heart of the keystone. This was the sort of thing that amused Boldt—private jokes that others might not get at all. The Boldts, who spoke German at home, when first hearing the name "Hart Island," probably thought of it as "Stag Island." Probably to them, that reference was more imprinted than the English words which sounded the same, "Heart Island."

"Stags may be a hunting motif but surely are less romantic than hearts. The verbal joke undercuts the romance, doesn't it?"

"Of course—and speaking of 'the romance,' Clover Boldt Baird must be here for lunch. I meant to point out her white Caddy convertible in the handicapped parking place. She's able to drive it herself, you know—had it specially made with hand controls, since her legs are paralyzed. But back to the 'romance' business: I'm skeptical about the place being a gift to Louise, hers to have the way she wanted. Heart Island doesn't strike me as being very 'feminine,' if I may be permitted gender stereotyping. The first construction project on her island was a tower—surely a male symbol, if ever there was one. And what was it for? To house George's pet fowl. I see him taking over the development of the island from the very outset."

Pete dug into his bag and took a Xeroxed clipping from a folder. Looking over the top of his glasses, he read: "During their first summer on their newly acquired island, the Boldts occupied the old Hart house. Guests at the grand hotels of Alexandria Bay, surprised to be awakened by (quote) 'the lusty crow of the chanticleer' and by 'the cackle of hens' heard across the calm water of the channel at dawn, 'are issuing complaints.' Those peculiar Boldts had built a 'Hennery,' of all things—a stone tower full of 'Plymouth Rocks, White Leghorns, Brown Leghorns, Brahmins, and in fact every other species of domestic fowl known to the civilized world'! The Boldts thereafter never failed to keep the local community amused by their antics."

"Is the Hennery still there?"

"Sure. It's that odd stone tower in the Italian Garden—but a tower is hardly the most practical arrangement for a chicken house. At the top was a wooden dovecote—that's a large bird house for pigeons, you know—surmounted by a conical roof, clad with wood shingles." Another sip of tonic seemed to inspire him. "It was prophetic, of course, that the first project should be a stone tower. If we're talking symbols, the tower should be foremost. Louise probably regarded the tower, as did most native-born Americans of the time, as a romantic element of

The Hennery

Wellesley House, a 56-room residence where George Boldt visited during his last years, was the centerpiece of his Wellesley Island estate. The Ice House, all that remains, is the small stone structure at the end of the pier. The stables appear at left. Note the length of the lower building roof, which disappears out of the photograph. The long pier reached deep water to accommodate yachts and many boats. Boldt was host to large parties at Wellesley House. The bridge at the right crossed an entry canal into the system of waterways that extended through the estate, reaching the main farm complex on the other side of the island. Elaborate flower gardens adjoined the gazebo at the end of the bridge. The Tennis House appears beyond the gazebo.

fantasy, recalling enchanted castles of fairy tales. For immigrant George, however, the meaning was far more genuine. He had lived in an Old World where there were genuine towers, where they meant something real, like power.”

“A chicken coop in the formal Italian Garden?”

“Oh, the Hennery was going to be demolished. Now what do they do? Should it be removed, if they really intend to ‘finish’ the place? That’s the sort of quandary they got themselves into over there. But I digress. Back to the tower symbol:

“The meaning to Boldt of the tower was made evident by the original figure that topped the tallest tower of the Castle—if we’re to believe a very odd, but apparently well-informed account. The main tower is now surmounted by a big weather-vane, recently restored, based on old photos. That feature may not have been original, however, but rather added after a valuable bronze statue was removed. What was there originally? “A brazen statue of a man standing over a lion.”

“Weird.”

“Yes, and what are we to make of that? The reference, of course, would have been generally to conquest, relating it to the arch-of-triumph motif. More particularly, the symbolism probably representing the Boldt name, which means ‘bold.’ But, I ask you, does all this reference to conquest seem very feminine? Would a woman who wanted a fantasy castle decorated with hearts have thought of putting a man standing over a dead lion atop its tallest tower?” Pete flagged the waiter for another round of drinks.

12. Some exercise was advised following our long repast, so after lunch we left the car to explore on foot. On arrival at the Ice House Pete and I prudently declined refreshments offered by Bud and Eleanor Forrest. The Forrests had adapted the stone building rising from the water as a delightful cottage. The Ice House was where ice cut from the River was stored to serve nearby Wellesley House, George Boldt's summer home during his last decades, they explained. Our hosts had collected historic momentos, such as Boldt china with a clover design, discarded by Clover Boldt Miles Johaneson. "That may be the very china made for her when a youngster, used in the Alster Tower," Pete suggested.

"You think so?" Eleanor Forrest was pleased. "I hadn't thought much about the Boldts or anybody actually *living* on Heart Island."

"But they did, for several years before beginning the Castle project. The Alster Tower was finished before they moved over to Belle Isle. The odd structure—hardly a 'house'—was really a sort of playhouse for the youngsters, you know. It had a charming, open kitchen—very modern in that sense—where the young people could prepare their own meals, without servants hovering around. I'll bet the china was used there. It's too casual in character for the Boldts' regular dining room. You don't think it was used here, at Wellesley House in later years?"

"No, at Hopewell Hall—at least that's where it came from," Eleanor explained. "We rescued what was left on its way to the dump."

"Clover Boldt wasn't very sentimental about the past. Too bad she didn't care more, and save more," Pete lamented.

"But someone, saved scrapbooks." Bud picked up a large volume from the coffee table, containing copies of photographs showing vanished Wellesley House. I was intrigued, explaining that my work on Courtney's play was expanding into a potential book about the Boldts. I asked where they got the volume. "The original album was George Boldt's—had 'G.B.' stamped on the leather cover. Ed Noble may have got it when he bought the property. There were still some personal effects here in Wellesley House then. I suppose Noble offered the keepsake to Clover, and she probably told him to keep it himself if he wanted it. She didn't."

We stepped back outside to see the lawn where Wellesley House stood. "I remember this place as a youngster," Pete said. "Noble had let it go, so it wasn't very inviting. Finally he demolished it. Wellesley House had fifty-six rooms, so by room count it was actually about two-thirds the size of the Castle. I suppose it seemed impractical to maintain, but imagine what it would be today if restored like Hart House and operated as an inn."

Bud reminded the professor, "You know that Wellesley House briefly served as an inn?"

"Oh yes, when Clover didn't want to use this place herself, she tried that operation—or was it after Noble acquired the property? I don't recall."

As we departed from the Ice House, Eleanor insisted, "You write that book—the real Boldt story for me." She pointed across the water, from the same point where George Boldt himself had looked at Boldt Castle during his last summer visits. "I want to know what went on over there!"

We followed an old concrete walk along a canal defined by concrete walls, now broken. These overgrown embankments had once presented elaborate floral displays, Pete explained. The walks atop them had connected pergolas, marble seats, and decorative footbridges. But now, to provide access to modern condominium units on Tennis Island, the developer had replaced a light pedestrian span (where Gus Miles had proposed to Clover, I learned) with a vehicular roadway. Earth fill now blocked the main canal, reduced at his point to an impassible culvert. The canals no longer provided an enchanting tour; rather, the extensive canal system was mostly sluggish backwater, green with weeds and algae.

But suddenly a stunning apparition transformed the depressing landscape. Rising from the water, a monster from the deep bristled with spiky roofs and towers, crustaceans on a great whale. The gigantic Boldt Yacht House, restored, was sensational, looking like it appeared a century ago, at the height of the Gilded Age.

"Wow."

"Yes, indeed. Some think this is Bill Hewitt's best work here—he had freer rein than on the Castle, probably. It's inventive architecture, for sure. Nothing like it elsewhere—in the whole world, fair to say. Yacht houses were something of a local building type. Tides make them less practical on the seacoast, but few inland waters had the great steam yachts of the St. Lawrence. Because of the severe winter, when the water freezes, it was desired to raise the big boats out of the water, and to protect them for half a year under cover. There were once many large yacht houses here. This is the only one left, at least of this size—but it was always the most spectacular of all."

"It's very sculptural."

"Like the Castle, it was intended to be a landmark, visible from great distances across the water. From the Castle, it was to be viewed from the large covered terrace outside the dining room and then, framed by the broad plate-glass bay window of the Dining Room. At the twilight dinner hour, towers and cupolas, together with the rigging of tall-masted yacht and railings of colossal houseboat, would be silhouetted against the sunset, then suddenly sparkle with hundreds of lights, reflected in the water."

Alongside the boat house portion of the building was a wing, dominated by a five-story tower, ninety-six feet high. On the other side, at the rear corner, was a second tower, and atop the highest central roof rose the tallest element, a cupola with conical roof, terminating in a large weathervane. Steeply pitched roofs and

Boldt Yacht House, estate superintendent's quarters

The Boldt Yacht House viewed from Heart Island

angular skyline likewise recalled the Castle, although materials and construction are different. The interior was equally astonishing.

"Look at the size of those doors! They must be in the Guinness Book of Records as the world's largest."

"The doors were said to be so large, so heavy, that they had to be opened and closed in sections, pivoted on giant, strap hinges of iron, moved by machine."

"Do they still work?"

"Yes, they were restored to working order."

"And the height—it's like a cathedral inside."

"Yes, the largest slip was for the major Boldt yacht, enabled to enter with tall masts and rigging standing. Designed and built by Herreshof, the alluring, white 'Louise,' was a lovely boat, curvaceous with clipper bow and fantail stern. The adjoining slip, with doors not quite so tall, was for a steam yacht with two stacks, the fast 'Presto,' acquired for the Boldt's son. A third, lower opening was for the steam yacht, 'Clover,' named for the Boldt's daughter. This was a Three Bears' yacht house, but soon

In the Boldt Yacht House is the Boldt's "Number 3," one of twenty identical, numbered boats built in 1909 by Leyare of Ogdensburg for racing by members of the Thousand Islands Yacht Club. The boat, later called "This" (a partner to "That"), was acquired with the Boldt property by Edward J. Noble, who renamed it "June II." His daughter, June Noble Larkin, contributed to restoration of the Yacht House. Subsequently the boat was renamed "Yesterday" by Jim and Tony Lewis, who donated it to the Shipyard Museum, Clayton, which has loaned it for display in the Yacht House. The boat was converted into a split cockpit runabout in the 1930's. Its length is twenty-eight feet, beam five feet.

it was too small. An addition provided the broadest opening, serving the gigantic houseboat, 'La Duchesse.' The wide spans required the many steel lattice trusses. Seventy tons of steel were used to frame the vast spaces, sixty-four feet—that's seven stories—high. The steel structure was prefabricated in New York City, brought on barges through the canal, and assembled here."

There is something surreal about a boathouse, a building on the water, with a liquid floor. It breathes. Not only does the breeze sweep through it, but within, lapping water echoes through lofty spaces, as in the belly of a great whale.

"This was a busy place, a hundred years ago. There were officers and crews of the many Boldt boats—and the fleet usually numbered fifteen or so. Then there was a team of craftsmen who worked in the shop. Here boats, including famous racing craft such as the 'P.D.Q.s,' were built.

"What does 'P.D.Q.' stand for?"

"'Pretty Damned Quick.' Fred Adams ran the boat operations, and he designed many of the new boats. Captains of the yachts were local men, who know the River, so they commuted to work from the Bay, but many young hands lived in quarters in the Yacht House. Some crewmen had to be on call around the clock, as steam engines had to be fired up at any hour, and launches always be available on call, with so many people living on the Boldt islands. The estate superintendent lived in a large, attached house.

"On each side of the slips screw jacks enabled large vessels to be lifted out of the water, which froze during the winter. A metal funnel could be lowered over the smokestack of the 'Louise', connected to the rooftop cupola, so that the large steam

Boat building in the Boldt Yacht House

Hart House, the original cottage on Heart Island,
dismantled and reconstructed on Wellesley Island as the Golf House

vessel could be fired up within the building. Large coal bins made up part of the big structure."

Shimmering sunlight, reflected from water below, dappled warmly glowing varnished wood surfaces of the cavernous interior. The marvelous space housed a collection of period pleasure craft, including some of the Boldt boats on loan from the Antique Boat Museum. Nowadays most visitors arrived at the Yacht House on a shuttle boat from Heart Island.

When we came to sprawling Hart House on the nearby golf links, Pete pulled another old photo from his trusty satchel. "Look at that gazebo atop the tower," Sure enough, the pavilion was just as it appeared in old photographs of Heart Island. "The present building is comprised, at least in part, of the original cottage of Congressman Hart. The Boldts had enlarged the old frame house on Heart Island, then dismantled it to make way for construction of the Castle. See that curved verandah? It's a motif seen on old photos of the Hart house. And these seem to be the same sort of roofs, supposedly 'Swiss' in style. Compare these roofs with the photo."

Hart House, like the Yacht House, had been refurbished in recent years. Similar to most other Boldt structures on Wellesley Island, Hart House was clad with weathered wood shingles. "You see how they turned the building around," Pete noted, "so the porch no longer faces the water. Here it's oriented to the links because this became the Boldts' golf clubhouse. When the Danielsons got it, the place was pretty seedy. During later decades it had served as staff quarters for the Thousand Island Club. In converting the building to a bed-and-breakfast inn, Dudley and Kathy didn't aim for an authentic restoration—for instance, the wall between the large living room and verandah was largely removed to create an even larger space. Some big mirrored walls seem incongruous, but Danielson's traditional furnishings make the place inviting".

The extent of the canals, as we walked atop embankments along them, was evidence of the long and costly campaign to improve this land—much of which had been marshy when acquired by Boldt, Pete explained. "They say that he kept a crew constantly at work for years, digging these canals. Supposedly there was no master plan. Boldt would simply come up now and then and point with his cane, 'Dig over that way.' He might have hoped to connect to the Lake of the Isles, but never made it. The main farm complex is over there, with a large staff house facing that body of water." After a mile or so of hiking a dusty road in the mid-afternoon sun, Pete lugging his leather bag, we abandoned the notion of visiting the farm complex where only few of Boldt's farm buildings remain, he explained, together with the staff house, all again clad in weather wood shingles.

On the way back to the T.I. Club Pete explained that through dozens of purchases over the years Boldt put together his 3000-acre Wellesley Island Farm. It was a business enterprise, he informed me—and as I was the professor's captive student, I learned more than I needed to know about its operation. "There actually were three farms, the 'Front' and 'Back' farms, as well as the 'Browning Farm.'" Among other things, this was the largest poultry operation in New York State. Vast flocks of geese, turkey, ducks chicken, pheasant and quail provided fowl for the kitchens of the Waldorf-Astoria. Pete stopped, put down his bag, lifted his baseball cap to mop his brow and then, to my surprise, dug into his portable file. The professor was irrepressible. Undaunted by the heat and glare, he pushed up his glasses and read: 'At Thanksgiving time, 1864 pounds of Wellesley Island turkey went to the Waldorf'. Isn't that something?"

"I'll bet they gobbled it up."

"What? Oh." He smiled wanly, but went back to his folder. Levity wasn't going to

The Wellesley Island Farm Complex
The large Farm House appears directly below the water standpipe

dissuade him. "I quote," he continued, "'Sheep and hogs are raised, for lamb and pork, as well as dairy and beef cattle'. Imagine. There was a butcher shop to dress meat and poultry, which then was ferried across the River to be carried by electric trolley to a refrigerated railroad car waiting on the tracks at Redwood. Would you believe that?"

"I'm beginning to believe anything about these Boldts."

"The Wellesley Island ham was particularly savored by the New York City clientele."

"I'll bet they made pigs of themselves." It was getting very hot.

"And listen to this: 'Many acres of plowed land [provide] many varieties of farm produce for shipment to New York.' Model dairies display 'the latest sanitary devices and every care is given to the production of milk, which more than meets the most exacting test.' At the creamery, machines prepare butter."

"Quite a spread. Do you suppose all Boldt's visitors had to get this tour, together with the full lecture?" Pete had reverted to his teaching mode. He was oblivious to heat or ribbing.

"Oh, yes, indeed. The farm complex was more than utilitarian, you see, but functioned as a sort of zoo, with interesting animals and notably many species of fowl on view in pens. Many of the birds were gorgeous and exotic, like peacocks, more decorative than useful. " He was fanning himself with his file folder, as his glasses continued to slide down his nose. "You remember that the Hennery on Heart Island had been Boldt's first project on the River. He had this fascination with birds."

"With a lot of things, apparently."

"Yes, fancy fowl had been one of his interests since his boyhood on rural Rügen." I recognized the professor's far-away look. No stopping him now. "In some of the large, fenced pens, the ground was white with chickens; in others great gaggles of geese swarmed. Birds were countless, numbering not in hundreds, but thousands. Feathers floated in an air charged with cackles, quacks, gobbles and hisses."

"Not music to my ears. I'm with those folks over at the Alexandria Bay hotels who objected to the racket.""

Coming to a bridge over one of the canals I extended my arm to halt Pete, who fell silent. I saw, only a few yards away, what at first seemed to be a statue in the water. Then, more surprising, the figure stirred, silently unfolding great wings. It was the biggest bird I had ever seen. We watched, entranced, as it slowly waved the wings, then nosily flapped them, lifting long legs from the water as it rose and majestically climbed skyward.

"What was that?"

"You're a city boy, aren't you? Just a heron—a Great Blue. They're common here. They have a large rookery over on Ironsides Island."

Mercifully, we returned to the shade of trees that lined the road, planted by Boldt a century earlier. I asked Pete how many employees it took to keep Boldt's Thousand Islands operation going.

"I haven't a total, but surely it ran to hundreds. There were some 150 men employed in quarrying, transporting, and laying up the granite masonry for the Castle, during those years. There were servants in all these houses—lots of them—and all sorts of other staff. He had the boat crews, the boat-building team, a canal-digging team, for instance. I never tried to estimate how many people Boldt employed up here. He even had his own fire department, which conducted drills regularly. All this required a lot of organization, but Boldt was a genius at organization.

"There were four operating divisions, each with managers and employees. First, there was the farm, then there was the fleet of boats, third the golf, tennis, and polo facilities (including the stables), and fourth, the several residences. Managers of all four divisions reported to the superintendent of the Boldt estate. From the Yacht House the superintendent directed an operations and maintenance crew. Licensed engineers were required, not merely to operate the steam engines of each yacht, but to be on duty around the clock, to operate the steam plants at Heart Island, and during the day, at the Yacht House. An electrical engineer and his assistant were on the staff as well. A bookkeeper tended the accounts and payrolls. Boldt was very attentive to detail, and caught the smallest error. The superintendent directed the many carpenters, handymen and night watchmen who were required to maintain the many buildings on several islands."

Golfers came into view. "Was Boldt a golfer?" I asked. Pete laughed.

"Can you imagine him devoting much time to hitting a little ball around a big field? Probably he didn't practice enough to become proficient, but in fact Boldt was said to be an enthusiast. Probably his interest was largely vicarious; his daughter Clover was the pro—a tournament-class golfer."

"Was this golf course early, historically?"

"Not the earliest in the U.S. or Canada, certainly, but one of the top-flight for its early date. It was 'supposed to be the longest in the world, and one of the three best in the United States.' The course attracted regular visitors, some of who lodged at the Hart House. You have to remember that the Golf Club operated in conjunction with the nearby Yacht Club, which provided more extensive dining and socializing.

The Boldt golf course, the eighth or "Windmill Hole"

Also, Boldt himself was a great host, who often entertained large gatherings lavishly at Wellesley House, as Clover did at Hopewell Hall. The Boldts were pivotal to many events that attracted interest and visitors to the Thousand Islands, such as the Gold Cup Power Boat Races, the polo matches, tennis tournaments. Clover One was a proficient—'lightening fast'—tennis player. Tournament class, in fact. These clay courts supplemented private grass courts at the Tennis House, an appendage to Wellesley House. You see the more public Tennis Loggia over there, across the course. It used to be a massive colonnade where observers in wicker arm chairs followed matches on the many clay courts, situated in a large, fenced enclosure behind it. Unfortunately, in later years it was enclosed to make a sort of motel out of it. Ugh. On the water side, the long structure overlooked a sunken parterre of flowers."

"I'll bet Boldt didn't play tennis."

"No, George Boldt probably wasn't to be seen on the tennis courts. He probably didn't race the fast boats he built either. It was Clover and her husband who raced fast boats. And Boldt surely didn't play polo. He merely paid the bills. Polo was an exceedingly costly pastime favored by Clover's first husband, Graham Miles."

"Why so costly? He had plenty of land here for a field."

Stables at Wellesley House

The dovecote in the tower was motifs favored by the Boldts. The horse is
"Jack," personal mount of Boldt's granddaughter, Clover, when a child.

"It's the polo ponies—they don't come cheap, and the Boldts as usual required the
best. They had railroad cars full of fine mounts delivered, when Gus took up polo."

"With his characteristic application, within a few years he 'made the Thousand Islands one of the polo centers of the east.' Folks laughed when he brought the first polo ponies to the River. But the next year they took him seriously, when he had a train bring thirty more in special cars. It was quite a day at the Bay, when all those ponies were rounded up, onto the barges! Boldt built a new polo stable, a practice field and another big, regulation field. Boldt engaged a fellow from Aiken, South Carolina to train the polo ponies. The games drew a large gallery."

"I saw at the Castle a photo of George and Louise Boldt, both on horseback, their children along side. They were horsy people?"

"Were they! Wellesley Island Farms at one time had a hundred and twenty horses, the number declining by 1910 (due to increased use of the internal combustion engine) to fifty-eight. Shortly after Boldt's death, the stable housed one stallion, twelve horses, eighteen mares and seven colts—a total of thirty-eight, plus an ass and twenty-one mules. The family's personal mounts were housed at the Wellesley House stables. The estate provided a track and bridal paths. In later years, Louise enjoyed driving these in her pony cart. The Boldts were also enthusiasts of early automobiles, building hard-surface roads on Wellesley Island for this purpose, contributing $5000 for the one that connected the Boldt estate to the Thousand Island Park community six miles away, at the western end of the large island."

The Chalet today

We walked down a drive to the Chalet. "There was an old farmhouse here," Pete explained. "Boldt replaced it with this villa that had fourteen bedrooms and six baths. He rented the place to celebrities like Geraldine Farrar, the opera star. It's been condominiumized now with some change of character. Over there on Florence Island was another 'palatial' Boldt home. And that cottage over there, believe it or not, was once the Birches, summer home of George Boldt, Jr. and his family. In more recent times it was cut down in size, the upper floors removed. These houses all were self-sufficient, having docks, boat houses and gardens. Each was served by its own domestic staff, although the main estate crews provided building maintenance. Smaller cottages were scattered about. The Tennis House, the most notable of these, was integral to the main residence and gardens of Wellesley House, serving as a guesthouse. At the Play Pavilion nearby there was a small theater, where Boldt in later years entertained guests with current motion picture films, brought from New York City."

"It's hard to put all this together. It seems so sprawling, so disorganized."

"Well, it was Boldt's way to improvise without much of a master plan. But when Wellesley House was here as the centerpiece, the Wellesley Island estate seemed more coherent. There were extensive gardens around the main house. Boldt had another passion. . . ."

"I don't doubt it."

"Yes—flowers. He always had 'two or three gardeners' following him about the grounds, as he pointed with his cane. So as to be always available, the head gardener lived near Wellesley House, in a cottage close to the range of greenhouses here. They not merely provided the Boldt properties on the River with seedlings and cut flowers, but also sent large quantities of seasonal blooms to New York City along

Post card view of Wellesley House gardens

The long pergola at left was flanked by huge perennial borders. Its wide walk led from the main house over the canal bridge to the towered playhouse where motion pictures were shown. Tennis House and its courts were off to the left. Heart Island appears in the distance.

with weekly shipments of farm produce. The most elaborate flower gardens were close at hand, along the canals near Wellesley House.

13.   Walking with Meg from the office toward her home, it was apparent why she had decided to put down roots here. This was a charming village, surrounded by water on three sides. Unlike the Bay, Clayton seemed fairly quiet, even at the height of the season. Riverside Drive was exceptionally wide, having once, she told me, been a parkway, with a median strip of lawn and flowers. Unfortunately the feature had been removed to allow diagonal parking, but the street was still spacious, with intermittent views of the blue river seen through slots between three-story brick commercial structures, little changed from the nineteenth century. Meg didn't stroll, as I was wont, but walked briskly. Making the effort to keep pace, I tried to continue our conversation.

    "Courtney envisions opening the second act with a scene in the Shell Room of the Alster Tower. I took a look at it, when I went to Heart Island. They're restoring it, you know. The Boldts actually had finished it, and lived there, I understand."

Alster Tower

"Yes, the Alster Tower was completed, furnished, and occupied by the Boldts. It was never their summer home, though. They always lived in other, larger houses nearby. The Alster Tower was intended, and always was used, as a sort of casino or game pavilion."

"I've heard it called the Playhouse for the children."

"The children were a little old for kiddies' playhouses—not that teenagers couldn't have fun, of course."

"It's a fun place."

"Sure is." She waved to friends in a passing car. "It was all very ingenious, and there was extraordinary woodwork. I recall a large, pocketed sliding glass door, for example. It was curved —one of a kind. There were few straight or parallel lines in the whole building. No square rooms or right angles. And the section! Marvelous manipulation of space, with split levels and overlapping volumes. Did you notice how the major area, the "Shell Room"—the one you're interested in—is linked visually to four secondary spaces?"

"I guess I've forgotten, if I did know. What are they?"

"The library, billiard room with bowling alley, café-grill—that had an open kitchen (very modern for the time)."

"Pete mentioned that."

"The forth space was a more formal dining room. It's all marvelously integrated: several floor levels meet within, connected by short flights of steps, entwined about massive round columns. I hope your staging can recreate something of the fantastic quality of the interior." We turned the corner, onto a tree-line street that connected a central park with the River.

"Was it called the Shell Room because the ceiling was shaped like a giant sea shell?"

"Yes—the roof, actually, built of structural tile vaults, carried on iron or steel I-beams. The upper roof surface was wild—like walking on the high seas. Nothing was level—almost made you seasick. Great. The whole surface was covered with lead. The valuable material disappeared, of course—mostly stolen, I think, but some of it may have gone, like much of the plumbing, for the two war efforts. After the lead was removed, water leakage ruined the interiors, before they put on some composition gunk. It's not quite the same. Nothing over there seems to be."

"What do you think of all the buildings, architecturally?"

"Oh, what a big question! And I'm almost home. How can I generalize, in a few words? Surely, taken as a whole (including the great Yacht House, almost unique as a survival of a rare building type) the ensemble is absolutely unmatched and irreplaceable—one of the great historic landmarks of the nation, surely. The Alster Tower, like the Yacht House, is absolutely unique—very imaginative and also architectural adroit. Its form doesn't follow any historic precedent so much as the form follows the nature of the material, stone. The shape tapers like a candle,, because a tower (particularly if laid up of rough masonry) ought to have thicker walls at its base. It's a folly, of course, with only one room on each of the upper floors, accessible by exterior stone steps. The rooms get smaller on the upper stories. Diminished size of the tower at the top, together with reduced scale of openings and use of smaller stone higher on the tower, enhances the perspective illusion of height, as well as suggesting stability. It's very clever. The masonry base merges almost imperceptibly into the natural landscape of granite and foliage. It shows real mastery.

Scenic and constructive intentions coincided, accounting in large part for the synergistic quality of this remarkable building. It's great, really."

"That's real critical acclaim. Who gets the credit?"

"I suspect it wasn't Hewitt, architect of the other buildings. But save that for another time."

"Do you think the other buildings—by Hewitt, I suppose—are so remarkable?"

"Architecturally, the Boldt projects are uneven, for many reasons, which require a long narrative of how the estate evolved over the years. The architects—William Hewitt, principally—were very adroit. The design of the castle is really a marvel, especially given the conditions presented the architect and Boldts' curious point of departure. Although they dismantled the old frame house, almost as large as the present structure, and had it moved across the ice to make two large summer homes on Wellesley Island (one still extant) the Boldts didn't give Hewitt carte blanche to design a new building. Instead they insisted on rebuilding the general configuration of the old frame house. I suppose the Boldts were familiar with that arrangement, and so were more confident about what they would get. George was something of a frustrated architect himself, I expect, but he did have ability 'to stand upon the blueprint,' as Oscar put it. Yes, the Boldts were tough clients, with ideas of their own. Of course, they were more limited in their imagination than an architect might be." A big black Lab came bounding to welcome her. I had to side step, as he pranced around us.

"The present Castle is much like the old frame house, then?"

"Yes, very much like it, in its basic arrangement. Even the highest tower recalls the one in the same position, similar in design, on the frame house—the portion that went over to become Wellesley House, where George Boldt spent his last summers."

"But the Castle must be much larger."

"Not so much as you might think. Most of the footprint is the same, with some expansion around the southwest corner, where you find the Reception Room now. The rotunda was a new idea, expanding the size. And the structure became far larger in cubage because of having so many floors cover the whole area. There are five stories now, requiring an elevator—five main levels. There are actually seven stories in all, if you count all three levels of attics under the high roofs, and of the highest tower."

"They seem to have wanted visibility, from some distance, to be seen rising above the treetops."

"Yes, even the old house had some of that landmark quality, since it had very steep roofs and the tower—a functional water tower, originally—like many of these island towers. The tower became a characteristic Thousand Islands motif—hence the popular term "castle" given to some of the grander, masonry summer homes. I think there are nine towers on Heart Island alone—and another tall one on the yacht house. . . and then there was one on Wellesley House, and on the stables. . . . Boldt had this thing about towers."

"Phallic, perhaps?."

Meg laughed. "Goes with the heart motif. One writer called the place 'randy'."

"Yes, that pair of pyramidal roofs on the main front does seem rather. . . mammary." Meg scowled, so I punted feebly. "But he surely had an edifice complex." She kicked it back one better:

"You mean an erection complex." Grinning, she covered her eyes in mock chagrin. "All those towers—I mean, he loved to build things, of course."

"Why did they rebuild, if the new structure was to be not very different from the old, wooden house?"

"Who knows? They wanted stone, not wood. Fire is a big concern on these islands, and Charles Emery had recently built his stone chateau here at Clayton, now demolished, alas. It was on the island where you still see the tall tower, right across from town. No doubt the Boldts wanted to surpass his splendid trophy house. The Boldts built the Alster Tower of stone while their own cottage was still wooden." We paused at the corner of another shady street. "At some point we think that they engaged a gang of Italian stonemasons, who built all sorts of gazebos and landscape follies around the island. These same masons may have adorned other islands, which have similar stone work. The Boldts added a fireproof stone kitchen wing to the frame house, before deciding to rebuild the whole place in steel and masonry construction. Durability is why the Castle survived a half century of neglect." She glanced at her watch. "But this is my turn, and the children are waiting. That's our house—guess which one the architect owns. The one with the funny colors, of course."

"One last question, if you have a moment: why do you think the Castle became so huge?"

"Surely the Boldts added more guestrooms, when they became socially ambitious in their entertaining there. On occasion they had the likes of the Vice President and Attorney General over there—even John Jacob Astor once—but the Boldts really didn't move in that set. Boldt had merely new money, and also served the very rich at his hotels. The Boldts couldn't expect to be regarded as social equals to the second and third generation of families like the Vanderbilts and Astors. Up here George and Louise Boldt were really big frogs in a small pond. Most Islander families at the turn of the century were new-rich, and not very genteel, I suspect. Boldt himself was not well educated, you know—but was an avid reader, talented in many fields, and clearly very intelligent—and even sentimental."

"Pete seems skeptical about all the heart business—the love story of Heart Island. You aren't?"

"Pete knows very well that Boldt was not an insensitive Prussian autocrat, because he told me himself that George Boldt often shed tears, sometimes merely on hearing music. He sang and was a self-taught pianist. He had a strong aesthetic impulse, which contributed to this success, of course. He appreciated paintings, collected porcelain and pottery, and loved flowers—and may have been the first to introduce them to commercial hotels. Cut flowers—roses especially—were almost a trademark of the Waldorf." She glanced at her watch again. "But gotta run. Come see me again."

14.   Courtney was at last to be found at the piano keyboard. He really did compose, as evidenced by papers strewn across the folded music rack. I wondered how he got that big grand back and forth to this island—and up and over the rocky path—every summer. He didn't want to chat, however, but wanted to get down to business. As

soon as I walked in he asked, "Recap the first act for me, will you? Are we all set to go to Heart Island for the second-act opener?"

"Sure. Our fairy godmother, scheming May, has realized our hero's fantasy. She passes the local frog, Bart, off as visiting prince, and cons the New Rich into welcoming him as Old Money. Bart meets Mary, supposed to be one of the privileged set, only to learn that she, too, is trying to break into this league." Courtney, elbow on the music rack, scratched his gray hair skeptically.

"Sort of a wedding of *Pygmalion* and the *House of Mirth*."

"Yeah. With the *Wizard of Oz* thrown in."

"George Boldt is the wizard?"

"You got it."

So what's the cliffhanger for the first-act finale. Gotta leave 'em hanging, you know."

"Well, there's curiosity about Boldt Castle, abandoned the previous year. No one has been allowed over there since Louise Boldt (supposedly) died and all work stopped. When Clover offers to open the Alster Tower for a party, everyone is dying to get over there."

"That's a cliffhanger? How about our love interest? Got the triangle working?"

"Well, our ingenue has set her sights on the comic heir presumptive to a new fortune—an effete fob, practicing to be a patrician—but our diamond-in-the-rough hero, the local boy Bart, distracts her from her mission. At this point, she wonders if our phony prince would be as good a catch—as good a provider, that is. She wonders if his 'old money' might be pretty well depleted. Bart doesn't reveal his humble identity until the climatic Alster Tower scene. Of course, everybody knows throughout who will get the girl, who will come to her senses (with the help of the good fairy, May) so that's not really suspenseful."

"There's got to be the ol' twisteroo someplace. This is pretty pat stuff. Why don't you just read Noel Coward's 'Conversation Piece' and swipe that plot? Pretty clever double twist there, as I recall."

"That can come later in the second act. I think we're OK to open it at the Alster Tower."

"Well, then, about that pivotal party scene: try to visualize a sort of high-class amateur hour—performers on that balcony above the bowling alley, guests assembled in the

Shell Room. I see—and hear—Clover and Estelle, entertain the guests, each singing short, amusing character pieces. One, "Poor Little Clover," may be a parody of the Gilbert and Sullivan ditty about Little Buttercup. Clover is complaining that she lost her childhood to premature social demands. She dislikes her obligation to serve as the Boldt hostess in her mother's absence. Pete tells me that George presided over sort of a captain's table at the Waldorf, where the original ballroom served as his private dining room after the Astoria portion was added with its larger ballroom. The Boldts invited distinguished hotel guests to dine with them in their private quarters regularly. Clover was pressed into service when Louise was ailing and trav-elling for her health in later years, and after her mother died. Clover was a sturdy, athletic girl, a fair Nordic type, contrasted with dark, glamorous Estelle, George Junior's wife. Estelle was a Mexican beauty, quite ravishing compared to plain Clo-ver. There was no love lost between the two. Clover, in fact, regarded Estelle as a big mistake—although she eventually made her own mistake, marrying an indolent sportsman playboy, to the disappointment of her workaholic father. She divorced Miles and remarried. At any rate, Estelle will do something Latin—a tango, per-haps. The tango came in a bit later, actually, and George was dismayed to see it danced at his hotel. He was more the Viennese waltz type, of course."

"Louise frequently was gone, you say, in later years? Travelling? George didn't go with her? Where did she go?"

"Well, she was up here much of the summer, of course. His visits were sporadic. He was ever engaged in his many business affairs. He liked to be present at the Waldorf to receive important visitors and attend major functions. He supposed the place couldn't run without him. And during the years while the Castle was rising, he was building the great Bellevue-Stratford in Philadelphia. He was one to attend to every detail, especially when it came to construction. He was keenly interested. So Louise probably saw him irregularly during her last years. While the Castle was rising, however, he did extend one of his European business trips to indulge in something of a buying spree with Louise. They had so many huge rooms to furnish. Boldt was a poor traveler, and didn't enjoy his trips abroad."

"Interesting. You say that she sometimes went off alone, however—to places other than up here?"

"Oh, I don't know. Ask Pete. I have this impression that she went to spas, espe-cially when she developed health problems. I recall hearing about Carlsbad—and Baden, I think. Of course, George may have been with her on some of these trips, as he occasionally went back to Germany on business, importing for his large hotel operations. He even had a separate importing company. But George would hardly be one to hang around spas for the duration of a 'cure'."

"I'm interested in this notion of Louise being left alone by a workaholic husband. Meg speculated about the hearts all over the place—that perhaps Boldt 'protesteth too much.' Pete seems to be of this mind as well."

"Lots of busy CEOs give their wives costly consolation prizes, you know. Heart Island may have been Louise's project, to keep her placated. But Boldt himself was passionately interested in building, so surely he was involved. In fact, it was pretty much a do-it-yourself project on a colossal scale. But we're off again, on a tangent. Let's get back to work."

15. Prof. Pete was still at his computer, exactly where I had left him three times before. The piles of plastic disk cases seemed even higher. "That must be a long book."

"History takes a long time, to produce a small product. The final publication is merely the tip of the iceberg, summarizing a lot of research."

"I'm feeling guilty about imposing on you so much."

"Obviously I enjoy sharing my special interests. There aren't many good listeners around here. Like most people, they want to talk about themselves. And they've heard all my stories."

I reminded Pete of his observation about unfavorable business conditions at the time when Boldt terminated work on the Heart Island project. I wondered if there might have been any connection with Louise's condition, since she seemed to be having some health prob-

The Bellevue-Stratford Hotel, Philadelphia

The Boldts' original Bellevue Hotel appears to the right before its demolition shortly after the new building was constructed,

lems at the time. What were the problems—psychological, perhaps? Did she drink?

"You're speculating," Pete suggested, but his frown was fleeting. "They said that Louise had been 'in delicate health' for some time. Locally they said that she had 'not enjoyed good health for nearly a year' before she died. Maybe Louise was distraught—by financial reversals that could have affected plans for completion of the Heart Island campaign. Her dream house down the drain—is that it?" He seemed intrigued. "Interesting idea. Hadn't thought of that before. That could account . . . ." His voice trailed off, and he began again: "Others have connected the building campaign with business conditions. It's not my original notion. I recall the view of one of Judge Merrick's descendents: Alden Merrick had been acquainted with Boldt. The lore in that family had it that Boldt paced his building program according to fluctuations of the stock market, where he was heavily invested. They regarded the tragic love story as sentimental nonsense. The Merricks thought that Boldt simply had cash-flow problems in 1904 and laid the workmen off. Could be, of course. There had been a 'Rich Man's Panic' shortly before Louise Boldt died."

"Now that's interesting. When was the panic?"

"It began during the summer of 1903, while Louise was on the River. She left early, during August, to go to Carlsbad."

"There may have been a connection?"

"Possibly. Boldt's financial difficulty may have affected plans for completion of the Castle—his immediate plans, at least. He was building the huge Bellevue-Stratford Hotel in Philadelphia at the time—a 3.5 million-dollar project. Ten years before the original Waldorf had opened just as a grave depression set in, leading to Boldt's breakdown. That brought the Boldts to the River in the first place. Now the Bellevue-Stratford was ready to open as another financial crisis struck. This must have affected their plans for the Castle—certainly their optimistic mood. Perhaps he considered it prudent to cut off the cash drain, and may have suggested this to Louise."

"He might have thought about stopping work even before Louise died?"

"Yes."

"That's not so romantic. Disappointment and worry may have contributed to Louise's condition, sending her abroad for a 'cure.' But even if a matter of practical economics, it's still tragic, in a sense, considering the heroic scale of the enterprise. But Boldt didn't go broke?"

"Hardly. But there were other grave crises and setbacks in the decades after Louise died. It was a bear market early in 1904, after Louise's death. Thereafter, Boldt no longer was amassing a great fortune at the incredible rate of the years over the turn of the century. Nevertheless, he kept buying property here and building, if on a much less ambitious scale. The farm was his main interest—the largest poultry operation in New York State at the time. He wasn't one to do things by halves."

"But did Louise drink? Courtney mentioned her going to European spas for a 'cure.' To dry out, perhaps?"

"Of course Louise drank. Everyone consumed vast quantities of wine with those interminable formal dinners, and Louise favored Manhattan cocktails. But I never heard that she had any serious drinking problem, like some other wives left here by successful but largely absent husbands."

"Were they drinking cocktails way back then? I thought that Manhattans might have come in the Roaring 'Twenties."

"We have an anecdote about Louise as a connoisseur of cocktails. She chided George that the Manhattans served at the Waldorf didn't compare with those at a rival hotel that she frequented, the Holland House. This was at a time when proper ladies (if they appeared in public dining rooms at all) drank cocktails decorously out of porcelain cups purported to contain afternoon tea."

"What do you suppose was the real purpose of that almost maniacal Heart Island project?"

"You don't ask easy questions. Purpose? Our own motives are always tangled, aren't they?—too complicated to unravel ourselves—so should historians speculate about motives of others? But of course we do. We should, however, recognize that there probably is no simple cause for any effect, especially when humans are the cause, because people aren't simple. The Boldts surely were not.

"More reasonably we may suppose there were several notions involved in the ambitious building campaign. One surely was social—not merely to establish visible social credentials for the Boldts, but to facilitate social life, in a communal sense. Surely Boldt Castle was to be for the Thousand Islands what the Breakers was to Newport and Whitehall to Palm Beach: the premier house at a resort colony of many important houses. As such these great houses were intended to provide focus to elite communities and to serve as their social centers."

"And to identify the owners as the host and hostess with the mostest."

" 'The mostest' was important, not merely as sociability, but as property. It's been said that 'the very notion of 'status'—i.e. social stratification based on consumption patterns of style of life—was born or invented in the nineteenth century.' As artists who employed a palette of consumerism to create a seductively attractive social milieu, George and Louise Boldt were masters. Remember that they had successfully made the Waldorf a social center for New York City."

"Too bad they never finished the project here."

"Pity. But the social center is only one aspect of a certain type of country house. We ought to place the Boldts' Thousand Islands estate in another category of country house. There were different species that developed at different times during the late nineteenth and early twentieth centuries."

"The trophy house, or power house?"

"Those were ego-serving aspects, to be sure, but I had in mind the functional distinction between a rural villa intended for occasional use, to provide recreation and entertainment, as contrasted with a large estate envisioned as a domain, a family seat for generations to come. Boldt's notion was quite different from that of most cottagers here, who didn't require thousands of acres and scores of buildings to enjoy a vacation of a few weeks during the summer."

"You think Boldt really thought his family would continue to be based here?"

"For generations yet unborn. That was the European model that he acquired as a boy, seeing the example of the lord of his home island. It's the model of the landed aristocracy, where the family fortune and states is based on a large property, identified by a great house."

"The English 'stately home.'"

"Or the German *Scholss*. This was a new idea that was emerging in America at the end of the nineteenth century—among a small class of people, of course. The American Revolution was far enough behind us for some Americans to look to England and the Continent for older traditions.

"Previously, many wealthy families had left the city by rail to visit vacation hotels or private country homes, principally to escape city heat during several weeks of the summer. Theirs were relatively simple 'cottages,' not 'castles.' Some families, like our Pullmans and Bournes, might have had more than one seasonal country house, each used only for a few weeks, but at different seasons. These folks generally didn't yet live in the suburbs year 'round, but resided in town houses to participate in urban society. The early suburbs—'streetcar suburbs'—of the period were quite

An aerial view before restoration of the Power House shows the Boldts' undeveloped Harbor Island directly behind Heart Island.

densely populated, mostly by families of moderate income, since houses there were built close together so as to allow many residents without their own horses and carriages to live within walking distance of commuter trolleys. Wealthy families relied upon steam railroad trains to give them access to more distant hinterlands. Once aboard a train, a family might travel a considerable distance to a country destination. An overnight trip, as from New York City to the Thousand Islands, might be more convenient in fact than a journey of several hours by horse and carriage during the day.

"Summer colonies of urban families who spent only a few weeks at each place tended to focus on a single activity, such as fishing at the Thousand Islands, racing at Saratoga, or mere socializing, as at Newport. A resort that was visited for merely a short stay didn't need to provide the wide range of amusements that might be required over a longer period, nor did summer homes at these resorts require many varied facilities for recreation. A summer house used only a few weeks of the year might suffice without extensive grounds for outdoor activities. A small Newport lot was considered sufficient even for a palatial house like the Breakers. Belcourt was only one of many large houses built at Newport on interior lots without waterfront.

"These earlier country places were 'cottages' or, in broader historical terminology, 'villas:' temporary, recreational residences in the country for city dwellers. A transformation occurred, generally in the 'nineties, when many affluent builders of country places looked to Europe and discovered the idea of the 'country house.' On the European model, it supplanted the city mansion as the family seat and as a monument to family attainment. Wood was transformed to masonry, and cottages moved from small lots in summer communities to vast domains, isolated in autocratic self-sufficiency, served by farms, even villages of dependent staff.

"Boldt Castle, together with the great Wellesley Island estate, clearly represented a very different notion than even the most ambitious of summer homes built nearby a few years earlier. The Pullmans only spent a few weeks on the River, devoting half the summer to the shore. Castle Rest was still a summer cottage. Boldt Castle, provided with an enormous heating plant to make it livable year 'round, was envisioned

as a different species. Unlike a summer cottage that was shuttered after a month or
so of use, a great country establishment would continue in operation whether the
family was in the city for much of the year, or travelling elsewhere for extended peri-
ods. A great country place was an institution that acquired a life of its own."

"Boldt was so busy in the City—it seems odd to develop such an elaborate operation
as one's permanent residence so far away from one's work."

"Ah, but Boldt knew it was here, going on living a life of its own, whether he was
here or not. And in truth he didn't spend much time up here. But simply knowing
that one's ideal place exists and awaits can provide psychic comfort—as a sort of
escape hatch."

"Strange."

"To us, perhaps. That's what makes it intriguing."

"But don't you think that the simple showplace aspect was most compelling? Pure
vanity?"

"No. I don't agree with simple-minded critics of the time like Veblen who saw only
'conspicuous consumption'—or even sometimes-perceptive Henry James who saw
rich Americans aping European nobility by building these great 'white elephants.'
Expatriate James brought a rather superficial disdain for all things American on his
last visit to his homeland, when he commented on these great country houses. In
the year Boldt Castle was abandoned, *House Beautiful* proclaimed, "It is the rich
man's duty to build the great house. . . . His house is in a measure public property"—as indeed Boldt Castle immediately became a tourist attraction and has continued to be an economic as well as cultural resource of the region. Probably better
attuned than Veblen and James were two other American contemporaries, Harry
Desmond and Herbert Croly. In their important, large opus, *Stately Homes in
America*, they criticized the critic, Henry James. They suggested that these buildings
weren't simply homage of uncultured Americans to their social betters in Europe,
and as such recognition of American inferiority. They observed that 'noble houses,
even when the nobleness is a reproduction, in some measure oblige; and Americans
want them because they feel the need and the value of the intellectual obligation.'"

"Intellectual obligation? Really? Sounds like reaching a bit."

"Perhaps, but consider what Desmond and Croly really meant by this. Newly rich
Americans were often all-at-sea, wondering what their wealth meant. Some thought
that a fortune ought to yield more than mere display. The rewards of achievement
ought to be not mere quantity of possessions, but quality of life. The builders of

stately homes wanted to live up to their new houses. The palaces were a challenge, not easy to live in, but castle builders wanted to find a finer way of life. They looked to the best architects, not merely to provide them with glamorous stage settings on which to strut, but to give them an environment of excellence, in which to excel. They wanted from their house and its designer more than comfort and ostentation; they wanted what was fine in life."

"You don't think they bought antiques and art simply because it was supposed to show good taste?"

"No, not always. The great collectors, like Henry Clay Frick and Andrew Mellon, were genuinely crazy about paintings. Without such patrons who endowed great museums with their personal collections, our whole culture would be poorer. Great architecture, too, requires great patrons. The relationship is reciprocal. Poor surroundings affect occupants adversely, but a finer place for living contributes to a finer life. Architecture, landscape architecture, fine and decorative arts, enrich and ennoble those who live in a truly great house. Life in a work of art may become a work of art."

I sensed that the professor had given this lecture before. With a cautious smile I ventured a reservation. "The new rich wanting their lives, their very persona, to be transformed by their architects reminds me of that earlier hope, that the ruthless Victorian businessman might be saved by his wife's benevolent goodness."

Pete laughed. "The architect as redeemer. Tell that one to Meg."

I continued to be a difficult student. "Not all critics were so accommodating about America's borrowing culture from Europe, were they?"

"No, but William Dean Howells observed that 'with the abundance of money, the imitation (of European culture) is simply inevitable.' New wealth enabled many American families to discover Europe first hand. The notion of 'educating' themselves and the public was involved. European decorative art was readily acquired by traveling Americans. European craftsmanship in the building trades was becoming available at home. Desmond and Croly thought it right that wealthy patrons ought to establish high standards of quality in their buildings, to be emulated by others. That was what money was for—at least for some who had it. Those who didn't might simply regard the big spenders as ostentatious New Rich. Old Money might be contemptuous of the upwardly mobile. The Boldts were really on the make, lower-upper-class, aspiring to the top rung of the ladder."

"Why," I asked, "when they had ample means at their disposal to pursue alternative, less rigorously demanding ways of living, did they lead such complicated, difficult lives? They could have been lounging on a beach instead of worrying about all the social obligations, all this stuff, and all the staff required to keep it going."

Detail of Italian Garden terrace wall

"Yes," Pete agreed, "they did seek difficult challenges. Alva Vanderbilt complained that there was 'no tougher job than a society leader's.' Surely life in Boldt Castle wouldn't have been easy. Why did they opt for this? Perhaps because 'they [felt] the need,' as Desmond and Croly sensed—a need, as another critic said, to fill a 'terrible vacancy.' The stratosphere is a great void. What was achievement for? Accomplishment ought to provide a better life, not merely more stuff—a life that was more fulfilling, ennobled by quality. In short, they wanted to become people of quality.

"A contemporary commentator asked, 'Who knows how to be rich in America? Plenty of people know how to get money; but . . . to be rich properly is, indeed, a fine art. It requires culture, imagination, and character.' Simply building a fine house didn't guarantee results. Even Desmond and Croly recognized 'the fact which stares one in the face in considering these residences is the incongruity between the scenery and the actors.'"

"Yes," I reflected, "the immigrant boy and tavern-keeper's daughter finally building their colossal castle. Surely there were many factors involved in the Boldts' attitude about their ambitious project, and I'll accept these notions as plausible. But I sense the need for something less general, more personal. The place and the campaign to build it were so idiosyncratic. There had to be something more unique about the Boldts and their motivation."

Pete took off his glasses, wiped his brow, and the lecture was over. Now came the informal discussion period. "You know, motivations are conjectural," he observed. "Historians have to be wary about rushing in where novelists have no fear of treading. I had thought, were I to write about it, an ironic title for the book might be 'A Place of Our Own'. Despite the Boldts' lavish trappings of success, one of the things Louise missed, I think, was a real home—a permanent place to call her own. They lived at the Waldorf after they moved to New York, you may recall. They had private quarters, to be sure—but frequently they gave up their own suite to important guests and moved into transients' rooms. And George was always at work, living there. There was no escape to a place Louise could call her own. That's was what Heart Island was supposed to be."

"A consolation prize?"

"You might look at it that way."

"Was it consolation for anything else missing—love, perhaps?"

"Who can know about that? If one were to seek Louise's rival, one might speculate most reasonably that it was George's work. Despite the vast establishment here, George rarely came for more than a few days at a time, and only a few times a season. Suppose Louise hadn't died, and the Castle had been completed: I can't imagine George Boldt changing his ways to spend more time here, even with his own ticker tape and direct telegraph line to the city. Can you picture Louise rattling around in that Castle alone? But of course there would be guests. Lots of guests, in all those rooms. But being on call as a constant hostess? That had been her job. A strange price to pay for sudden wealth. Louise may have been motivated to move out of the hotel, but where to? A colossal house that was a virtual hotel."

"Do you think Louise was unhappy?"

"I hadn't thought of it that way, exactly. But there's that anecdote about Mrs. Vanderbilt, coming back from Europe to behold the stupendous palace that Hunt, her architect built for her, the Breakers, at Newport. They say that she burst into tears, crying, 'This isn't what I wanted at all!' Would Louise have been happy, living in her chateau, or was it George's ambition to house her in a castle? Was Louise already unhappy, and the building project an attempt to give her some positive interest? Who knows? She may have been discontented, perhaps, without knowing why. How ironic, to have so much that everyone else envied, yet to need so much that others already had, and took for granted."

"Like . . . ?"

"We're speculating again—but like a simple home, unburdened by floors full of guests and servants, and by an onerous regimen of prescribed formality. She might have been happier with Courtney's place, if not with my modest digs here. I suspect that Louise fell in love with the old frame cottage, but George may have wanted to transform it into a castle—a trophy house, a prodigy showplace. That may be why the new building initially followed the configuration of the old cottage plan so closely, to reassure Louise. Perhaps she was led to believe that the change would be slight, the new place much like the old. Possibly, on their return from the season in Europe, she was stunned—became alarmed—to see what actually was happening."

"It was incredible. It could have been like the homecoming of Mrs. Vanderbilt."

"Yes."

"And this could help explain the mystery."

"The mystery?"

"Of Boldt Castle—and what happened to Louise Boldt."

16.   Courtney's woodpile was higher when next I saw it, vestigial fragments of noble white pine neatly piled to the roof of the wood shelter. This time I found the composer, similar attired—or rather similarly without attire except for dirty shorts and shoes—dragging large branches, laden with luxurious boughs of long needles that would have decorated a dozen houses at Christmas time.

"Do you do everything around this big place by yourself?"

"Not as much as needs doing, but it's hard to get help during the short season, and I don't like to have work done when I'm not here to check—too much "fixin' up," if you know what I mean. Once we arrived, expecting to see the house trim repainted the same dark green—and were horrified to find it a luminous turquoise. Had to do it all over. We have eighty-seven windows in the main house alone."

"Do you spend all summer washing windows?"

"Not me, but we do have help in the house, you know. But what have you been up to? More Boldt research, I'll bet. The summer's fleeting, and we've got to get our play done. I hope you've not been distracted by starting that Boldt book you threatened to write."

"Oh, but I've been working on our book, too." He frowned at the qualifying adverb. "I found a song that May Irwin actually wrote—composed music as well as lyrics. Bet you don't know this one!"

"What is it?"

""It's fortuitous, that's what it is. It has the black connection, and is pointed counterpoint for the Boldt connection."

"Yes?"

"The subtitle is 'A Negro Hymn'."

"Oh, lord."

"But there's the connection with Ben, the black waiter, but this is really the voice of May, Bart's fairy godmother and guardian angel when our hero has found his way out to the enchanted islands."

"OK, so what's the song?"

"The real name? 'Live Humble.' Imagine May—or a duet of May and Ben—singing that to the Boldts and their guests."

17. "I'm wondering," I mused to Meg, "how Boldt Castle compares in size and importance to other great houses of America."

"It wasn't the only 'castle' on the River, you know, or even the first. That was Castle Rest, built in 1888 by George M. Pullman, the Chicago railroad-car manufacturer. A local reporter in 1890 gushed that it was 'perhaps the most costly summer home ever constructed in the Western Hemisphere.' That may have overstated the claim, but it was an ambitious and important building. During the decade of the 1890s wooden cottages here and elsewhere were supplanted by stone châteaux." She opened a folder to a Xerox. "Here's an early observation about these stately homes of the 'nineties:

> The typical country residence of the New York millionaire . . . remained a [seasonal] villa . . . but it became an elaborate, costly and even palatial villa. The type passed quickly from informality to formality, . . . from a complete lack of social pretension to a conspicuous assertion of social position.

Boldt Castle was exceptionally grand, for sure, but not really unique. Here, look at this." She withdrew a faded old photograph from her folder. "Here's Carleton Villa, the imposing Wycoff summer home on Carleton Island. That's off Cape Vincent. Quite a place, eh? It was thought to be the most expensive residence on the St. Lawrence in the 'nineties. Probably was. It cost more than $200,000, equiva-

Carleton Villa

lent today to more than three million, but was surpassed by Boldt Castle, constructed at the turn of the century. Castle Rest must have cost as much as Carleton Villa, but was even more pivotal architecturally."

"Castle Rest is gone now, isn't it?"

"Yes, dynamited by the family when the locals refused to lower taxes on the vacant building. Carleton Villa is a ruin, which may collapse altogether shortly. The transition from wood to stone, from cottage to castle, occurred here, as elsewhere in the Northeast, more or less in the 1890s. Architects of shingle-clad cottages built in the 'eighties had employed rustic stone occasionally, but mostly for ancillary, decorative elements. In 1888, for Castle Rest, S. S. Beman designed a massive five-story stone tower as the principal element of the house, much of which was shingle-clad. The service wing and powerhouse were both masonry structures. A few years later, Charles Emery built a sandstone 'castle' on Calumet Island, across from Clayton. The many-towered chateau greeted the Boldts when they first arrived at the Clayton railroad depot. No doubt George Boldt had these three monumental houses in mind when he said he intended to build the finest house on the St. Lawrence River."

"How about palatial homes at Newport and elsewhere?"

"In size, or cost, you mean—or architecturally? Comprehensive surveys have regarded Boldt Castle as one of the nation's most important residential buildings. Surely its size alone ranks it in the fore. Counting rooms is an inexact measure, since some may count bathrooms and corridors, even closets, to exaggerate reputed size of a house. Others may count only the principle rooms, excluding service elements. Nevertheless, in general terms, probably Biltmore was virtually in a class by itself as the largest house ever constructed in the United States, with a reputed 250 rooms. Otto Kahn's place on Long Island, Oheka, is said to be the second largest with 127 rooms."

"How many rooms in Boldt Castle?"

"The Castle was also supposed to contain 127 rooms, but they may have been counted differently. An article when construction began gave the number of rooms in Boldt Castle as 127, but thirty of these were said to be bathrooms, reducing the number to 97."

"Thirty bathrooms?"

"Yes, thirty, but one author gave ninety as the number of rooms plus thirty-one bath rooms. By my own count, on the floor directly above the main level there are seventeen large rooms, not including obvious bathrooms, closets, and corridors. There are the same number of rooms on the third floor, which is identical to the second, and twelve on the fourth, and one on the fifth floor. This brings the total number of major rooms, above the main floor, to forty seven."

"That's a lot of bedrooms."

"But the rooms weren't all for sleeping. Two were designated as common spaces—the Roof Garden and Reading Room on the fourth floor, and another large space up there, by tradition, was supposed to have been intended as a 'studio'—sometimes said to be for George, Jr. (although I never heard he had any artistic inclination. It might have been more of an overflow dormitory for his male college chums, who might come in numbers). Ten to sixteen of these rooms probably would have been allocated to servants. If we deduct three chambers clearly designated on the plan for Mr. and Mrs. Boldt and daughter Clover, twenty-five to thirty-one bedrooms remain for visitors. Some of the rooms could be thrown together to form suites for families, or providing sitting rooms or else sleeping rooms for guest's personal attendants. Guests in this league sometimes brought a nursemaid, a lady's maid, or a valet, or all three. This makes room designation difficult, as well as an estimate of number of guests that might be accommodated. Furthermore, double occupancy wasn't normally anticipated in this set, where husband and wife might be provided separate sleeping rooms (as indeed George and Louise Boldt had) but couples might share a connecting sitting room. According to one account, 'the building will contain twenty-seven suites of [guest] rooms.' But I count only twenty-five to thirty-one guest bedrooms, not that many suites of rooms."

"I'm interested in imagining the kind of life that would have gone on in such a place—and how Louise Boldt might have fit into it. I suppose twenty-five or thirty guest rooms might not mean as many as fifty or sixty guests?"

Carleton Villa Today

After more than a century, one of the landmark buildings of the Thousand Islands stands in ruinous condition. The Wycoff house has lost its great tower, seen in the picture on page 83.

"No, that would be only with double occupancy of all the rooms, and without some being used as sitting rooms or without guests' servants occupying some of the rooms. I expect that twelve to fifteen couples would be more like the usual guest list."

"How does this compare with house parties at other country places of this class?"

"Biltmore, for comparison, has thirty-four 'master bedrooms.' Similarly, that great house might accommodate some fifteen or so visiting couples in regal Vanderbilt style—and indeed Boldt Castle might have entertained the same number."

"Twenty-five or thirty guest bedrooms still seems rather institutional—not much of a real home. Are we sure this wasn't supposed to be an exclusive hotel?"

"George Boldt denied that rumor at the time. The size of the dining room appears to confirm that it wasn't to serve as a conventional restaurant. The room seems designed to serve a single group together at one long table. The convention of the time in this set was to entertain as many as twenty-four at dinner, but the Boldts always did things in a big way. In the remarkable Boldt china collection was a set of Sèvres porcelain for forty-eight places, especially commissioned. In New York Louise commonly entertained as many as thirty-eight guests for dinner, fifty for buffet suppers, and three to four hundred at receptions."

"How do you know that?"

"The food was prepared by the Waldorf-Astoria kitchens, and the menus are in the New York Public Library Archives. So if the Boldts were accustomed to dinner parties for as many as thirty-eight guests, bedrooms for thirty or so guests might be consistent, allowing for some local folks to be invited for dinner as well.

"The Castle dining room really isn't so huge as you might expect, given the number of other rooms. The Boldt dining room isn't all that much larger than that at Fulford Place at Brockville, for example, which regularly accommodated a conventional number of twenty-four at table. "

"So you envision about fifteen couples as guests normally?"

"We know that Louise entertained fifteen couples at dinner parties up here while the Castle was being built. It's my considered opinion that a dozen or more couples would have been the rule. Of course, we haven't even talked about bedrooms in the Alster Tower, but I expect that they may have been more intended for the younger generation that might be bored with the dressy and interminable formal receptions and dinners. Others have given higher estimates of the number of guests to be accommodated in the Castle. The *Architectural Record* article, written while Boldt was still alive, said that the Castle was unusual for its "unusually large number of apartments [that] accommodate fifty or more guests, besides family [and] servants. But I think the writer, probably unaccustomed to the generous life style of these great houses, made a common mistake of thinking that every guest room would be shared by a couple, like a commercial middle-class hotel. On that basis, the twenty-five or thirty guest bed rooms could house fifty or more visitors."

"So, to get back to the question, then, how does the Castle compare in size to Biltmore and other great houses in America?"

"Oh, you want me to say it's number two or three, don't you? It's not so simple. We don't have good statistics, and when we do get definite numbers, we don't know how they were figured. Here's the best I can do:

"On the main level the Castle has fifteen major rooms—again not counting closets and corridors. Perhaps nine or ten rooms in the lower level would have been finished spaces. This would bring the total number of designated 'rooms' only to

The dining room has received some temporary finishes, not of the quality anticipated had the room been completed. Furnishings are not original but suggest scale. A barren appearance is attributable largely to the absence of carpet and window draperies.

about seventy-two—still no mean number. So some fifty-five of the 127 rooms originally counted then must have been secondary spaces, such as stairwells, passages, and many service and storage rooms. The Bridge Authority supposes that the place has 'over 120' rooms."

"You said that the place on Long Island, number two, had 127 rooms? So Boldt Castle comes close to Oheka as the second largest house in America?"

"If you consider that the Boldts had so many other buildings on the estate, it might well exceed Oheka. George Boldt, Jr., while a bachelor, may have occupied the Alster Tower together with his friends. If we throw in the 56-room Wellesley House, the Tennis House, the Chalet, Florence Island, the Birches, the Golf House, Hopewell Hall (no mean cottage). . . to say nothing of the great houseboat, the yachts, and other staff houses, or the farmhouse and ancillary buildings, the Boldt estate complex probably was one of the grandest in America."

"So we might safely say that Boldt Castle, if not number two, was at least number three in importance?"

"Not so fast. There were many large houses built between the 'nineties and the Great Depression of the 1930s—sometimes called 'the Country Place Era.' Many were comparable in size to each other, averaging about a hundred rooms. I've compiled a list, which you can have—make it a footnote or appendix to your book, if you like. There are, let's see, nine more important country houses that seem comparable—and the list might be expanded."

"Where are these places?"

"Oh, two outside Philadelphia, a couple at Newport, another on the Hudson, and one each in California, the Berkshires, Palm Beach, and Lake Forest, near Chicago. But such a selection is tentative—more representative than definitive. I think it's more prudent to say that the Boldt estate was among the most ambitious private properties ever developed in this country. Shortly after the Castle was built it was recognized in a national architectural journal as being 'among the most important dwellings in America.'"

18.   Courtney's island should have satisfied anyone. Who would trade a Heron for a Heart Island? Who would give up the natural quality, like a serene Japanese garden, with gray and orange lichens on pink granite rocks, combined with clinging ferns? Who would need an artificial Italian Garden with massed beds of flowers, raised on a massive masonry terrace? Why Italian fountains, when surrounded by American water?

Courtney didn't need to ponder that question long. "That's easy. Our situation was different. The second generation of my family was already here when the Boldts arrived," Courtney recalled. "If not so rich, we were secure—financially, but more importantly, socially. Island families of our vintage didn't need to prove anything to anyone. As the Brahmin matron commented, when asked what sort of fashionable chapeau she would acquire for a forthcoming event, 'Boston ladies *have* their hats.' We didn't need new chapeaux or new chateaux. We came here to fish."

"Somehow I can't see Boldt sitting out with a fish pole." Courtney smiled agreement. His notion of patrician reserve required modesty about his property, which was in fact a rare survival of the sort of grand country house now difficult and costly to maintain. I was a mere "caller," a day visitor, not a houseguest. I didn't participate in family's social circle, but as merely a business associate was booked into a nearby hotel. I never got to the upper floors of Courtney's place, but there must have been eight or ten bedrooms on the second floor (still occupied by the extended family and guests) plus a warren of smaller servants' rooms under the roof on the third floor—rarely used now because they were so warm. Courtney's grandparents had brought a staff of twelve with them. The crew had been comprised of local men. Their quarters at the boathouse were favored now by the younger generation. The family now affected a "camp" mystique, albeit surrounded by valuable nineteenth-century antiques on worn oriental carpets.

"How did your family regard the Boldts?"

"With consternation, amusement—but not without wonder, and perhaps even awe, to be honest. The Boldt project surely had everyone bowled over, even if the old-timers feigned disdain for new exhibitionism."

"Did the Boldts fit in—to Thousand Islands society, I mean?"

"Well, in a sense, the Boldts invented society here. You see, for the first three or four decades, families here came to get away from urban 'society'—'high society,' that is. There was enough of that during the winter in New York and Chicago. There wasn't much socializing among islanders until the heyday at the turn of the century, and the Boldts were central to forming a social colony here. Until they came, the island establishments were more like the Great Camps of the nearby Adirondacks, where old New York families escaped, to hide from view amid thousands of acres of wilderness. Similarly, an island with a cottage large enough to carry on a continual house party was its own community."

"Your family got to know the Boldts?"

"The Boldts made a point of getting to know us, you might say. But the summer is so short; one doesn't see neighbors all that much. We all belonged to the Yacht Club, of course, and everyone was acquainted with one another. There were naturally lots of dinner parties and outings on one island or another and on boats."

"Why did the Boldts settle here, if they sought sociability? Why not Newport?"

"Newport was beyond them. After all, Caroline Astor—"*The*" Mrs. Astor— was in full sway there, at Beechwood—an old cottage, not much larger than this place, and not nearly so grand as Boldt Castle. But the Astors owned the Waldorf-Astoria, you know. Boldt served the likes of the Astors."

"I thought Boldt owned the hotel, which was where he made his fortune."

"Yes, that's a common supposition. In truth, he wouldn't have been nearly such a big spender, had his money been tied up in that property. He put it to better use, investing a fantastic cash flow in the Bull Market, which parlayed it into more cash. That's another story, and quite a story—get Peter to tell it. He's better informed. The Boldts wanted to turn the Thousand Islands into another Newport—a sort of

Postcard view of Belle Isle, built by the Boldts and sold to the Peacocks of Pittsburgh

second class Newport for third class millionaires. But really, the idea wasn't theirs. Several Islander families courted the Boldts and entertained them here, because they wanted to establish a social colony. The Boldts were seen as contributors. Boldt was widely acquainted with the rich and famous, of course, because of his business. Several folks in the Alexandria Bay neighborhood wanted to build a clubhouse. They sought subscribers, and they introduced the visiting Boldts at a large, community reception. This was just after he opened the Waldorf. It was a shrewd move for those interested in development of our resort. Boldt not only came with great largesse himself, contributing to the club, but brought other prominent and expansive New Yorkers."

"Pete pointed out the island where the club house used to stand."

"Yes, Welcome Island—the big old barn of a place is gone now. Went in the Depression."

"You remember it?"

"I was a youngster, and the glory days were long past by the 'thirties. I remember the shaggy, shingled building abandoned, looking sad. But I still have Dad's navy blue blazer with the Yacht Club crest, and we still have club burgees—the little pennants, you know—for our boats down in the boathouse. Somewhere we even have the old membership lists (a register of yachts, actually)—attractive little booklets printed annually. Sort of an Island Social Register of the time."

"Your family must have had a large boat, too, judging from the size of your boathouse."

"Oh, everyone did, before the First World War. Then the government acquired the larger ones, for the war effort. They never came back. The age of steam was over, anyway."

"I've looked at the photos on the wall. They were all steam yachts, apparently, as all had smoke stacks."

"Yes, the era of the larger yachts—there were dozens here over a hundred feet long—was prior to the internal combustion engine—which was just coming in. The Boldts built roads on Wellesley Island for the new novelty, automobiles. The new-fangled contraptions were for the kids. George and Louise were horse people, you know."

"Yes, Pete told me."

"Very fine horses. I think my grandfather admired the polo ponies more than anything else the Boldts displayed so conspicuously. Boldt was quite a horseman himself. He rode regularly in Central Park. Louise, in later years, contented herself mostly with a pony cart. The whole family was horsy. They had a polo field, after Clover married, and polo ponies. The matches brought a lively crew of young men, to the delight of all the young ladies."

"Heron Island didn't have one of the tall boathouses, did it?"

"No, our family wasn't into the showy masted yachts. Neither were the Bournes nor Pullman-Lowdens. That was more the Emery-Boldt-Peacock crowd. New money."

"But your yacht house is big."

"The boats were big enough to carry a whole house party on an island tour, and the boathouses also were large because they often housed the crew, as well. You see, it took ten or more hands to operate the big boats, and if the crew were to be on call at the whim of the owner, they had to reside in yacht-house quarters. The skipper was generally a local man, who knew the River, and he would live in town, but be expected to rush over on a moment's notice."

"Did the Boldts dominate Island society?"

"Oh, no. They simply put on the grandest show. Others were really more prominent nationally and, I suppose, far richer."

"Who?"

"Oh, Commodore Bourne, down at Dark Island Castle. Probably he had the greatest fortune—Singer Sewing Machine money."

"Commodore?"

"Of the New York Yacht Club. George Pullman, the railroad car manufacturer, who built Castle Rest, led the Chicago contingent. Probably both Bourne and Pullman outclassed Boldt financially. They both built marvelous summer homes here, but had other seasonal homes, one on Long Island's North Shore and the other at Long Branch in Jersey. They weren't driven like Boldt to spend vast sums on one grandiose project. Boldt was obsessive. I suppose he had recollections of aristocratic country seats of noble families in Germany. Most other Islanders came here to escape from chores, but Boldt created a vast rural estate, with a huge farm operation. He was compulsive about work. But why are we talking about the Boldts all the time? Is your mind on that book, instead of ours?"

"No, I've brought some first-act revisions. I'll give you a recap: Bart, our hero, is passed off by May as a visiting scion of Old Money and so becomes the fraudulent houseguest of a comic fop, the heir-presumptive to New Money. The inane young man regards this as a social coup. Mary appears on the scene; she turns out to be (she hopes) the 'fiancée' of Bart's host. It's clear that she's looking for 'a good provider,' as she puts it. Obviously her silly intended is no match for the local boy romantically. No suspense here, of course, about what will happen. We've got to play it for the laughs. There's interaction between May and Fay to enliven it—catty, comic stuff between two rival stage stars, right?

"Here's my next thought: let's get Bart, a local mechanic incognito, involved in the Gold Cup Races—we can build to the big event at the end of the second act. Bart will be offstage driving one of the powerboats—but there will be lots of noise and suspense until he reappears. He loses the race, but wins the girl. Like it?"

"There's got to be more to fill up a second act than an offstage race. You didn't mention my Alster Tower scene. You've got to get everyone over to Heart Island somehow, where Clover and Estelle can sing my numbers. This will be a big musical scene. That's where the climax should be, not some offstage race."

"I'll work on it."

19.   I finally caught Professor Pete away from his computer. He was on a narrow dock appended to his boathouse, seated in a vintage Lyman, puttering with its outboard motor.

"We were just talking about yachts, over at Heron Island."

"This is as close as I'll ever get, to a yacht, or to an antique boat. I envy Courtney his collection of skiffs and runabouts."

"The Boldts obviously had a collection of boats, judging from the size of the yacht house."

"Oh, of course. They had his-and-hers yachts, one might say. But really, the parents favored the big steam yacht, the "Louise," and the kids used smaller boats. They had lots of them—built racing craft in the yacht house shop, in fact. Clover and Gus Miles were into racing. We had the international Gold Cup power boat races here, after the turn of the century, you know."

"Yes, I heard about them, but don't know much."

"You must visit the Antique Boat Museum at Clayton—and look at Roger Lucas's compilation of pictures of Boldt boats, a whole volume devoted to the subject."

Bow of houseboat "La Duchesse" and yacht "Louise" at the Boldt Yacht House, being expanded at right to provide an additional berth for the great houseboat

"Do they have any Boldt boats at the Museum?"

"Yes, some on loan at the Yacht House, and they'll be getting the great Boldt house-boat, 'La Duchesse.' Andy McNally is leaving it to them. The McNallys are an old Island family, part of the Chicago contingent. It's the map-publishing family, you know—Rand McNally."

"I saw 'La Duchesse' on the island tour. With all these buildings, why on earth did the Boldts need a huge houseboat, pray tell?"

"Did they *need* any of this stuff? Like the Castle, the houseboat was unfinished when Louise died."

"Did Boldt use it later?"

"Can you imagine him sitting aboard a houseboat? Doing what? He probably went aboard once in a while to check its maintenance. He thrived on that sort of thing."

"The houseboat was restored by McNally?"

Afterdeck of the houseboat "La Duchesse"

"He got it from Ed Noble—the Life Savers man who bought most of the Boldt property here, you know. The houseboat had sunk inside its berth in the Boldt yacht house. McNally had it raised, and a whole new steel hull rebuilt. It's quite something. Have you ever seen a boat with fireplaces aboard?"

"No, really?"

"Yes, and a Tiffany stained-glass skylight, bronze door handles especially cast with the Boldt crest—you ought to see it. 'La Duchesse' was said to be the largest house-boat in the world. I'll introduce you to Andy."

20.   Andy McNally, an affable fellow with white hair but ruddy color, came through the garden carrying a bucket. "Been berrying," he said. "Want some?" So much for formalities. He lurched into a guided tour of his vegetables and flowers, of far less interest to me than the great, white backdrop of floating building, with large glass windows, striped awnings, flowers in tubs and boxes, and an inviting gangplank. The McNally family summer home was nearby, now occupied by the younger generation, Andy explained. He preferred to live aboard the houseboat. I didn't ask, but supposed he planned to give the huge vessel to the Antique Boat Museum in part because it might be more than his family might want to maintain in the long haul. His larger motivation however was altruistic; he knew how much the unique Boldt relic appealed to the public.

Saloon of the houseboat "La Duchesse," moored in canal with Wellesley House seen though windows. A stained glass skylight illuminates the piano in the alcove, with the spacious dancing deck beyond.

We passed through a covered rear deck, large enough for a dancing party, but now filled with wicker furniture. "This was made large enough for dancing, almost eighteen by fifty feet, with no columns or other obstructions. But too noisy out here," he explained. Fiberglass speed boats and jet skis flitted about, while a huge freighter approached.

"Can that ship get through this narrow channel?"

"Yes, without making as much noise as these little waterbugs." At the end of the deck, flanking a bay window, were matched doors with stained glass panels containing the Boldt emblem. He held a screen door open for me. The large "saloon," as I suppose one calls a genuine drawing room aboard a boat, was paneled in dark Mahogany with fluted Ionic pilasters, the room lightened by a beamed ceiling painted white. The glow of the stained glass skylight in the bay window fell on one end, while a formal fireplace terminated the room. We sat down on a sofa, across the room from a large sheet of glass, now covered with a translucent blind to filter the late morning sun. "I'd never guess I wasn't on terra firma."

"You will, in a moment." Then came the roll. "That's the wash of the freighter you saw passing." There was a sort of puffing sound beyond the shaded window. "When two of them meet in this channel, they sound the horns to confirm on which side of one another they'll pass. It's noisier then—most noticeably in the middle of the night!"

I noticed the paintings, gilded frames contrasting with the dark wood walls. "Thousand Islands scenes, aren't they? Very attractive."

"Impressionist, from the turn of the century. My parents picked them up locally, from a visiting artist—not well known today. But if you're interested in paintings, I'll show you their best discovery. Come." On our way he explained that this level had, opening off a central stair corridor, an original den and smoking room, together with one bed room and two baths. He led me down a flight of stairs, into a formal paneled dining room. Over the fireplace was a larger framed canvas—the view from an elevated island of other islands, receding into the distance.

"Inness," Andy stated.

"George Inness? You don't leave that here all winter!"

"Of course not. I wrap it up and hand carry it with me in the plane, back to Chicago. But tell me again what you're up to."

Climbing the stairs back to the saloon, I explained that my official mission here was Courtney's play, but my interest in the Boldts was turning into another project, a book about Boldt Castle—and I was hoping to interest Clover Boldt Baird in the project. "But who will buy your book? Why, even Clover isn't interested in finding out much about her grandparents. If the family doesn't care, who will?" I mentioned the increasing number of visitors to Heart Island. "But they're content with the legend," Andy protested. "Why would they buy a book, to tell them what they already get free over there?"

"I think there's more to the story, something different that hasn't been told. Maybe Mrs. Baird can help."

"Oh? I doubt it. We've been here as long as the Boldts, and I don't recall hearing much different, except that Boldt may have been concerned about his cash flow when the market decline after the turn of the century. He was rather profligate, obviously, carrying huge payrolls up here, digging canals and reclaiming marshes, as well as starting new building projects all the time. But we all know that. So what's new?"

Saloon of "La Duchesse," the Boldt-McNally houseboat

"I won't know until I find it. But I don't think that much searching has been done."

"There's that Lucas fellow. He's produced those booklets, several of them, about the Boldt projects. Carries them around in the trunk of his car, leaving them on consignment at newsstands. I suppose he sells some, for all his exertion. You're not about to do that?"

"No. I thought that a regional publisher, perhaps a nearby university press, might be interested. Syracuse or Cornell, maybe. This will be more than another picture book."

"Well, good luck. We're always interested in local history, and surely will buy some copies. The family, I mean. Rand McNally doesn't do conventional trade books, you know."

"Of course." A middle-aged woman in white uniform stepped in to remind Mr. McNally that his lunch and the *New York Times* were on the dining table, which was my clue to depart.

21.   I found myself looking forward to the short drive to the comfortable village of Clayton, and mounted the narrow, steep stairs with pleasant anticipation. I found Meg perched on a stool, sketching on a short roll of yellow tracing paper. Without the now familiar kerchief, she tossed her blond hair, brushing it back as she rose to greet me.

"What shall we talk about this morning?"

"I've read that Boldt Castle is a replica of a historic building on the Rhine."

"Nonsense."

"What about this business of Boldt seeing castles on the Rhine when a boy?"

"He didn't live anywhere near the Rhine, but on an island in the Baltic Sea. Probably, like many tourists, he saw the Rhine River landmarks in later years. I suppose he went there to buy wine in quantity for his hotels. There's some similarity between the Castle's main tower and one on a well-known *Schloss* on the Rhine. That form doesn't seem very French, as does much of the exterior detail on the castle—much of it in a *François Premier* style apparently preferred by the architect, who surely looked at Chambord and other chateaux of the period. Perhaps Boldt brought back a German postcard as a model for the main tower."

"Boldt's own taste ran to the Germanic rather than French?"

"Naturally, I suppose. He was born German. Hardenbergh, of German Dutch descent, had designed the original Waldorf Hotel in a neo-German Renaissance mode. Astor, who owned the property, was himself similarly of German descent. But I wouldn't characterize Boldt Castle as a whole as being specifically German in style. It's a creative synthesis of many things. There's more French about it, perhaps, than German—William Hewitt traveled in Europe and probably saw French chateaux, and the Bellevue-Stratford, designed for Boldt concurrent with the Castle is French Renaissance in style—but of course Boldt Castle is really an American fantasy."

"You told me that the Boldts were probably involved in the design. They weren't ones to leave everything to their architect but wanted to have things exactly their own way, right? "

The original Waldorf Hotel, on the site of William Waldorf Astor's Fifth Avenue residence at 33rd Street, Henry J. Hardenbergh, architect

"Sure. Here's an example: we know, from the architect's two designs for the Arch of Triumph and flanking colonnades, that Hewitt favored something more stylistically correct and finished, whereas the Boldts insisted on something more romantic and rustic. In fact, it was said that the 'architects [made] each drawing exactly as George suggested." The Boldts were intensely interested in these projects, but the Castle grew to such a colossal project that it might have been beyond them to control. They went abroad for a period when many decisions probably were made. I suspect that what they got wasn't exactly what they anticipated. An article that appeared when the castle project first was announced suggested that the character would be more medieval and fake-antique. I recall mention of rough stone being "mossy." Instead, they got crisply cut new granite, carefully laid up. The French chateau forms and the French Renaissance detail of roof dormers and chimneys probably wasn't recognized by the Boldts, whose own taste may have been closer to the fantastic Alster Tower.

"Even if fictitious and inauthentic, choice of style was important. At the time, important houses in this league were being built in many styles. Which to choose? As one writer observed, 'An upper-middle class house is a visible symbol of economic power. A symbol is like a word. One must know what it means, and that can only be done through memory. Thus the house, as symbol, must be in a known style with known connotations.' That was penned by an architect who had done many houses. He knew his clientele. He went on to say, "If (a house) is in a new style, one can not readily tell how expressive it is, or what class lives in it. Considerable experience is necessary before it becomes generally known to be cheap or costly, upper, middle, or lower class. This fact tends to make the upper-middle class extremely conservative, particularly as regards style. The style must be an old one, with clear honorific overtones...."

Biltmore

"The chateau style, with these high, steep roofs and towers, was in favor then?"

"Of course, Frederick Vanderbilt's 'Biltmore' in North Carolina, the largest house in America, was in this mode, as was 'Oheka,' Otto Kahn's place on Long Island, said to be the second largest. Kahn was Jewish. Perhaps the continental character appealed to those who didn't identify themselves with the wasp establishment. The Jewish Rothschild's Waddeston Manor in England was incongruously in the French chateau mode. Harbor Hill, Clarence Mackay's elegant house on Long Island was of this style—he was Irving Berlin's alienated father-in-law, you recall. Mackay was a Catholic (Irish, I suppose) who was socially insecure, so he cut off his daughter and

Oheka

her Jewish husband. I suppose that the mainline English Georgian tradition appealed less to those not to-the-establishment-born than a Continental style."

"What do you think might have been early influences that Boldt may have brought from his German childhood?"

"You mean architectural influences? Obviously more important were broader personal experiences that shaped his character." She went to the window, where the air conditioning unit was merely whirring, and flipped a dial. Now it rumbled ominously. "Sorry. Early morning is quieter, but it gets hot early. You were saying?"

"Let's start with the more particular matter of influential buildings he might have known."

"The island of Rügen [she pronounced it "Roor-gen"] isn't known for its important buildings. It was a rural backwater, isolated in the Baltic Sea, except for one aspect: it was an emerging summer resort for the city of Berlin."

"Aha!"

"Yes, and Rügen was much like the Thousand Islands in many ways, with granite outcroppings, northern woodlands, a deeply broken shoreline, with many promontories, bays, and wetlands—and many smaller islands around the big one. Surely the similar character of the Thousand Islands struck a chord with Boldt."

"Were there hotels and summer homes on his native island?"

"Don't visualize a colony of weekend commuters. Berliners didn't maintain cottages on the island, but rather they spent quiet vacations at modest hotels—and there weren't many of those. The enclave was very low key, but toney. Very genteel. Elizabeth von Arnim—delightful novelist (I've read all of her stuff)—described quiet life in these hotels later in the century, when the resort still was little developed. The watering hole was largely the invention of the local lord, the Graf, or Count, who later became the Prince of Putbus. Like most early nineteenth century resorts it was envisioned as a health spa, where the newly urban affluent went purportedly with serious intent of physical rejuvenation. I don't imagine that Putbus, the resort town, was exactly the fast lane. Pretty sleepy, by our standards, no doubt."

"And so Boldt may have been influenced by the hotel culture of the resort, directing him toward his primary vocation as *hôtelier*."

"Probably. He left at age thirteen, when young men not destined for college left school and began a trade apprenticeship. Apparently George Boldt's father was something of a superintendent or business manager for the count, perhaps even operating a hotel establishment."

"Have you seen the resort buildings?"

"Some old engravings. The early ones were tastefully neo-classical in style, as one might imagine. They were built in Germany's Beidermeir period, roughly corresponding to our Greek Revival episode."

"There isn't much neo-classical about Heart Island."

"No, except the Triumphal Arch and Peristyle. Those planned colonnades did recall a waterside villa on Rügen, where similar colonnades connected detached buildings. But of course the more direct model for the Arch of Triumph and flanking colonnades was the Chicago World's Fair, which was opening about the same time as the Waldorf. It's interesting that Hewitt originally proposed a more correct classical style for the feature. Apparently the Boldts rejected it, preferring a more rustic interpretation, rendering it less incompatible with the nearby Alster Tower. Here, I'll show you the original design."

"And I thought those two pyramidal roofs on the castle were mammary. Look at those two domed pavilions!"

Meg laughed. "I hadn't thought of them that way, but they *are* called "temples of love," you know."

"I don't suppose Boldt saw anything like that back in Germany—but he probably was impressed by the house of Count, or Prince. It must have been an imposing residence."

"Well, considering it was an island in the Baltic Sea, perhaps it was imposing. Probably young Boldt found it impressive. The villa was large for the place, but not nearly so grand as Boldt Castle. Not so interesting, really."

"Was there any similarity?"

"Not much, except it was rather roofy, like most older German buildings built before the classical revival. They all have steep, red tile roofs there—like the Castle. Before Boldt left Rügen, a "big, fantastic' new hotel was built near the famous cliffs on the island, which probably impressed young George. What may really be pertinent is a *Jagdscholoss*, or hunting castle that the Graf built in his shooting preserve.

He commissioned Germany's preeminent important architect of the time, Karl Friedrich Schinkel, to design a romantic folly. It was, oddly, not in the prevailing neo-classic style of the period, which was the specialty of the architect. It was rather—would you believe—a stone mini-castle?"

"Now we're getting some place."

"Yes. Like the Alster Tower (and unlike most German buildings, and virtually every structure on Rügen) it didn't have steep roofs—or even any visible roofs. Like the Alster Tower, it was dominated by a central shaft of many stories, rising to an observation deck behind stone battlements."

"You have a picture?"

"Here—but see, there isn't any specific resemblance, beyond the notion of the basic form."

Jagdschloss Granitz, Rügen

"The Alster Tower really seems more interesting—more inventive, doesn't it?"

"I agree. Romantic castles weren't really Schinkel's *métier*."

"Have you found any other models for Boldt buildings?"

"Well, there's a curious connection—coincidental, perhaps—but intriguing. Kaiser Wilhelm's mother, Princess Victoria of England (Queen Victoria's daughter), who became Kaiserin of Germany, built a retirement villa in her later years that bears some semblance. It was constructed shortly before Boldt Castle. Possibly the Boldts saw it on one of their European treks."

"The Boldts wouldn't have visited royalty?"

"Probably not, but Boldt knew Vicki's brother-in-law, Prince Henry, who had stayed at the Waldorf. Boldt always tried to be personally attentive to important guests. He may even have met Vicki and Fritz much earlier. They visited Rügen when he was a youngster, sojourning there on the royal yacht during their honeymoon."

"Probably the great yacht made an indelible impression on the boy."

"Yes, and possibly—although it seems a remote possibility—young Boldt was introduced by the Graf to the important visitors. Perhaps Boldt retained a personal sense of identification with the Kaiser and Kaiserin, in contrast to their son, who became

Kaiser Wilhelm. Wilhelm, a difficult and perhaps unbalanced man, became alienated from his widowed mother, in large part because she was English. The First World War, you recall. Her husband Fritz was briefly Kaiser before his early death. He had been progressive in his views and was recalled by the liberal faction in Germany as the lost hope.

Friedrichshof, Kronberg

"This is a picture of Vicki's rural retreat, Friedrichsfhof. See, it's chateauesque. There's some similarity to the elevation of Boldt Castle that faces the main channel. And the tall tower appears about where it would be on Boldt Castle. Furthermore, there's an arch of triumph on that side. One doesn't often find classical triumphal arches on romantic castles, in Europe or in America. All in the all, the coincidences are remarkable."

"Was there any particular occasion when the Boldts might have visited the place?"

"Vicki built it near a spa—a resort town, and we know that Louise favored these spas."

"Why do you suppose the triumphal arch appeared on the German model?"

"That's clear—it's inscribed as a memorial to Vicki's husband, Fritz. It was a sentimental gesture."

"And the Heart Island arch carries a carved heart."

"So it does. And—this is eerie—Louise's health was waning when they erected the monument at Heart Island."

"And so the Heart Island arch turned into a memorial—not of a wife to her husband, but a husband to his wife."

"Indeed."

22.   I was feeling increasingly guilty that I wasn't staying back in that hotel room, where I should be, working on Courtney's play. But the River was so inviting, and my boat was waiting—and there was so much to learn. I promised myself I wouldn't stay long, whenever I called on Meg or Pete—just a few questions. But the conversations were engrossing. I had envisioned an expense-paid vacation at an attractive

resort, but this rushing about trying to write a book while committed to completing a play was hardly relaxing.

I was headed for Pete's again, but steered my little aluminum boat past the great arch at Heart Island. It appeared different now, after talking about it. I pictured a June day when a group stood on the Heart Island, looking across the lagoon, to this strange mass of stone: long-gowned ladies wearing broad-brimmed hats lavishly adorned with feathers, carrying frilled parasols. The gents, carrying walking sticks, wore jackets and straw skimmers. All watched as a block and tackle creaked on a wooden derrick, raising the granite hart. There was an appreciative murmur and a few gloved hands clapped as the large stone was set in place.

Which of those figures was Louise Boldt and which George Boldt? Yes, they must be the couple in the center, holding hands. What were they thinking?

Boldt Castle from the northeast

"Pete, Meg was telling me something about Rügen—aspects of the place that might have contributed to Boldt's values, tastes, and motivation."

"Yes, we've talked about the place and its building precedents, like the Schinkel hunting lodge."

"But why did Boldt call his building the "Alster Tower?" Is there a Rügen connection?"

"No, I believe the reference is to the Alster River that flows through Hamburg."

"Why Hamburg? That's on the mainland, not even near Rügen, is it?"

Not close, but probably the closest port of transatlantic emigration. The Hamburg-America Line was based there, and possibly George Boldt, perhaps Louise's parents, too, had departed for America from Hamburg. Probably he passed through that port city several times on subsequent trips abroad, occasionally with his wife, Louise. Furthermore, the association of the name 'Alster' with the German city of Hamburg seems almost certain. 'Alster' is no English word, nor a German noun, other than as a place name. 'Alster' is no place in Rügen. The name refers to only one place in Germany: it's the name of that river which flows through Hamburg."

"The Alster Tower

"Is there any sort of mini-castle on that river that might have served as a model?"

"I've asked over there, and drawn a blank. What there is, or was, was an upscale neighborhood of suburban villas, built on the shores of the river and little lakes that it connected—sort of like Grosse Pointe, next to Detroit. I've found a few villas that were towered, but none that were as rustic or original as Boldt's project. But there's another, more fascinating account of its origin. This story has come down as oral tradition:

They say Boldt Castle copied some castle on the Rhine. That's not right. It was the Alster Tower, not Boldt Castle, and it wasn't some old castle, but a new one. Boldt saw a hunting lodge that the Kaiser was building. It looked like a castle, but was smaller—just a vacation place. Boldt got an idea. He was always one to act, sometimes impulsively. He paid some workman to copy the plans for the building, brought them back and gave them to Seth Pope, who worked his crews in shifts to build quickly a scaled-down version of the Kaiser's castle. Then Boldt had McIntyre, the photographer, take a picture of the outside as soon as it was up. From a distance out on the water the real size wasn't obvious. Boldt then sent the picture to the Kaiser, with a note: "See, in America we finish your castle before you!"

"Wonderful. Sounds nutty enough to be plausible."

"Plausibly in character, given Boldt's complex personality and taste for the elaborate joke."

"Did he have a sense of humor?"

"Yes, of a dry, ironic sort. Here is an account of his style: he would 'shake his head slowly, wink a liquid blue eye very slowly, and remark . . . .' Boldt had this manner of cocking his head to one side, when introducing a story. Tastes have changed today, and some of his wit may seem beyond the pale. Asked how many 'colored folks' had patronized the Waldorf-Astoria, he said that he had only seen two, in one of the restaurants. 'When they glanced at the prices on the bill of fare, they both turned white.' Of course, he wouldn't tell that story today. Boldt was very fond of Al Smith—which tells you something about his lighter side, if you have any recollection of that colorful politician. Once when some of his staff leaked a funny but disrespectful story to the press, they feared Boldt's reaction (remember he had a temper). 'What would the Old Man say?' Failing to evade the boss in the lobby after the paper appeared, the Assistant Steward was queried: "Oh, Mr. Doyle, did you see the *Sun* today?" Doyle feigned ignorance. "Well, it's the funniest thing you ever saw. A story about one of our bellboys. I was so amused by it that I sent a copy to Mr. Astor who, I know, will get a good laugh out of it".' Here's another good one: at an annual Christmas party for hotel employees, Boldt announced (with the accent he still had at the time), 'Boys, dis is your night. Have as good a time as possible. You can even get trunk if you vish. . . .' Then he asked everyone to tell a story. One fellow rose to tell about getting fired regularly by 'dat old son of a bitch down der'.' He only had to walk out the back door and around to the front, however, to 'strikes de old man an' gets de job back. Dat's what I t'ink o' dat old son of a bitch.' Embarrassed laughter dwindled to a hush, all eyes on Boldt, who 'almost invariably proved himself master of a situation.' Now he jumped up, held out his hand and said, with a hearty laugh, "Vest, py golly, you're de only man dat undershtands me!'

"Boldt surely was affable, as he had to be in his role as host. Doubtless he heard and endured endless jocularity. There are no reports of his being a raconteur, however. Basically, he was serious minded—an industrious German worker, if that isn't too much of a stereotype. But even hard working Germans enjoy their glass of wine or beer-hall merriment.

"Yes, I can envision the Alster Tower as an elaborate joke. Boldt's replica may have been reduced in scale—like the Disney mock villages constructed three-fifths ordinary size, better to relate them to children. And would Boldt have the audacity to send such a message to the Kaiser? Is that in character for a man some regarded as a snob? Boldt still visited Germany occasionally, and in his business would be careful not to give offense to any prestigious personage. But who knows? The fellow who told the story originally, Alden Merrick's grandfather, knew Boldt—better than any of us."

"Great story. Was the building actually built so quickly?"

"Good question. In reality, the building took two years to finish—a fact that does not, on the face of it, seem to be in accord with crews working overtime to complete the structure. It was the exterior, however, that supposedly was rushed. Interior finishing, with hand-carved wood, elaborate plaster work, stained glass and Venetian chandeliers, surely occupied the greater portion of that interval; the stone shell of the Tower might have been raised much more quickly."

"But factually you have found the Hamburg connection, suggested by the Alster name, to be a dead end?"

"Not exactly. Probably the city had special significance for George Boldt, since he left his homeland from that port. More particularly, regarding the name, there's another intriguing bit of historical trivia than may fit into the puzzle. You see, over a period of years after his father (Vicki's Fritz) died, young Kaiser Wilhelm made a grand tour of German cities. To honor him, the City of Hamburg erected a reception pavilion. Probably it wasn't intended to be a permanent facility, so it has disappeared, but I wonder if it wasn't a miniature castle. On one of his wine-buying trips, Boldt, passing through Hamburg again as the German port of entry and departure, might have seen the work in progress, or the preliminary sketches, and even have acquired plans. Perhaps that's the origin of the story. I need to dig further to

A panoramic photograph taken from the tower of the Thousand Islands House, Alexandria Bay. Belle Isle is left of center, with the white house; Wellesley house is directly behind, with bridge and Tennis House to the right, with Play House and greenhouses farther to the right. To the left of Belle Isle, behind Boldt's wooded Friendly Island is the Chalet, and farther to the left appears The Birches, behind St. Elmo Island, which largely obscures the Boldt Pier. Its roof barely appears above the trees. The farm water standpipe appears above Belle Isle, with the large Farm House to the left.

learn where this pavilion was built, and what happened to it. There must be photographs. I wouldn't be surprised to find that it was constructed in the scenic Alster River and lake quarter, but was removed for subsequent development."

"Maybe that building inspired the Alster Tower. That could have started the story about copying the Kaiser's building. It would account for the 'Alster' name."

"Exactly—but its just a hunch. But wait, there's something more." He unfolded a clipping and read: "A high stone tower . . . is now about finished and is one of the strange sights on this end of the River." But that's from June of 1899. Here's the other that I really want, from August of that year:

> The famous Alster Tower is perhaps the most elaborate and unique piece of architecture of its nature in the world. The building of the tower was begun two years ago this summer and has been progressing since. The work on the exterior is completed and the workmen will take away their tools from the interior about Saturday of this week. This will be the completion of an idea born while Mr. Boldt was in Germany a few years ago. He was in attendance at a reception given the Emperor in a town built especially for the occasion in Alster Bay and the complete detail of this castle suggested the building of one similar in character. This tower is product of Mr. Boldt's architectural taste and sense of the beautiful and is unique in every particular. The shell room is the largest in the tower. This is finished in antique stuccowork and is most elaborately decorated. The Venetian room is perhaps the most beautiful of its kind outside the Italian borders. It is

Gilbert Rafferty's Isle Imperial appears at left, with its yacht house directly behind on Wellesley Island. To the right is the Belle Isle (Peacock) Yacht House and next the Boldt Yacht House with the houseboat La Duchesse and yacht Louise. Heart Island appears at the right, with the cottage community of Westminster Park behind it. Boldt's Harbor Island appears behind the Power House at the extreme right. The photograph is dated 1912. The stern of an excursion boat appears at the left bottom of the print, with black smoke billowing cloud from its steam engine.

purely Italian in all its appointments, the hanging chandeliers and all having been imported direct from Venice. The interior hall work is all hand carved. There is a billiard room and a bowling alley in the tower and rooms above for Mr. Boldt, Jr., and a delightful kitchen for Miss Clover Boldt. The chinaware is marked with sweet clover in harmony with her name."

"Why, that's the china that Eleanor Forrest has!"

Pete shared my delight with his smile. "Yes."

"That reference seems sufficient for me. It doesn't mention Hamburg by name, but speaks of an 'Alster Bay.'"

"That might be one of the city lakes made by damming the river; but still it doesn't quite do it. That slight inaccuracy makes the account suspect, but we wonder where a newspaper reporter got such specific information about the name 'Alster.' The Hamburg connection resonates with me, as a historian, for another reason. Hamburg, a principal member of the Hanseatic League, had been a free city. It was a city of business men, hence was politically liberal, as opposed to the rural domains of conservative landed nobles, such as of Count Malte von Putbus of Rügen, George Boldt's island home in the Baltic Sea. Hamburg had long been a European commercial center, and when the United States became independent, trade between that city and America contributed to the economic prosperity of Hamburg. Upscale residential neighborhoods along the Alster River and its lakes represented this new urban wealth—Boldt's economic and social milieu.

"The city not only had a transportation and trading link with the United States; it had a ideological bond. Unlike Boldt's Prussia, independent Hamburg retained a liberal constitution after the failed revolutions of 1848, remaining something of a model for many Germans of the emerging Middle Class. In many ways Hamburg was the most American of German cities at the time."

"You're inclined to accept the story about the Kaiser's mini-castle—or, rather, which one of the two versions?"

"The anecdote about Boldt's joke on the Kaiser may not be altogether inconsistent with the newspaper account except in details. I have a problem with a key sentence written by the journalist: 'He was in attendance at a reception given the Emperor *in a town* built especially for the occasion in Alster Bay and the complete detail of *this castle* suggested the building of one similar in character.' Note that the journalist first mentions 'a town' being built, but then refers to 'this castle.' That doesn't make much sense. Then what does this mean: 'the complete detail of this castle suggested the building of one similar in character.' The journalist had just stressed that the Alster Tower represented Boldt's personal taste, but how could the building result from much personal involvement if it replicated the 'complete detail' of the model?

"This is where we historians have to get out the magnifying glass. Bear with me. The journalist did say that 'the complete detail of this castle suggested the building of one *similar* in character.' Similar, not identical—but if only similar, why mention 'the complete detail'? That phrase, 'complete detail' really doesn't seem to fit the context. Here's what I think, trying to guess what the reporter's hasty, sloppy writing meant. The writer may have had in mind construction drawings that provided 'complete detail[s]' of the model building, and the reporter might have been alluding to construction drawings that Boldt had obtained in Hamburg. When Boldt reduced the scale of the building, it became merely 'similar' rather than identical. This seems plausible, as the Alster Tower evidences sophisticated taste, attuned to current Art Nouveau developments on the continent. It would be surprising indeed to confirm that the Ogdensburg builder, Seth Pope, was its designer.

"Furthermore, the newspaper article has a ring of credibility. Consider other facts mentioned. Daughter Clover Boldt was fourteen years old at the time, a teenager rather than a little girl, but the kitchenette might have been intended for her use, particularly when the Alster Tower was planned two years earlier and she was but twelve years old. The china with the clover pattern did indeed exist—we may have seen a few pieces over at the Forrests'. Other items in the same article aren't only informative, but seem verified:

'One of the most beautiful spots (on the island) is the rough stone pavilion located on the lawn. This is roofed with Brazilian bark, which is durable for a century and is a convenient place for the orchestra when lawn parties and teas are given.'

Reconstructed gazebo

"I remember that bark—not on the roof, but covering the interior ceiling. The gazebo, near the Alster Tower, has been restored. The reporter furthermore was privy to personal items, such as the scheduled visit to Heart Island of the U. S. Attorney General and Boldt's plans to go abroad the following summer. This suggests that the informant might have been Boldt himself, or someone close to him who was well-informed."

23. Courtney's big boathouse, like most, was fairly dark, lit only by small, cobwebby windows and doors open to the River. Sunlight is the enemy of polished varnish, which gleamed on an array of wooden boats. In contrast to dull, weathered wood surfaces of the building interior, faded life jackets hanging on pegs, next to worn paddles and old bait cans, the seductively curvaceous boats glowed brown and black like a museum gallery of fine Beidermeir furniture, highlighted with the glint of brass and chrome. Sunlight entering the open doors, reflected from the watery floor of the room, dappled the trusses overhead with shimmering light. A magical place.

"Our older, family boats are at the Antique Boat Museum in Clayton," Courtney explained. "My parents acquired these here back in the 'thirties and 'forties, when many families were giving up their island places. Few local folks had money to spend on luxuries and, during the war, fuel was rationed. I remember them buying this job when I was a kid. Four hundred dollars." It was a double-cockpit runabout with red leather upholstery. "Today it's an antique itself."

"Four hundred dollars! That's a couple of nights at a local hotel these days."

"But a lot of money during the Depression. There was some criticism of our arrogance, continuing to live extravagantly with servants and all, but we gave employment to a lot of local folk when they needed it. The place was sad—grim, when I was a boy. I remember when the old Yacht Club building went up for tax sale—I think it went for only a few hundred dollars, but was pretty useless at the time—big barn of a building with huge rooms. It was demolished."

"You explained that your family never had one of the tall-masted yachts. But still it must have been a big steam yacht?"

"Commodious, you might say, but not grandiose. My family, I suppose, thought the sea monsters ostentatious—which they surely were. That was the whole idea. We use to say, 'the smaller the fortune the larger the yacht.' There was some truth to that. Commodore Bourne didn't have a huge vessel here—only at his Long Island estate, I think—he bought the ocean-going craft from the King of Belgium. George Pullman didn't even bother maintaining a large yacht. He simply rented one while here. The Boldts' 'Louise' was in the luxury yacht class, but really not big, compared to most of them. The largest by far was the Laughlins' 'Carona.' They had a fairly modest cottage, but dominated the River with the colossal ship, which had such a large draft that it could only run up and down the main channel. The Laughlins had to build the long pier at the Bay, in order to go to town. They called it the 'Carona Pier'."

"Who were the Laughlins?"

"Philadelphia and Pittsburgh family, steel—Jones and Laughlin Steel. Charles Emery's yacht, 'Calumet,' second largest on the River, was only six and a half feet shorter than Laughlin's 'Corona.' At least a dozen other Islanders' yachts exceeded a hundred feet in length.

"Are any of the big steam yachts still around?"

"Not here, certainly. One is still extant, I understand, being restored over on the New England coast. The 'Magadoma' was the Fulford yacht."

"Who was Fulford?"

"Pink Pills for Pale People. The Fulfords' place was—is—at Brockville, now open as a museum house, with all the original contents. Too bad they didn't keep the yacht, which ought to come back to the River some day. Fulford Place is worth a visit. The Heart Island people should take a look, if they want to see authentic interiors of the period."

"They're not Victorian?"

"No, not at all. Edwardian. They have a drawing room full of French furniture. That's what the Boldts probably had in mind for the Castle's elegant reception room, which is similar in character."

"The Fulford house is smaller than Boldt Castle?"

"Of course, with fewer rooms, but those rooms aren't much smaller. I recall the dining room being almost as large as the Castle's—and ours, in fact. Formal dinner parties, requiring maid service, are a thing of the past up here. We still have all that china and silver gathering dust in the pantry."

"Was there much socializing among Islander families?'

"Some coming and going, of course—but not as much as you might think. When you have a country house full of your own guests, you don't do much calling on neighbors, and find it hard to get away from your island for other social events. The Yacht Club was for community affairs, when and if one could break away from entertaining one's own guests. The summer was so short—still is."

"Was the Thousand Islands Yacht Club exclusive?"

"I suppose that was relative, depending on who you were. It was a costly operation, so it required stiff fees, which was economically selective, of course."

"Was there snobbery—discrimination?"

"I would like to think not. But I don't ever remember seeing the Straus names or other prominent Jewish families on the membership role, now that you mention it. They may have preferred to keep to themselves, but when you're only up here a few weeks a year, and have your own house parties, that's not uncommon. Straus had a big yacht, I recall. But there were several yacht clubs, actually, perhaps because of incompatibility. The Thousand Island Yacht Club was largely comprised of families around Alexandria Bay, and was the most social in orientation. The Chippewa Bay club was more focussed on boating—Frontenac as well, which had a club house, although the grand hotel a few steps away on Round Island already served as a social center for the nearby islands—and, indeed, for the region. The long pier at Frontenac always was a showplace, lined with yachts. For many of the T.I. Club families, boats were mere trophies, operated by staff."

Frontenac Pier, Round Island

"The yachts weren't used much?"

"Not the use for which they were designed, distance cruising. Occasionally a family would take off for a short trip out on the Lake, or down to Quebec, but generally a yacht merely adorned one's island, to be admired like one's handsome villa and abundant flowerbeds, by throngs of tourists on passing tour boats. The yacht might carry a whole house party to one of the grand hotels, which had fine cuisine and annual balls and other social events, or to the Club, or to the golf links on Wellesley Island, or some other golf course—or to the club's tennis courts or the polo field. Mrs. Peacock took her houseguests out on the 'Irene' every afternoon for tea. But the staterooms on these big boats were rarely occupied, and the galleys rarely used. Nevertheless, there would be a crew of maybe eight or twelve men at the ready all the time."

"You mentioned balls. Was the drill dressy here?"

"Of course. Changing clothes several times a day was the principle occupation. That's why we have such large walk-in closets. Guests came with trunks, sometimes attended by valets and ladies' maids. Women actually brought their jewels. Imagine—today when we run around in jeans and shorts, with nothing on all those closet shelves but extra bath towels. In those days, even though some families, like ours, were more interested in outdoor than indoor sports, we would all dress for dinner, and dress to the nines for the gala events at the Yacht Club or the grand hotels. That's when the jewels came out—only a few times each season."

"I envision 'My Fair Lady'."

"Got it. The same period—Edwardian—and the same fabulous attire—those colossal hats and sumptuous gowns. Our show will be a costly production, I fear, but gorgeous. But there should be a distinction between our characters' dress: Clover, for example, being raised to suppose privilege her due, was less interested in personal display, whereas her sister-in-law, Estelle, being new to it all, dressed to kill. Again, May, an earthy gal who preferred operating her farm here to socializing at the yacht club, wouldn't put on the dog like Fay, an upwardly mobile Broadway star. Keep in mind the contrast between these pairs."

"Also our hero and protagonist," I added.

"Well, not exactly, in the same sense," Courtney cautioned. "They're a contrasting pair, of course—the poor boy, Horatio-Alger type, and the spoiled-brat Rich Kid. This Cinderella business requires the local boy to aspire to be what the other guy is, however, so the costumes and manners can't be so different."

"But the Clayton fellow is more awkward in his new clothes and manners."

"Yes, and his host is pretentious in his, so we do have the contrast there," Courtney agreed. "Keep in mind, though, that when we come to the moment of truth, when Bart reveals his true identity, he will shed the phony clothes and manners."

"Right. And gets the girl, who comes to her senses and bids goodbye to her 'good provider'."

"Of course."

"Not exactly revolutionary, Courtney."

"Audiences like the tried and true, believe me. Psychic security, confirming that all is right with a stable world. No surprises."

24. Courtney agreed with my notion to end the play with the Gold Cup race held here in 1905. Our hero, the local fellow whose fairy godmother, May Irwin, had arranged for him to pass as a houseguest at one of the island villas, evidences inclination for things mechanical. As this isn't common in this high-toned crowd, Bart is

appointed to drive the powerful boat built by a syndicate of wealthy islanders to, represent the Thousand Island Yacht Club. Up to this point my collaborator was agreeable. Courtney thought, however, that our Horatio-Alger hero simply *had* to win the race—he declared than an audience would demand it. I argued, to the contrary, that this would push our period literary parody too far. Winning the race would be too predictable, too blatantly cornball, for an audience today. Besides, I argued, the point might be better made that winning the race was merely a matter of throwing superfluous wealth at powerful engines, whereas the grace with which our humble but noble hero took defeat would show his real stuff—to Mary, in particular. Her shock of recognition shatters her own fantasy about the privileged life on these islands. Love for one another triumphs, defeating selfish materialism. Poor but happy, arm-and-arm the lovers exit into the sunset. If Courtney wanted cliché, I could deliver cliché. But Courtney couldn't buy this resolution; he supposed that

our audience would find it a downer if the hero didn't win the race. He envisioned a finale with the fraudulent couple accepted into the alien world of the privileged islanders, amidst general cheering. The question, whether philosophical or theatrical, was left hanging, but regardless I needed to know more about powerboat racing.

Clover and Gus racing the PDQ V

The Antique Boat Museum at Clayton was a larger version of Courtney's boathouse. If the modern metal shed was less romantic than the aged wooden barn, the contents were even more spectacular. Where else would one ever see at one glance such an expanse of gleaming wood? Like most visitors, I suppose, given our consumerist culture, I couldn't resist playing the shopper, deliberating about which of the gorgeous boats I might choose, were one mine to have. It's a game not to be missed. A nineteenth-century naphtha launch with scalloped canopy was a charmer—a cute put-put—but who could resist a powerful, Gatsby-era, triple-cockpit runabout, thirty-feet or so long, of gleaming mahogany with tufted, white leather upholstery?

The Gold Cup racers weren't even contenders. They weren't pleasure boats, nor were they ravishing craft designed to elicit envy. They had no purpose other than winning a race. They were minimal, utilitarian containers for engines—and the engines of the time seem quaint by modern standards. It's difficult to recognize what marvels they were as the twentieth century opened, and to imagine the international interest in the powerboat races. The Duke of Westminster sent a contender across the Atlantic to participate at the Thousand Islands.

After visiting the wooden boats of the past, nearby marinas full of white plastic boats appear banal. Surely all these mass-produced, high-powered, low-maintenance craft gave much pleasure to many people today, and are indeed practical, but they seem inertly robotic compared to living wood. Courtney introduced me to owners of a modern craft of a class rightly called a 'yacht,' a class far less common on the River today than a century ago. Surely the vessel wasn't built for economy; nevertheless its hull was still fiberglass—even though it had bathrooms (hardly "heads") clad in marble and a large living room (hardly a "saloon") with Chinese décor. The owners lived aboard the yacht during the summer, when it was moored next to a new house built for the 'shoulder seasons.' The comfortable house served for the few weeks while the skipper was en route to and from Florida with the yacht. The owners flew back and forth seasonally.

If miniature in size compared to big plastic boats, Courtney's labor-intensive little wooden boats seemed equally luxurious. Having learned more about boating on the River, I asked him if his family participated in racing.

"We were never in the Gold Cup league," Courtney commented, "but we did have one of the one-class boats built by Leyare. Because of the problem of handicapping a variety of craft, the club decided to commission construction of a fleet of identical boats, carrying only numbers rather than names, so that members could race more competitively. Skill in handling would count more than mere horsepower. There are still a few of the old numbered boats around. The Boldts would have had number 13, of course. Everything was number 13 with them. They were odd about such things. But they got number 3, since they were early on the list."

"Boldt came over when thirteen years old, I understand."

"Yes, that was the connection, of course. I suppose that Boldt figured the number was lucky rather than unlucky for him."

25. Pete's island place was a common "camp," not a commodious "country house," like Courtney's, and surely not a commanding "castle" like Boldt's. The differences weren't merely of size and pretension, but of ways of life. Like Courtney's larger

summer home, however, the professor's cabin was venerable. Similarly, the interior was dark but warm in character, all surfaces were wood, and the place smelled of aged wood, warmed by the sun, smoked by a century of wood burning on the stone hearth. If anything, Pete had even more vintage photographs on the walls, and piles of them on table tops, including old stereopticon cards with a viewer. "Your place reminds me of Courtney's," I commented. He laughed.

"We're not in that league. We don't dress for dinner over here—but I suppose they don't over there anymore, either."

"Heron Island has a bigger house, but there's a similar character—a good fit, I suppose."

"I have to squint to see the similarity in our chateaux—but I know what you mean. Our places, like most of the rickety old buildings up here, are mellow, to the point of being seedy. I don't suppose Courtney has added a piece of furniture to the big house over there during his lifetime. He doesn't notice the stuffing coming out of the upholstery. That's the way it's always been, in his mind."

"Still, it must be very costly to keep that kind of place going, even without buying new furniture. He says they have to wash eighty-some windows every summer."

"Yes, the folks that pass in the tour boats hear their guides over the loudspeakers exclaim breathlessly about 'Millionaire's Row.' They suppose that money is no object to people who live in those places. But it's all relative. Courtney probably is strapped, just to keep his island as it is. His burden is probably the same as mine, relative to our means. We all have a tendency to live at the very limit of our means, don't we?"

"Even the Boldts?"

"Especially the Boldts, I would say. That may be the reason why Courtney's family has enjoyed Heron Island for so many generations, in contrast to the sudden deflating of the Boldt fantasy. Courtney doesn't spend a dime more than he has to. He can't afford to indulge in extravagance, I'll wager."

"He could sell any one of those antique boats for thousands of dollars."

"Many thousands, yes. But he doesn't want the money; he wants Heron Island as it is. Old money seems to survive because those who have inherited it regard it differently from the way the new rich regard sudden wealth; old money is not to be spent, you see. Courtney has Heron Island because his family hasn't been living off its principal, spending capital like the profligate Boldts."

"What was the compelling need? It does seem odd that the Boldts owned Harbor Island, right next to Heart, which is a beautiful, wild island like Heron. Instead of appreciating that sort of natural quality, enjoying a comfortable house like Courtney's, they wanted an unlivable castle, and needed for some reason to transform Heart Island with retaining walls and terraces—even changing its shape!"

"Yes, and changing half of Wellesley Island. As someone said of Boldt, "He was forever turning water into land, or land into water." I suppose the challenge appealed to him, reclaiming the marshes, recreating a landscape."

"There's something godlike about reinventing the landscape."

"Ah, my friend, you're getting close."

"Close? To what?"

"You're a writer; you want to write about the Boldt mystery—the Great American Tragedy, no? Then recall classical Greek tragedy. But before the thunderbolt from Olympus struck, Boldt must have derived great satisfaction to stroll along those canal-side walks, embellished with lawns and gardens, and think, 'I made all this.'"

"He had enormous creative drive."

"Irrepressible—compulsive. Fortunately, he had fair taste, but he made some mistakes. Wellesley House wasn't a great success. Nary a breeze in there. Mosquito gulch. They may have been one reason Clover didn't want the place. "

"Do you remember seeing Wellesley House?"

"Only after Ed Noble owned it, before he had it razed. It was a big, empty house—run down, but not really in bad shape. Courtney may have known it before Noble bought the Boldt estate—but only as a youngster, I suppose."

"I'd be interested in the character of the place, to compare with Boldt Castle—and the interiors, especially."

"Here are photos copied from that old Boldt album we saw at the Forrests'. You can see that there's nothing Victorian about the rooms—but these pictures may represent the place a decade or so after the Castle was built. The most attractive room, as I remember it, was a large sunroom with windows on three sides and a big stone fireplace on the fourth side. It was bright and airy—nothing dark or gloomy about it."

"What did Boldt intend to do with another big house, in addition to the Castle?"

"Oh, he had lots of houses. Was mad about them. He rationalized his building mania as a real-estate venture, but needless to say rentals from these properties for a few weeks of the year couldn't begin to pay back the investment. Did we talk about his last great project—the hotel over by the T.I. Club?"

"You mentioned it."

"It would have been quite a place—maybe it would have revived the waning prestige of the resort after two of the grand hotels burned, a few years before he died. I've seen the architect's drawings. It was to be a multi-storied, fireproof hotel. The steel was erected but construction problems delayed completion. When Boldt died, as World War I broke out, the steel framing for the structure was pulled down. The scrap served the war effort. And there was still another ambitious, unfinished building project. Would you believe that when he died he was building another big house? In Montecito, California—near Santa Barbara. He never lived in that one either."

"Did Louise Boldt ever get to live in any of these houses?"

"Well, she did enjoy the old place on Heart Island for five or six summers, before they launched the great Castle project, and they used the fine Belle Island house for several seasons while the Castle was rising. But the houseboat was still being completed when Louise Boldt died. And they had just moved from the hotel quarters into a New York townhouse when she died, just after New Year's. She had finally escaped from the public life in that grand hotel."

"You don't think she enjoyed the glamour of the Waldorf-Astoria?"

"Nice place to visit, but live there? What a *vida loca*. It was one of the most hectic spots in Manhattan. A mob scene. One of Boldt's close associates observed, 'living with Mr. Boldt was very much like being a gold fish in a glass bowl.' If life at the Waldorf-Astoria had once seemed glamorous, it must have paled. Those who live at length in hotels, a contemporary observed, 'tend to become either blasé or urbane,... accustomed to living in public, eating in public, and all but sleeping in public.' Just as it was ironic that she didn't live to see her dream Castle complete, so after years of living in the Waldorf-Astoria when she finally got a place of her own in the city she died within a month."

"Do you think there was some connection between these projects—a New York town house and the Castle—and her failing health, and death?"

Pete adjusted his spectacles thoughtfully. "Yes. I suspect there was."

The Waldorf-Astoria, New York City, on the Fifth Avenue site of the Empire State Building. The original Waldorf Hotel is the lower portion at the left. The Astoria addition on 34th Street made this the largest hotel in the world.

I waited for more, but nothing came, so I proposed my own scenario: "Here's how I'm thinking it might have gone: George, minting money, is consumed with urgent business affairs. He's just finished enlarging the Waldorf-Astoria into the largest hotel in the world, and now is building the Bellevue-Stratford in Philadelphia. He's there often, and doubly pressed when back in New York. This is the time of life when their children were leaving the nest. Louise, having less interaction now with husband and children, began to have health problems. Psychosomatic? Depression? Who knows? George feels remiss for not giving Louise what she missed: his attention, mostly, but as recompense, he promises her something else she has missed, a place of her own, away from the public stage of the grand hotel—the New York town house, but even more her dream house, the Castle. So far so good?"

"Plausible."

"I picture Louise's health gradually failing, while George feels unable to help adequately. As compensation he pours millions into her pet project up here. It fits with the tragic love story, deepening the tragedy, doesn't it?"

"Wait a minute. Does health fail gradually from depression? You're missing something."

"How?"

"There's one small problem."

"What's that?"

"Louise didn't gradually fade away. She went suddenly. Louise died by her own hand."

26. Pete then insisted I would have to get it directly from Clover Boldt Baird—that he never should have let that much slip, and that he was *not* to be quoted (as I do here—but I get ahead of myself). Courtney was picking up the tab for my summer venture, and I owned him the book for his play. I found myself where 'two roads diverged.' Which road to pursue? Idle curiosity brought me to this point, but now further travel on the Boldt route would require a serious commitment of time and energy. To get to Mrs. Baird, I would have to proffer some bait. I heard the cash register jingling again, as I heard it when Courtney had told me about the quarter-million paid admissions annually at Boldt Castle. I didn't agonize much about the decision but immediately began drafting some evocative material to send to her: a beginning segment and some key sketches of her grandparents' story.

My first attempt began by describing the tall freestanding, four-sided clock that we see today in the center of the Waldorf-Astoria lobby on Park Avenue—quite a marvel. Flash back to 1893: after the closing of the Chicago World's Fair, a huge crate arrives at the new Waldorf Hotel on Fifth Avenue. George and Louise watch as workmen pry apart the planks, exposing the gleaming gold object. Then flash to the Empire State Building standing on the site today. A cinemagraphic sort of strategy continued, laden with Proustean memory tricks.

Receiving an initial installment, Mrs. Baird did write back, as anticipated—if only to suggest that I tell it straight. Jumping backward and forward in time confused her. Just tell the story from the beginning, she recommended.

My first inclination was defensive, to explain that the clock was like Proust's Madeleine, that seemingly inconsequential little teacake that sets in motion the French novelist's epical cycle of novels, *In Search of Lost Time*. The odd clock meant several things. It served as a *momento mori*, a reminder of how these dumb things that we humans make eventually survive us. Here was this anachronistic Victorian survivor, now centerpiece of the 1930's Art Deco lobby of the new Waldorf-Astoria, an already-historic twentieth-century building. Generations of the rich and famous, and generations of those who came to see the rich and famous, had wondered at the marvel. That long procession of people was gone now, replaced by others who still kept coming along as the time machine ticks on. Its four clocks face in four directions, telling four different times at four different places on the globe. What's the correct time? There are different truths, seen by different viewers from different vantage-points.

But then I figured I was just a journalist, not a literary artist. No cinematic tricks, just tell the story—from the beginning, she required. And so I began, not in New York City, but on the Baltic island of Rügen. From Pete, from the Internet, and as the product of two-hour drives down to the Syracuse University Library, I was learning something about the place, about the social and cultural milieu there in the early nineteenth century. One

The clock from the 1893 Chicago World's Fair, installed by the Boldts in the original Waldorf Hotel, now centerpiece of the lobby in the Waldorf-Astoria, Park Avenue, New York City.

could place the Boldts with some confidence in a general way, as being in that small class that would have been "*Bürgers*" or *bourgeois*, had there been a *Burg* or city on the island—a sort of "middle class," neither agrarian nor aristocratic. George's mother apparently was of more rustic stock—a photograph showed her smoking the farm wife's clay pipe. (I learned this subsequently from Clover Boldt, who had the photo in a family album, until "the local thief stole the irreplaceable volume"—a neighbor whom she suspected but didn't have evidence to charge). The Boldts, however, were a family that had been neither farmers nor shopkeepers, but of the *Ritter* class—the free knights of feudal time. Unless (like many Prussians in this situation) one opted for a military career, the job market for knight-errants was severely depressed in the early nineteenth century. The vocation of George's father seems to have been, by grace of the local Prince, that of a minor bureaucrat in a provincial island town, his income probably augmented by modest commercial enterprise. Of necessity, he may have been 'in trade,' to use that British Upper Class term of contempt.

Why did thirteen-year old Georg Karl Boldt come alone to America? That's one of the great mysteries of this tale. Did he run away (as some had said) or, if not, what did his father foresee, what did he wish, for his son? Americans can hardly appreciate the powerful, unyielding sense of social predestination implied by the German term, *Stand*. Its implication in the early nineteenth century was more that of "caste" even than "class." In traditional Germany, one's proper place was predetermined by birth. One's future was predestined. Peasants—or even *Bürgers*—didn't aspire to be princes—to build lordly castles. We might call the Rügen Boldts "marginal" socially, hanging onto the fringe of landed gentry, retaining vestiges of ancient honor, but without the property that provided economic status.

Georg Karl Boldt's father apparently worked for the Graf von Putbus—virtually the only game in town. We don't know his role, but as the island wasn't large, we can be fairly certain that young Georg Boldt knew the culture of the resort community nurtured by the Count. Probably he was familiar with the new hotel facilities that were attracting affluent Berliners, and even a few international visitors like Thomas Carlyle. Perhaps his future vocation was determined at an early age. Possibly he was even employed as a bell boy or kitchen helper before coming to America. Regardless, Rügen was a sociable place, noted for "a generous hospitality . . ., which involved a great deal of visiting and fed a spirit of conviviality." Indeed, "the word 'home' as we understand it in the English-speaking world, does not exist in Prussia. . . . Instead of taking a friend home, one takes him to a *Stammtisch* or club-table." It was in places of public socializing that one formed personal bonds. And so the twig was bent.

Why did young Georg leave? Are we to believe, as told so consistently, even during his lifetime, that he came alone, at the age of thirteen? Why?

Very quickly, the notion of a biography of George Charles Boldt faltered. The most important things are unknown and probably unknowable. Had he siblings? What was his family life, his relation with parents? Did he run away? From what?

What I know now I didn't discover in those few summer months, but have continued to learn. Cultural tradition and particular conditions of Prussia at the time provide some context. Thirteen was an age when boys might begin an apprenticeship, often leaving home to work for, and learn from, an established craftsman—or possibly a *hôtelier*, were hotel management one's ambition. Career opportunities on an out-of-the-way island are limited. The principle exports of many small islands are their youngsters.

The Germans were methodical about record keeping, and an exit permit would have been required for Boldt to emigrate—but the government archives have no record of Boldt departing. Why?

Young men were being conscripted for military service, as Bismarck sent an army into Denmark, beginning his imperialist strategy. The people of Rügen, who lived on a neighboring island in the Baltic Sea, didn't regard the Danes as the enemy. Traditionally there had been affinity between these maritime people. Furthermore, the Boldts probably had been partial to the young king, Fritz, who had visited their island before he recently died as a young man. King Friedrich III had been progressive in his views (his enemies contending his English wife influenced him). Probably middle-class Berliners who sojourned on Rügen deplored the regressive polices of his successor, who increasingly empowered the ambitious, militaristic Bismarck.

It appears that young Boldt, like many others, slipped away without official approval. Was he merely a draft-dodger? Avoidance of military service, especially in a cause he didn't support, may have been a factor.

But why New York? Germans had been emigrating to America for some time, especially since Junker repression of a liberal movement in1848, when large numbers of disappointed Germans came, many settling in a German-American community in New York City. Probably Boldt had relatives or family acquaintances already here, perhaps agreeing to take the youngster in. The notion of the brave lad facing the unknown all by himself may be overly dramatized, but still one must be struck by a boy leaving home for the New World at age thirteen.

Probably Boldt sailed in 1864 from Rügen to Hamburg, taking a trans-Atlantic ship from there to New York City. From his arrival in America, the story may be reconstructed more confidently. We know where young Georg, now George, was first employed, and can track his career thereafter. We know how he met Louise, and can follow their family moves from Philadelphia to New York to the Thousand Islands. But the most important factors, questions of personal relationships and internal motivations, can never be known. The prospect of a Boldt biography wasn't propitious.

Having scrapped the Proustian overture, my second submission found more favor with Mrs. Baird. An evocation of a Hans Christian Anderson sort of Rügen, storks nesting on the chimneys of steep, tile-roofed houses, young Georg peering from the casement window of his sloped-ceiling bedroom to watch for ships on the endless sea, appealed to her. A poet herself, she particularly liked the image of the younger tot transfixed by gilded swan necks, legs of an ornate table he discovered when Papa took him to visit the Graf at his Schloss. She was enchanted by the lad's exploration of the bird-filled marshes of his island. It was going very well, she thought. I was a bit concerned that I knew so little about the real people, so had to write mostly about a place largely imagined from my reading. Rügen was in Communist East Germany at the time, and was virtually inaccessible to westerners.

Another installment depicted the heroic lad of thirteen arriving alone, disembarking from a tall-masted ship at Castle Garden, the immigration depot at the Battery, on the southern tip of Manhattan, then walking up bustling Broadway with its fashionable Ladies' Mile and recruiting stations during the Civil War. Mrs. Baird endorsed the Horatio-Alger aspect of her grandfather, when he began his spectacular rise by peeling vegetables at the small Merchants' Exchange Hotel.

I could crank out one of these sketches a week, between my other interviews and, I confess, minimal work on the play. Needless to say, the TV in my hotel room never was turned on. The fourth installment mailed to Mrs. Baird wasn't received with the same approval, however. As our lad became a young man, his granddaughter found some of the personality traits that made Boldt an achiever less ingratiating than his boyish pluck. When managing a large resort hotel at Cornwall-on-Hudson he had a falling out with the owner. He quit impulsively, stormed out, leaving a hotel full of guests. Boldt was an emotional man, with a temper—a "man of wrath," as they say in German. His granddaughter didn't care for that aspect of his personality. She was quite pointed. "I cannot endorse this," she stated. That terminated the sending of installments back and forth, but we didn't end our communication. The ice had been broken, she knew I could write, and indeed was writing this book. I suspected that I would in time discuss with her a suppressed version of Louise Boldt's death.

27. Pete was a sanguine sort of guy, but I sensed that his patience with seeing me pop into his workroom every couple of days must have been wearing thin. Fearing an eventual objection, I tried to defuse it. "Look, Pete, you're being overly generous, feeding me so much of your research. You ought to have a stake in my book, somehow. At least I'll credit you for your contribution—or maybe you'd like to be a co-author."

"No way. I'm a terrible collaborator. I couldn't work with Courtney, the way you do. And as for giving me credit . . ." He laughed. "Do you think I want to be responsible for your mistakes?"

"You don't mind continuing to help me this way?"

"When I start to mind, I'll let you know." He smiled amiably, so I pressed ahead.

"What sort of relationship do you suppose they had—George and Louise?," I asked Pete. "What would have been usual, at least, for the time?"

"That depends on several variables, like class. Rural Americans in the Midwest, for instance, differed from, say, some wealthy easterners. Already, before the turn of the century, some prominent socialites were divorcing and remarrying without incurring approbation. It was accepted that some upper class men weren't sterling family men, and even that not all wives were homebodies. The mores were very different, for different groups, and so one shouldn't generalize. The sudden change in standards, as the Boldts rose so propulsively through the social strata, probably was part of the problem."

"Then you, too, suspect there may have been a problem?"

"Becoming so very rich so very suddenly had to be a problem. 'The Hazard of New Fortunes,' as Howells put it. Do you know that George Boldt had a vervous breakdown after opening the Waldorf, when the deep depression of the 'nineties set in, and he had mortgaged everything he owned? He had far more employees on his payroll than he had guests at his new hotel. One Sunday the hotel register showed forty guests. On the payroll there were 970 employees. New Yorkers laughed or sighed at 'Boldt's Folly.' Boldt had borrowed heavily to furnish and equip the large facility. He discovered the kitchen was poorly planned and needed extensive alteration. Extreme stress and consequent depression brought him and his family to the Thousand Islands within months of the hotel's opening, after he was advised by his doctor and friends to recuperate. George Boldt later recalled that during the first four months after opening the Waldorf, he had lost $192,000, equivalent to more than three million dollars today. He was sure he had made a dreadful mistake, and would be ruined, taking his family down with him. That was 1893. Only five years later George was building the Astoria addition to the Waldorf, making it the world's largest hotel (while maintaining the illusion that it was ultra-exclusive). He then quickly went on to build the huge Bellevue-Stratford in Philadelphia, at the same time Boldt Castle was rising. This all happened within seven years—from despair over financial ruin to amassing a multi-million dollar fortune. Those were incredible years, and must have had great impact upon the Boldts personally."

" How did Boldt parlay so much money, so fast?"

"Boldt's income was so exceptional as to be considered newsworthy. His salary alone was twenty times that of the President of the United States. The President wasn't underpaid; the Chief Executive's salary was about that of most business executives in large corporations. Boldt was simply doing twenty times as well.

    "Another executive's annual stipend, only three times the salary of the President of the United States, was reported as an 'extraordinary annual salary.' Astonishing indeed was George Boldt's: in 1903 the New York World announced: '$500,000 per Year, Boldt's Modest Salary.' Six years later, his 1910 salary, again said to be $500,000, made him 'one of the highest paid men in the United States,' or 'the largest salaried man in this country, if not the world.' In modern dollars, his salary was more like eight and a quarter million a year.

    "Surely this salary put Boldt in quite a different class from most business executives at the time. Eldridge Gary, Chairman of 'the world's first billion-dollar corporation,' United States Steel, earned only $100,000, a fifth as much as Boldt."

"Did many other businessmen in the nation draw as much as Boldt?"

"A few, but not many. Not as salary, nor even as income from investments. With tongue in cheek, one commentator said that the very rich considered 'thirty to forty thousand per year . . . decent poverty.' That amount would be more like a half million or 660 K per annum today. This range was fairly typical of a top business executive's salary at the time, making him comfortably affluent, surely, but not 'really rich' to the Really Rich. The same observer at the time regarded three to four hundred thousand per annum as 'easy circumstances'—middling rich, at least. That would be a modern income ranging from 4 to 6.6 million. Boldt was doing even better, drawing the equivalent of 8.8 million dollars a year in *salary*, without considering income from his many investments. Even beyond his regular pay, it was said that he was 'making more money outside the hotel than in it, in real estate, chiefly,' from which he was thought to have made a million dollars in 1903 alone. Given this torrent of revenue, the lavish expenditure of the Boldts at the Thousand Islands may begin to appear plausible. By 1910, Boldt's fortune was estimated to be 'several times the desired one million,' which is to say, in our terms today, he had accumulated a fortune approaching fifty million dollars. Boldt was indeed a 'capitalist.'

"The Boldts were the richest family here?"

"No, by no means, only the most extravagant. Expenditure is no measure of wealth. In fact, George Boldt appeared on neither 1892 nor 1902 lists of American millionaires, although twenty other Islanders were listed. The Pullmans, for example, surely were wealthier in terms of assets than the Boldts, but it does not necessarily follow that the disposable income of one family was greater than that of the other. The Pullman wealth was largely tied up as capital investment whereas the Boldts actually owned relatively little. They had a cash flow, however, that was truly phenomenal.

"Boldt made a great deal of money in a short time, and spent a great deal. On George Boldt's death, his estate was surprisingly small—only a couple million. The Pullman estate was almost nine times Boldt's when probated. One of the Hayden brothers at Fairyland left an estate even larger than Pullman's. There were others: Charles Emery of Calumet Island left more than twice George Boldt's estate. But in a different class altogether was Frederick Bourne of Dark Island. His estate was twenty-two times Boldt's. So you see the Boldts really were trying to keep up with the bigger fish, which may account for their big splash in the pond. One can still almost hear some other Islanders after Boldt's death exclaiming (recalling old John D. Rockefeller's remark, on learning the amount of the late J. P. Morgan's estate) 'Why, to think . . . he was hardly rich at all!'"

"So there really were quite a few others here that were wealthier than the Boldts?"

"I think there were two distinct classes of wealth here, the super-rich—the Bournes, Haydens, Packer-Wilburs, Pullman-Lowdens, Bradleys—and then the merely rich: the Emerys, Boldts, and many other multi-millionaire Islanders. In the first class, Bourne was probably worth 500 million, Hayden, 400 million, Packer and Pullman, both 300 million. Then there was a big break between the super-rich and the merely rich, like Emery, with 83 million, and Boldt, a mere 33 million. So, you see, the Boldts weren't the largest frogs, even in the small pond of the Thousand Islands!"

"A lot of money concentrated in one place—and I had hardly heard of the place when I came."

"Oh yes, the Islands were awash in money a century ago, but so was the nation. But our Islanders weren't even among the really rich in America at the turn of the century, families like the Astors, Vanderbilts and Rockefellers, whose fortunes were measured in our terms not in hundreds of millions but in billions of dollars.

"John Jacob Astor, who built the Astoria portion of Boldt's hotel, was hardly salaried, but for purpose of comparison, income from his investments in 1905 was thought to be more than three million dollars. Today that would be more like fifty million dollars a year, which is to say that he was taking in annually as much as Boldt accumulated in a lifetime. J. J. Astor's expatriate cousin in England, Viscount William Waldorf Astor, was supposed to have an income double that, amounting to a hundred million modern dollars a year. Andrew Carnegie was drawing every two weeks more than Boldt made in a year. To us, looking at their incredible expenditure here, the Boldts seem to have been very rich. It's all relative. To the Boldts themselves, looking at their neighbors, the Bournes and Pullmans nearby, let alone their New York City sponsors, the Astors, they didn't consider themselves very rich at all."

"Do you suppose it made a difference, once one became a mega-millionaire— who had more or less money?"

"Of course it did. Money is power, despite the amusing observation of John Jacob Astor (as one imagines him counseling George Boldt, with a sigh, when his up-wardly-mobile friend made his first million): "A man who has a million dollars is as well off as if he were rich.""

"But how about those strikers at the Pullman plant?" Pullman was the most famous man here at the time of the famous Pullman Strike at his railroad car works, when the President sent in the U.S. Army. It was a national crisis, threatening shutdown of all the nation's railroads."

"Ah, so. And not just the strikers; there were about two million children under age fourteen working full time. As critics of the capitalist system were quick to point out, the average factory worker at this time was paid little more than $500 per year, equivalent today to about eight thousand dollars. Boldt was earning a thousand times the salary of the typical American industrial worker. The Boldts' family income, if not the family's accumulated wealth, placed them among about 32,000 families in America—not a select club, perhaps, but more so when one realizes that this comprised but .001 per cent of the population, or one out of 873,000 families.

"Today the prominent landmark buildings left by the Boldts give the impression that they were the most eminent Islanders of the time. This was not so. In their day the Boldts were neither the wealthiest nor the most famou of Islanders. Better known, and more remembered nationally than even the super-rich like the Bournes and Pullmans, were nationally prominent authors like J.G. Holland, journalists like Arthur Brisbane, and theatrical celebrities like May Irwin. The Boldts were really trying to make it into this league. The Pullmans were from Chicago; the most prominent New Yorker family on the River wasn't the Boldt family, but probably the Bournes, of Dark Island, or perhaps the Nathan Straus family, of Belora, Cherry Island (even though they were Jewish). Nathan Straus, a great philanthropist, was probably the most distinguished man on the River at the time."

"The children were still young during the seven years when the Boldt fortune escalated and they developed Heart Island?"

"They were all young—Louise in her thirties during this decade, and the children still teenagers during the Heart Island development years. 'Cricket,' as they called George, Jr., was just twenty when they removed the old frame house and began construction of the Castle. Clover was still a teenager."

"How old was Louise when she died?"

"Only forty-one."

"Wasn't it unusual for a woman so young, with all the advantages of health care that money could provide, to die at such an early age?"

"It's odd that there was so little comment on her passing, and so few questions."

"A conspiracy of silence?"

Pete shrugged. "Who knows?"

"Speaking as an architect, Meg suggested that some clients undertake ambitious house-building campaigns in order to try to save a marriage."

He smiled. "That may be on the mark."

"Possibly the marriage was strained, right? We were getting around to that before, when you talked about Louise wanting a real home of her own, away from the hotel—but the Castle was turning into a virtual hotel."

"Yes, *probably* the marriage was strained, I would say. Do you know that Louise always referred to her husband as 'Mr. Boldt'? That was in public, of course, and may not have been so unusual for the time. But Boldt was totally consumed by his spectacular business projects. It wasn't just building and opening the grand hotels, and hobnobbing with world celebrities, but he was a player in the heady bull market at the end of the 'nineties, when his investments were parlaying his fortune. Home life had to be pretty dull by comparison, if he had any home life—if they had any home. We talked about their living in the hotel. Louise was supposed to be regularly on stage, dressed in fabulous Worth gowns, entertaining famous guests in their private hotel dining room."

"Did she find that distasteful?"

"I suppose the glamour wore thin. Being a "princess" or, at her age, a "queen," may be more pleasant as a fantasy than as a job description. But it wasn't so much that Louise disliked the limelight as the fact that the role she was so elaborately costumed to play had become insubstantial. You see, Louise was a tavern-keeper's daughter who went into tavern-keeping herself. It was her alliance with George Boldt that had initiated his independent proprietorship of a hotel, and Louise had been a working wife, his real partner in developing their little Bellevue Hotel in Philadelphia. They said that Louise was 'a sharer in her husband's business, ran the cashier's desk,' and 'that she 'had worked with him for years and knew the hotel business as well as he did.'

"After the move to New York, for initial planning and decorating of the Waldorf, Louise was part of the team—she decorated all the guestrooms herself, you know. Then the Waldorf opened. Louise had been the hostess at their Bellevue, but no more. She was out."

"Why?"

"George hired Oscar—her rival—to serve as official greeter. It was a fateful juncture, and George seemed to intuit this himself. He carefully arranged to hire Oscar on the thirteenth of the month. Thirteen was his "lucky' number, you know. Oscar became his stand-in, now that George himself was becoming the executive of a large business—and when the far larger Astoria addition made this Big Business indeed. 'Oscar-of-the-Waldorf'—that used to be a household name in America. Oscar was far better known than Boldt himself, for he developed a public persona identified with the grand hotel and so became a celebrity in his own right, a 'tremendous drawing card.' Oscar was really a glorified headwaiter, as the public saw him, a sort of famous greeter of famous people. To be admitted to the Palm Garden by Oscar was regarded as an achievement; to be greeted by name was regarded as an ultimate social attainment. Americans even thought that Oscar was responsible for the quality of Waldorf cuisine, and Oscar wrote an enormous cookbook, but he had nothing to do with the kitchen. Beyond his image as guardian of the velvet rope, his real business was more as the banquet manager, and banquets were then, as now, big business at the Waldorf-Astoria.

"Louise resented Oscar, you suppose?"

"I don't think she was the sort of person to be jealous or harbor grudges. Oscar recalled only pleasant relations with Louise, whom he liked personally. What dismayed Louise was being put out to pasture. I suspect that Heart Island was her compensation."

"Like the obligatory gift from Tiffany's—to redress an extramarital affair?"

"That's an analogy, certainly."

"Getting back to their personal relationship, do you suppose that there were infidelities? You know the local stories."

"Yes, we hear them all the time." He smiled, peering over his glasses. "You're the journalist, aren't you? Sniffing about."

"My job."

"A historian's too. But we have no reason to suspect any affairs, despite that old canard about her running off with the chauffeur, or whatever."

"Don't you think that persistent folk lore may have some basis, even if inaccurate?"

"Basis, yes. Boldt wasn't universally loved up here. He had a falling out and fired an estate superintendent, a local man well known and liked—took him to court for theft—painful business for all concerned, and the family is still here. Prominent local folks."

"No midlife crises for George—or Louise?"

"I wouldn't suppose there weren't crises, given their strange life. But I picture him totally obsessed with his work—fully engaged in business and all this building. His vocation required odd hours. A great hotel is in full gear in the evening. He got his kicks from gambling venture capital, playing the market. Because of his business, buying enormous quantities of food, he was a commodity trader, you know."

"What was Louise doing in the meantime?"

"There were the children—but as they moved upward socially, the kids had to go off to the right schools: Lawrenceville for Cricket, Miss Spence's for Clover. They were no longer children at home during the Castle campaign. I suppose the project was

Louise's preoccupation, being left in an empty nest by a distracted husband. I see where you're going, though. George would leave Louise up here all week, or for weeks at a time. Indeed, there have been Island wives, left up here for the season, who have found amusement locally—not merely playing golf with other CEO's wives. One could always engage a professional guide to take one fishing—or whatever—every day."

"You don't suppose that Louise developed an attachment with someone here, which might have been the origin of the elopement tale—if not a chauffeur, then someone else?"

"Surely there were plenty of men on the Boldt payroll here—hundreds, probably during those years. There were at least sixty men at the Oak Island quarry alone, as pictured in a remarkable group photograph. By some accounts about a hundred and fifty were engaged there. Stone masons right off the boat from Italy worked on the Heart Island project. There were gardeners, stable grooms, sailors—men everywhere, while George was away greeting presidents and princes, while watching his ticker tape in the City. Your plot is plausible, but there's no reason to think it probable. No, rather than 'the other man' or 'other woman' angle, there was that even more dangerous protagonist: success."

Closing my laptop, I ventured again, "Pete, you're writing this book for me. Think about how we might work together on it."

"Oh, I'm enjoying this. At my stage of life, when you look at all the boxes full of paper, and now all the disks piling up, you realize that this stuff ought to be of some use. No sense saving it for that book that will never be written. I didn't tell you before, but I checked up on you. I've read your stuff. I think my material will be in good hands."

Pete was marvelously informative about the economic basis for the Boldt Castle phenomena. He provided more data than I cared to have about the relative financial worth of other island dwellers but, when I probed for more of a sense of the social dynamics of the summer colony, he suggested that I talk to a remarkable lady, Jean Hammond. "She's been here forever." He smiled knowingly. "And she's really something."

"That's what you said about Meg, and you sure were right. But this lady can't be 'something' in quite the same way."

"Imagine Meg a half-century from now and you'll get Jean."

28. Mrs. Hammond invited me to visit her at 'The Ledges,' a stone cottage within view
of Heart Island. I was astonished when she came to the door herself, almost dropping my laptop, tap recorder, and bunch of flowers. This could hardly be a woman
in her 'nineties. She had to be at least three decades younger—a trim, slight but
erect figure, beautifully coifed hair ringing a smiling face. She lived alone—at her
age!—in the comfortable one-floor house with lots of glass that she and her husband
had built. "We tore down the big house," she explained, "when it became impractical for the two of us. It was the same vintage as Courtney's. I don't know how he
does it. Works all summer over there, trying to keep the place going. This little
house was just right for the two of us, and now it suits me fine."

After I commented appreciatively on the tasteful surroundings, I asked if I might
tape our conversation. She frowned. "Don't turn that thing on. I'd rather speak
freely." Then she got directly to the point: "What would you like to know?"

"Well, as I told you, I'm interested in the Boldts and how they fit into Thousand
Islands society."

"But I was just a youngster when they arrived!" She smiled, trusting I would get the
joke. "My parents built a summer home on Sylvan Island—sold that to one of the
Wilbur boys from Sport Island when I moved here with my husband. People seem
to think I should know everything, since I've been around so long. But I haven't
been here forever. George Boldt was still at Wellesley House when I was a teenager,
but I never knew his wife, who died when I was a small child. Clover, of course, I
knew well, and so saw her father occasionally at Wellesley House, but he was a busy
man. And now I know Clover's daughter, our Clover, of course."

"Pete explained to me that the Boldts weren't the richest family here." Mrs.
Hammond didn't seem pleased with the observation, her smile disappearing.

"Really, I wouldn't know about that."

"He said that Commodore Bourne was certainly the wealthiest man here at the
time."

"It's pronounced 'Born.' Pete knows more than I about that. I knew Margie well,
of course. We played a lot of tennis, along with Clover—she was better than all of
us."

"Margie?"

"Marjorie Bourne. She was the Commodore's daughter. She retained Dark Island
after a quarrel with her brother over who would have it. Messy business. Needless

The Thousand Islands Yacht Club on Welcome Island, which obscures The Birches and Chalet.

to say, they weren't close. That wasn't unusual, however. There was always a lot of feuding here."

"I have the notion that the Thousand Islands Yacht Club was a real social community."

She laughed. "A small-town community, maybe—where everybody knew everyone else's business, and talked about whoever wasn't there that day."

"But it was the real social center, wasn't it?" She seemed puzzled.

"I never thought so. No, I wouldn't say that it was the 'center,' because there were many centers. There were even other yacht clubs, you know—and some rivalry between them. But the grand hotels really outdid the clubs for social events. Boldt, of course, managed to outdo the local hotels for special occasions, when he brought to the Yacht Club a decorator and carload of floral décor from the Waldorf. But we didn't spend all of our time at the Yacht Club. There were too many other places to go, and things to do. Some islands had their own ball rooms—if you could call them that—like the huge space over the boathouse at Ina Island."

"But at the Yacht Club, wouldn't I find the social leaders as regulars?" She looked even more puzzled.

"'Social leaders? You must have been reading about some other place. There weren't any 'leaders' here. Everybody was either quarreling, or too stubbornly independent to accept any 'leaders'."

"What was all the quarreling about?"

"Why, some of these people we just naturally pugnacious. Don't suppose that you're talking about ladies and gentlemen, back in that first generation. Some ladies, perhaps, and even a few gentlemen, but remember that these were self-made men, most of whom had clawed their way to the top. Take Gilbert Rafferty, for example—a quarrelsome Irishman, especially when in his cups. Always feuding."

"Who was he?"

"Imperial Island. Came from Pittsburgh, like my husband. Rafferty produced coke from coal."

"There were some Jewish families here, I understand."

"Yes. The Breitenbachs owned this place at one time."

"Courtney didn't recall whether any of those families belonged to the Thousand Islands Yacht Club." Mrs. Hammond looked surprised.

"But of course not. Courtney must have known that. There was another yacht club at Alexandria Bay. I think they participated in that. They kept pretty much to themselves, as I recall."

"I still can't get a handle on how the Boldts fit in. Would you find Clover regularly at the yacht club, as a real presence there?" Mrs. Hammond laughed.

"Oh, no!" She clapped her hands in delight. "That was Emma Hagan. Dear old Emma. She must have weighed three-hundred pounds. They had to devise a special arrangement for getting her in and out of boats. Emma had *her* chair on the verandah, right at the head of the steps, where everyone entering would have to acknowledge her commanding presence. We youngsters were told by our parents that we must *not* make fun of her—and she was so funny. In addition to being so corpulent, she had one wandering eye that was always looking somewhere else. But we had to keep a straight face and be courteous. I always curtseyed to Mrs. Hagan at the top of the steps, and she was always there—every day. Now, if you're looking for the real "presence" at the Yacht Club, she was it. Clover was elsewhere, playing golf or tennis, usually."

"So who was this Mrs. Hagan?"

"Ina Isle. She had been a laundress. Her husband invented and manufactured commercial laundry equipment. That's Thousand Islands 'society' for you!"

I left still marveling at Jean Hammond's remarkable vitality and charm, wondering if I could retain so much zest for life after another half-century of it. Of course, I wasn't in Mrs. Hammond's life situation. F. Scott Fitzgerald observed that "Living well is the best revenge." Mrs. Hammond seemed evidence that living well has its advantages.

29. Recalling my first sight of Boldt Castle, and thinking of illustrations for a possible book or article, I had asked if I might find somewhere a similar night view of the landmark, seen in the moonlight, across the water. Meg said there were zillions of images, to be found at several local archives. She vaguely recalled seeing a ghostly,

moonlit scene in a nineteen-twenties' tourist brochure, probably to be found at the Antique Boat Museum library, but she suggested more confidently that the prominent local painter, Michael Ringer, had done an evening scene of Heart Island, viewed from the Bay—probably much as I had seen it. I ought to drive to his studio—worth a visit, at any rate, she advised.

I was surprised to find no artist struggling in a garret—or a fiercely hot loft over a swayback boathouse, like Professor Pete's—but instead I found on Dingman Point a remarkable institution—a large, modern, air-conditioned structure housing an upscale gallery of Ringer art. Ringer himself, I discovered, is a regional institution—a "cultural treasure," as the Japanese might say about a nationally important artist. As a young man, he quickly produced a huge regional *oeuvre*, and quickly established a large regional following. He has appeared in a series of interviews on National Public Radio. Although he is prolific, his work is in high demand, new canvases fetching prices in the four to eight-thousand dollar range. Astutely, he has published costly art books that reproduce his work effectively, as well as moderately priced reproductions, engagement books, calendars, and even inexpensive post cards that feature his popular paintings. He not only paints, but also is casting bronze sculpture. Ringer is not merely a local artist, but a local industry.

The rather shrine-like gallery was hushed, oriental carpets on gleaming hardwood floors, fine woodwork, subdued and effective lighting. A new addition had sloped, soaring ceilings, with stained-glass panels. The place had more class than the most upscale of the resort hotels at nearby Alexandria Bay. Best of all, it was rich with immediately accessible and engaging art. Instantly, I fell into that private game of all covetous shoppers: which one would I buy, had I the means to have at least one of the works?

Ringer has an uncanny sense of place, living intimately with the River and knowing its many moods through the changes of season. He is a master of atmospheric water, whether seeing islands vanishing into distant haze, or vapor rising on a chill autumn morning. He loves boats—which is one reason Islanders love his work. He appreciates the charm of old cottages and decrepit boathouses. In a word, he knows and loves the River.

But I was looking for Heart Island. I didn't have to spend several thousand dollars for a painting. What I sought was available as a poster: Heart Island, just as I had first seen it—except earlier in the evening, with the sky still glowing with sunset. But there were the theatrical floodlights, the dark profile against the sky. It was right, and Michael generously allowed me to use it.

30. Meg had assembled pictures of the Alster Tower, which she compared with another building. "This was Castle Rest. See, the most striking feature was its tall stone tower, likewise rustic in character, similarly constructed of rough granite. Seth Pope, a local contractor, had built Castle Rest for George M. Pullman and then, a few years later, he built the Alster Tower for George C. Boldt. But Seth Pope wasn't the designer of the first work—that was Solon Spencer Beman, an important Chicago architect. Boldt probably admired Pullman's trophy house as well, and he did engage Seth Pope to provide something similar. But did he also commission Beman to design the Alster Tower? That's an intriguing question."

"Castle Rest is gone?"

"Tragic. The family blew it up, when the locals refused to lower taxes. The place had been unused for years, but maintained. The family argued that it no longer was useful as a residence, but offered to keep it up it as a memorial to George Pullman —if the heavy taxes would be abated. Castle Rest was an architectural landmark and a highlight of the boat tours here,—a real asset for the whole region. But the natives couldn't recognize that the days of soak-the-rich were over. So Castle Rest was dynamited."

"What a loss!"

"Not everyone thought so. Pete tells about trying to interest Grant Mitchell in historic preservation. Mitchell was a hotel owner at the Bay who was probably the major advocate of development at the time. He preceded Vince Dee as Chairman of the Bridge Authority. Mitchell was of the view that the Thousand Islands would be better off without all those old wrecks."

"Like Boldt Castle, I suppose."

"It *was* a wreck, before they rescued it from total ruin. Vince Dee, thank God, became Chairman of the Authority, which acquired Heart Island. Vince had more vision than his predecessor."

"Do you see resemblances between the Alster Tower and Castle Rest than might suggest attribution to Beman as the architect?"

"No, not really. In fact, Castle Rest does not even look like Beman work that I know, which was more conventionally Victorian in character—not very interesting, which Castle Rest surely was. Castle Rest was quite odd, really distinctive, in 1888. Possibly the distinction of both buildings has much to do with their common builder, Seth Pope. But we do know that Beman was architect of Castle Rest. That doesn't mean that Pope couldn't have contributed to the design—possibly he made the design proposal to Pullman, and Beman, who was Pullman's regular architect for this vast works, merely administered the contract, as he customarily did for Pullman." Meg got up and went to the window, to turn down the old air-conditioning unit, which in addition to whirring had begun to clatter. "I don't know which is worse, the heat or the noise."

"So there were 'castles' here before Boldt. The 'castle' idea wasn't his alone."

"No. Dark Island Castle came later, but probably the first thing the Boldts saw at the Thousand Islands, when they disembarked from the train at Clayton, was Charles Emery's shining new chateau across the water, on Calumet Island. It was a tow-

ered villa, built of raspberry-colored Potsdam sandstone, crowned with orange tile roofs—rather fruity. Vivid. And then, before arriving by steamboat at Alexandria Bay, they would have passed Castle Rest, darker, more brooding—invariably pointed out as the summer home of George M. Pullman. Probably by the time they landed at the Bay the castle notion was firmly im-

Calumet Castle as it appeared when the Boldts arrived. Subsequently a ball room addition to the left doubled its size.

planted. But of course, George recalled the fantasy castle built by the Graf von Putbus, his father's boss at Rügen, so the new images resonated with memory of his home island."

"That sort of dream castle probably impressed the youngster—perhaps indelibly, as a romantic ideal."

"Of course. The count's hunting castle was the genesis, indirectly. But not really the formal precedent. The Alster Tower is too different. We need to look at other models. You want the full architecture lecture?"

"Sure. "

"Castle Rest, only a few islands up the River, derived from the precedent of the German *Wohnturm*, or "living tower," which was the form of the Rügen mini-castle and might as well have been the model for the Kaiser's reception pavilion at Hamburg—Pete's pet theory, you know. Clearly, the Alster Tower owes something directly to the "German fortress" model, as Castle Rest was viewed at the time. Probably its tall, square, stone tower was the immediate impetus for the Boldt project. Again, a contemporary writer thought the Alster Tower resembled an 'old ruin from the Black Forest.'

"We know that Solon S. Beman designed Castle Rest for George M. Pullman, and that Seth Pope was the local contractor who built Pullman's stone tower. We do know as well that Seth Pope subsequently built the Alster Tower for the Boldts. What we don't know, in truth, is who designed the unique Alster Tower.

"One recent writer said that Seth Pope was 'architect' of the Alster Tower. This may have confused the roles of builder and architect. Formally, Alster Tower is an extremely complex conception. It's also a technical tour de force. It seems highly improbable that a local contractor, occupied at the time with a booming construction business, would have had either inclination or time, let alone ability, to design such an intensely manipulated small structure.

"If not Seth Pope, who might have been architect of the Alster Tower? Conceivably, if Boldt admired the Pullman's building, engaging its contractor, he might have commissioned its architect as well. Could Beman have designed the Alster Tower? Castle Rest, at least in its masonry portions, was similar in character. Beman designed the Pullman residence to merge, like the Alster Tower, imperceptibly into carefully preserved natural landscape. Castle Rest likewise employed uncut, rough granite, including some chunks of cyclopean size. Clearly, the romantic notion of a tall tower is common to both buildings. Castle Rest, beautifully composed and effective landmark that it was, even

Freighter passing the Alster Tower

though imaginative and innovative, never attained the quality of fantasy which so characterizes the Alster Tower. The imagination of its designer is of another order altogether; the Alster Tower appears much more improvisational, more spontaneous, more exuberant—on the edge, almost out of control. This doesn't look like the more conventional, disciplined hand of Solon Spencer Beman. Furthermore, Beman was in Chicago, far distant either from Boldt or from Heart Island, whereas the complexity of the Alster Tower suggests that in some measure it must have been improvised on the site."

"Could the Boldts themselves have been on the site to shape the building, contributing much of the design themselves?"

"Good thought. But George was so involved in his business, building and opening the great new Astoria portion of the hotel, that it seems unlikely he would be spending much time on Heart Island, designing day-by-day an extremely complicated structure as it rose. Louise might have been on hand to contribute more. It's not impossible that she directed Seth Pope, making decisions as the building evolved. But considerable foresight was required; some sort of planning had to be done in advance. This isn't the work of an amateur. As an architect, I see the hand of an architect at work.

"William Hewitt designed virtually all of the other structures on Heart Island, as well as other Boldt buildings on Wellesley Island. He began working on the Boldts' River projects as soon as they bought Heart Island. In 1895 he designed a rustic, stone Power House as a miniature castle—not built until years later. So why not attribute the Alster Tower, four years afterwards, to Hewitt?

"The firm of Hewitt and Hewitt, (later becoming Hewitt, Steven & Paist) although they exhibited other Heart Island designs, never showed a design, nor claimed authorship of the Alster Tower. Bill Hewitt in Philadelphia was remote from Alexandria Bay, and for sure the Alster Tower required involvement of the designer in its construction. Could this building have ever evolved on paper? Could its eccentric plans and sections even be drawn? It's really quite improvisational. While technically possible, the point rather is that this kind of design does not evolve on paper, with the T-square and triangle of a conventional architect. Furthermore, the style of the Alster Tower isn't really consistent with the other Hewitt buildings. Closest, perhaps, in character is the Powerhouse, but the Powerhouse, although built of rough granite masonry in a castellated style, is inherently different. Roofs dominate its formal conception, just as they do the Hewitt-designed Castle and Yacht House, as well as Wellesley House, probably all by the same hand. The Alster Tower, however, was never envisioned in the same formal language. Curiously, it has more or less flat roofs (undulating, actually) except for the porch wing, where a low-pitched gable is formed by massive slabs of stone. Whereas the Hewitt buildings rise with sheer walls abruptly from ground or water, the Alster Tower was intended to meld with the landscape, almost to dissolve as molten stone into the native bed of granite. Surely, this design may be regarded as "organic," in Antonio Gaudí's, if not exactly Frank Lloyd Wright's sense of that term. Actually, the intent is akin to Beman's Castle Rest which was integrated into the land."

"Barcelona is a long way from Alexandria Bay."

Meg laughed. "Oh, don't be such a stick-in-the-mud. You asked for the architectural history lecture. Now pay attention.

"The Catalan architect Antonio Gaudí could have been author of the Alster Tower. If you've climbed through the fantastic spires of his unfinished Barcelona Cathedral, you've sense the kinship of spirit, a similar sensation to climbing the stone stairway entwined about the exterior of the Alster Tower. Traversing the lead surface of the Alster Towers rolling roofs (and they were intended to be experienced

Climbers ascend the Alster Tower

on foot) reminds you of the Spanish architect's surreal roofscapes. His bizarre forms, embellished with bits of colored tile, broken crockery and other found objects, expressed the same fantastic impulse that gave form to the Alster Tower. The kinship is merely *Zeitgeist*, however. The similarity derived from a common *Art Nouveau* taste for the surreal and bizarre." Meg smiled. "You see, I paid attention in my art-history classes. You want more?"

"Okay."

"'Organic' in a rather literal sense, *l'Art Nouveau* endeavored to convey the dynamic quality of natural life, largely through use of fluid, curvilinear forms. Indeed, some writhing ironwork at the Alster Tower recalls that of the Paris Metro stations by Hector Guimard. Boldt himself had dining chairs of the style aboard 'La Duchesse.' The same serpentine quality pervades the interior design of the Alster Tower, particularly where walls, stairs and even doors are warped into curved shapes.

"The German equivalent of *l'Art Nouveau* was the *Jugendstil* (Young Style). More than decorative fashions, these contemporary movements sought *expression*, and were proto-Expressionist. What were they endeavoring to express? Perhaps what is verbally inexpressible, some sort of non-rational, spiritual dynamic.—How's that for art-historical rhetoric? And are you ready for this? Here's a great quote: Unlike conventional buildings that 'set limits to our world,' walls should 'seek to enclose the unlimited, towers seek to reach the heavens. On steps we ascend as if being carried upward—last symbol of our inner strivings.' Wow. Love that purple prose. But, more importantly, the Boldts probably would have loved it and, in truth, this might have served as the real program for the Alster Tower. That sort of expressionist impulse surely motivated its amorphous plan and section, its verticality and spiraling ascension. . . . Now how's that for today's architecture lecture?"

"Bravo. But who designed the Alster Tower?" She smiled and shrugged.

"Dunno."

31. "How could Boldt have amassed such wealth in so few years?" I asked Pete.

"Well, he fell into exceptional opportunities, time after time. Pure luck, perhaps—which may be why the Boldts were supposed to be superstitious about luck. You see, as a venture capitalist, Boldt didn't have to use his own capital. In the beginning, he didn't have any, to speak of. Boldt had the uncanny ability to use other people's money. There was plenty of money around, and he knew how to get hold of it. He was a gambler, and borrowed heavily. It paid off. But there were risks, and a high price to be paid in personal stress.

Dining saloon aboard "La Duchesse"

"Boldt's luck was in his connections, but in fairness his connections were based on his personal qualities that others admired. In truth, Boldt's phenomenal success derived not primarily from lucky breaks or instinctive shrewdness in recognizing and optimizing breaks, but indeed from his charisma. He was a charmer. Here's one capsule characterization: "modest, kindly, thoughtful, and refined." Although he developed very polished manners, it would be a mistake to think of Boldt as aloof or reserved. No, to the contrary, he was known for 'his never failing amiability.' A 'perpetually genial man,' he 'put on a fresh smile every morning.'

"Apparently his particular combination of personality traits won him not merely friends, but active proponents who volunteered assistance. First a regular customer at Parker's Restaurant, impressed by the 'suave and courteous' manner of Boldt, the pleasant cashier, decided to make the inexperienced young man manager of a large resort hotel—quite a leap professionally. Boldt then left that initial management position to accept a demotion, becoming a mere assistant steward at a small gentlemen's club—in effect a headwaiter, meeting the clubmen. That was a shrewd move, however, for it was the super-elite Philadelphia Club, the nation's oldest gentlemen's club, and it was the year of the Philadelphia World's Fair, when the club was thronged with visiting dignitaries. There he met important men and married his boss's daughter. Boldt learned much from his father-in-law and the experience at the Club. At the time, it was said, 'the master of the [commercial] hotel is generally too great a swell to attend to his guests, or look after the cooking and waiters.' The latter, however, was what Boldt did at the Club, for it was no commercial hotel—and its members wouldn't enter one. Boldt sensed such cultural nuances. He always had a keen social sense, deriving from his boyhood on Rügen, no doubt. The clubmen were more than pleased with Boldt at the Philadelphia Club. 'His name slowly began to assume as much importance as the Philadelphia Club itself.' Indeed, 'it was a forgone conclusion that Boldt would not long remain at the Philadelphia Club.'

"At the Philadelphia Club it was 'his charm' as well as 'his very apparent ability' that attracted the attention of 'a man of high social prestige and power,' Anthony J. Antelo, who became his second important booster. At the Club, Boldt began talking about 'a little hotel of his own.' He and Louise suspected that prospective patrons were 'tired of sitting in their own parlors.' They had noted Petrie's languishing restaurant, in a small hotel, as a perfect opportunity. It was Antelo, together with other clubmen, who put George and Louise Boldt in their small Bellevue Hotel."

The Bellevue Hotel, Philadelphia

"What more do we know about her role there? You said that she took care of the cashier's desk and learned the hotel business as well as her husband. But was she more than a helpmate?"

"Oh, yes. Yes, indeed. Louise not merely graced the little hotel with her personal charm. More importantly, they said, 'what she knew even better than her husband was feminine psychology. Through her years at the Hotel Bellevue, where she had been active in the supervision of that inn's service, she had not lost her understanding of the woman's mind.' Louise knew what other women wanted: to get out of the Victorian confinement of their houses. They craved the 'glamour of the crowd.' The flower-filled Bellevue was the model for the women-filled Waldorf. Louise's feminine taste and keen intuition were critical to building the Waldorf-Astoria as the unique institution it became and is today.

"In venturing out on his own, Boldt had 'no difficulty in raising money,' which was supplied by clubmen. The little Bellevue Hotel established the Boldts reputation. Much of their following came from the ranks of the Philadelphia Club, and the Boldts quickly became known for running an elite establishment, 'like an exclusive club.' It was 'more like a club than any hotel in the country.' Boldt played the 'role of old-time host.' 'His policy was to charge high prices for good things, which . . . preserved its exclusiveness.' Boldt's were the 'highest prices that Philadelphia ever heard of,' 'about thirty per cent higher than any other restaurant in Philadelphia.' As he would subsequently at the Waldorf, Boldt ran the inn on the European plan, without including meals with rooms—then a new practice in America. The Bellevue was 'always . . . the pet of [his] great heart [on which he] lavished his most loving care, . . . the most infinite attention.' The Boldts did 'the most astonishing things' to create new standards of food and service. The 'little hotel acquired national fame,' as 'prestige piled on prestige.' It became 'America's most famous little hotel and doubtless its best one.' The food was marvelous—Boldt engaged a fine European chef. Some visitors 'traveled a thousand miles to enjoy one of George C. Boldt's incomparable dinners.' It was discussed 'whenever American gourmets swapped tales of rare dishes.' The Bellevue became 'the best eating-place in America,' 'world famous for its cuisine.' In fact, Boldt sent his famous Terrapin à la Maryland to Buckingham Palace during Queen Victoria's reign. In return, the queen sent the chef an autographed photograph. It wasn't merely the food, however, but the service and ambiance as well that set it apart. And it wasn't merely the Boldts' personal attention to every guest, but that of all the staff. Indeed, the familiar tone was worthy of note: 'the servants are on terms of intimacy with many of the guests.' And then there were all those fresh flowers that the Boldts loved."

"I really want to stress Louise's contribution to their success, and her active involvement in the business. She was a working partner. This seems important to understanding her plight in later years, when she was shut out of the business. Have you anything more to substantiate her role?"

"Here are some more quotes: 'She was 'a great business help to him.' And another: 'What 'a great part this astute lady played in making the Waldorf the breathless wonder it was in the 1890s'! And here's a good one: 'Those who stood closest to him in all of his many activities are the first to aver that the greatest of his successes were due to the quick wit and unfailing good sense of his wife. "I'll ask Louise," was the most frequent response that he gave, when important matters were first put up to him for decision. In a cooperation that was hardly short of marvelous to those that really understood it, this man and his wife worked'."

"Couldn't ask for much more than that."

"No, there's little doubt that Louise became a real business partner. I expect she grew into that role, as she matured. After all, she was only fifteen when they wed. But participating in the male domain wasn't regarded as admirable in those days of 'separate spheres' for men and women. Being an equal to one's husband wasn't socially an advantage at the time when proper ladies were supposed to be kept enshrined as decorative trophies. But Louise was a German-American girl, brought up in a different culture. She was born in Philadelphia, but her parents spoke German at home, and so was she able to converse with George in his native tongue, which no doubt contributed to their mutual attraction."

"You say she was only fifteen years old when they married?"

Pete seemed delighted to reveal a little-known fact. "Yes, she was much younger than he, by almost eleven years—a child bride, by our standards. The difference is especially considerable, when one person is only fifteen and the other twenty-six. I expect that as she outgrew her girlishness, the relationship had to adjust, perhaps with some difficulty."

"Probably Boldt was paternalistic," I ventured, "at least at first, regarding her as childish?"

"That wasn't uncommon at the time, even for men who were neither Prussian nor considerably older than their young wives. You know Ibsen's 'Doll's House?' Imagine George and Louise as Torvald and Nora."

"I remember how that play turned out. She walked out on him."

"Yes. She grew up." Pete smiled, as if sharing a secret. ". . . That reminds me of one of the folk tales—that Louise left George."

"Do you suspect that he was domineering?"

"The family recollects that he was—but you may get to hear this from Clover herself, in time. Back in Prussia 'women, even of social position, were regarded as man's chattel.' We wouldn't have expected George to hold advanced views of feminism or to have accepted his wife as a working partner. This is one of many contrasting characterizations of the man that are hard to reconcile. We just heard about consulting his wife whenever he had an important decision to make. Is that what we expect of a Prussian autocrat? Boldt had many sides. I really suspect that he was both adoring and authoritarian—as one writer said paraphrasing Clover Two, "He was gentle and yet he was unyielding." The two aren't mutually exclusive in a man, particularly a Prussian—both devoted and demanding. He was an erratic, emotional man—a man of many parts, a sort of untutored polymath, both calculating and impulsive. He could be alternately authoritarian and strict, or considerate and charming. Fascinating character."

"Do you have accounts of the time, personal recollections, that convey his personality?"

"Oh, do I!" As Pete rummaged through his papers, lapping of water in the boathouse below accompanied the fading whine of a distant outboard motor. "I have dozens of characterizations left by those who knew him. I've tried to fit them together, like fragments of mosaic. Pasted together they run pages, however. I'll make a copy for you. Use whatever you like, or put the whole thing in an appendix. I don't think you want me to read them all aloud."

"Just give me one or two now, for flavor."

"Well, here's a sort of general characterization: 'So overwhelmingly great was Boldt's personality, . . . the innate lovableness of the man endeared him to every one with whom he came in contact. . . . Immensely popular, . . . he was the most charming and gentle of men, a lovable, simple person, . . . earnest and true, . . . [with a] personality that kept old friends, and made new ones. . . . You could not keep him from making friends. . . . [He] does not allow his wonderful energy to obscure his affability. . . . He nearly always smiles'."

"That's certainly complimentary."

"Oh, they all are, as I recall. Oscar penned many of the hero-worshiping compliments after Boldt's death—but 'the Chief,' as he called him, was gone, so the assistant's adulation wasn't self-serving. The consistency of the characterizations by many people seems to corroborate them."

"I'm having troubling reconciling this view of the 'loveable, simple person' with the splendor of his grandiose Castle."

"Well, here's another: 'Gentle, mild-mannered, unassuming, . . . modest in his demeanor, . . . [his] human quality [conveyed] the enthusiasms of the perpetual boy that he was at heart. . . .'"

"He was supposed to be 'unassuming, . . . modest in his demeanor'? The guy who built that monumental trophy house? This doesn't ring true."

"I'm not making this up. Here's the evidence."

"But everything seems contradictory. At one moment he's supposed to be dependent on his wife, but then he's domineering. Then he's your friendly nice guy, but turns into an authoritarian perfectionist, demanding of others. Was he schizoid—a Jeckyll-Hyde personality?"

"That I don't know, but he was a perfectionist, yes. Someone said, 'Perfection . . . was his religion.' You'll find the more you learn about George Boldt, the more intriguing he becomes. He was a very complex man—not the simple soul portrayed by Oscar in his book—I'll grant you that. It was his adoring Oscar who was the simple soul."

"Yes, as Leo Durocher said, 'Nice guys finish last,' I suppose?"

"Boldt knew how to be nice, when niceness paid. But there was much more to him. He had a temper and was stubborn—no pushover wimp. Remember, this was the kid who came alone to the streets of New York at age thirteen. You're right—for almost every one of his attributes, there was a contradictory one. But most of us are more than one simple person, aren't we? Boldt seemed to live several lives, as several different people."

"Multiple personalities. What do we know about Louise?"

"We have less about her, but the few characterizations portray her as a sweet person, likable. Here's one, written by a contemporary: a 'very charming woman she was, . . . his wife.' Although Boldt has been considered a snob, there's no suggestion that Louise was socially ambitions. She may have been miscast as the regal mistress of Boldt Castle. One wonders if that was a role she really wanted to play, or whether George assigned her that part. He might have thought that she deserved the pedestal, but life atop a column can be lonely."

"You say she wasn't sociable—a socialite?"

"Certainly she was socially adroit, self- assured when meeting even distinguished people. Having had much experience as a professional hostess, she was invariably pleasant, even with disagreeable people, even under adverse circumstances. In her business, she had to know how to handle rude and insolent people (as the new rich often are). Although skilled with personal relations superficially, I expect that she may have been rather naïve socially. Her father, after all, was once a tavern keeper, and her early formative experience probably was restricted to a small, German-American community. Beneath her social skill probably lurked considerable insecurity, especially when she rose socially. But we have to remember that her father became steward of the Philadelphia Club, and I suspect that the proud Papa showed off little Louise to charmed members of that ultra-exclusive coterie. That she as well as George became well liked there probably contributed to the great success of their first joint venture, the little Bellevue Hotel in Philadelphia.

"The Boldts' acquaintance with patrician Philadelphia was a real key to their success, leading to the Astor connection. They came to recognize 'class' and in Philadelphia learned to purvey the aura of the 'classy' to those whose had plenty of new money to spend. They applied their learning to cash in the 'gold rush' of new western fortunes pouring into New York City, where the action was. The Waldorf-Astoria 'began to fill up with recently manicured iron workers from Pittsburgh [the likes of Alex Peacock of Belle Island, 'shirtsleeve millionaires' who 'still smelled of burning coke'], loggers from Duluth, copper miners from Michigan, brewers from Milwaukee and St. Louis, and other gentry, who thought a cotillion was something to eat, but who could sign checks with numbers on them as long as a Santa Fe freight train.' The Boldts themselves were socially in this milieu of the New Rich. Boldt aspired to more, however. He cherished his personal friendship with Andrew D. White, President of Cornell University, and was extremely proud to serve on the Board of Trustees of the University, since he had so little formal education himself. He's memorialized by the Boldt Tower there, given by his daughter, and by the Boldt Memorial Dining Room—probably a gift of George Baker, a friend of Boldt and a major benefactor to Cornell, through Boldt's influence."

"In a sense, the Boldts were both 'marginal' socially?"

"Of course. Remember, they continued to speak German at home, until the advent of the First World War. They probably considered themselves marginal, knowing that others regarded them so. I think that they identified with other marginal families, like the Strauses over at Cherry Island. That Jewish family was likewise rich (Macy's Department Store) but at the fringe of the wasp establishment. Of course, Boldt could converse in German with many of the leading Jewish families of New York. But, needless to say, all of them craved acceptance. The Boldts weren't Lutheran, but were 'born again fashionable' as High Church Episcopalians. They named their daughter 'Clover' and adopted the nickname, 'Cricket' for their son. The English character of the Philadelphia Club and the Main Line rubbed off. No doubt young George, Jr. was nicknamed for that esoteric English sport played at Main Line clubs."

"Boldt Castle represents the American Dream, doesn't it? Poor immigrant boy builds a dream castle for his wife, the innkeeper's daughter."

"That's part of its mystique, surely. So much more moving than the palaces built by third-generation-rich Vanderbilts—not very interesting people, really".

"What do we know about the sort of guests the Boldts entertained here?"

"We only hear of the more notable visitors, of course, which probably gives a skewed impression, but one does suspect that the Boldts favored those bearing public credentials, whose status was recognizable. The Boldts were upwardly mobile, socially ambitious. George and Louise never made the New York City *Social Register*, you know, although their daughter eventually did. Fifty other New York City families at the Islands were listed, a hundred more were not."

"What did listing mean? Prominence, wealth?"

"Money had nothing whatsoever to do with qualifying; family was all. The *Social Register* stated, 'One must not be 'employed.' That left out a lot of folks. One genteel lady remembered that 'only those in the professions' were considered to be 'true gentlemen'; businessmen didn't qualify.

"Not all Islanders were inclined to be identified by the *Social Register*, which was anti-Semitic. Nevertheless, for many in America, especially the socially ambitious, as said at the time, 'the epitome of glamour was the *Social Register*.' No doubt the

The Boldt Pier, with houseboat "La Duchesse" at left.
The Thousand Islands Club was built behind the pier.

Boldts wanted in—as indeed Clover accomplished."

"You're suggesting that they were snobs?"

"I wouldn't be the first to call George Boldt a snob. After all, snobbery was his business. It was his instinct—his genius. That's what the little Bellevue and then the grand Waldorf-Astoria were all about. Snobbery came from Europe, from Rügen's vestigial feudalism of the Graf von Putbus, and made Boldt the American purveyor of aristocratic pretension in serving the rich and famous. His greatest contribution, you know, was turning the American hotel, which had been largely a necessary evil for travelers, when no wealthy American would consider staying at a commercial hotel, into an urban social center favored by the very rich. He himself said, 'Do you know, I would rather see Mrs. Astor sitting in my Palm Garden and drinking a cup of hot water, than view [ill-mannered "Bet-a-Million" Gates] in there eating the costliest dinner I could serve him!' Mrs. Astor represented what he wanted: social acceptance by the American elite of the American hotel."

"And he succeeded."

"With unbelievable success. As one wag put it, 'He purveyed exclusiveness to the masses.'"

"But how did he make so much money at it, so very quickly?"

"Ah, yes. We got off that track. You see, he had a likeable quality that endeared him to earlier patrons. First there was a New York City physician, a patron of Parker's restaurant, where George tended the cash register, who gave him his first big break, running the large resort hotel up the Hudson; then Louise's father, William Kehrer made him his assistant at the Philadelphia Club. This portrait photo [p. ix] was taken in 1876, the year he went to Philadelphia and met young Louise. Soon A. J. Antelo and other club men helped George and Louise get started at their little Bellevue."

"And then he charmed William Waldorf Astor, who appeared on that dark and stormy night to ask for a room there, when there was no room at the inn."

"Aha, so you've heard that one. Don't be so gullible."

"But its such a good anecdote: George and Louise Boldt give up their own quarters for Astor, who repaid them by building the Waldorf for them."

"It's a good story because it's oversimplified. Can you imagine the Astors patronizing a commercial hotel? That wasn't done in their set. Don't you suppose that many prominent families in Philadelphia would have welcomed them as houseguests?

There are other variants of the tale about the Boldts giving up their own room for a prominent visitor. One hears these stories even in Argentina. In fact, the Boldts frequently gave their private quarters to guests, even at the Waldorf-Astoria. But, in short, it wasn't Astor but Abner Bartlett, who was really the largest Fairy Godfather of the whole tale."

"I never heard of Abner Bartlett."

"No. He was an *éminance grise*, behind the scenes. Said to be 'as important in New York City in the 1880s and early 'nineties, in his way, as anyone,' Bartlett was an agent for William Waldorf Astor, who left America in a fit of pique when his fortune failed to buy his election to Congress. Astor bought an ancient castle and another stately home in England, where he established that branch of the family, becoming Viscount Astor. He was rather disinterested in his American holdings, largely Manhattan real estate, leaving business to agents. Abner Bartlett represented absent Waldorf Astor, whose communications from England were infrequent. Conscious of his responsibility, Bartlett was ever discreet in New York City, but went to Philadelphia to play. He discovered the elegant little 24-room Bellevue, favored of eminent gentlemen. The Boldts were known to be likewise discreet and to indulge guests with novel touches like fresh flowers and fruit in every room. By his own account, he was charmed not only by George, but also by Louise Boldt. As one writer put it, 'Abner Bartlett . . . a tall thin fellow elongated by his stovepipe hat and Henry Clay neckgear into a perfect picture of the bluenose, went occasionally to Philadelphia to enjoy himself.' Boldt himself said that his 'greatest leap up the ladder of fame and prosperity had its mainspring in a weakness of old Abner Bartlett for strong spirits.' The Boldts treated Bartlett very well. Boldt gave him his own apartment in the Bellevue—probably origin of the popular story. Shrewd move."

"So Bartlett recommended Boldt as proprietor of Astor's new hotel."

"Yes, but there's more to it. Life's not so simple. When Waldorf Astor's wife had a medical (or more probably a psychosomatic) problem requiring help, she went to Dr. Wier Mitchell, a Philadelphia physician was reputed to be the leading specialist. Dr. Mitchell's cure entailed confinement for a particular regimen. Rather than entering a hospital, Mrs. Astor moved into a suite of eight rooms at the Boldts' exclusive little Bellevue for an extended sojourn, where she 'recovered from a nervous breakdown under Mrs. Boldt's care.' This was a remarkable event, considering the abhorrence of commercial hotels by the social elite at the time. Boldt prepared a special diet and devised a special call bell for her use, but note that it was Louise Boldt who personally attended Mary Astor."

"So that's how the Astors came to know the Boldts."

"Yes, but there's still more to it. You see, Mrs. William Waldorf Astor was Mary Paul, a prominent belle of Philadelphia and Newport. Both her parents descended from colonial families, which distinguished them from New Money (enhancing Mary's eligibility to become Mrs. Astor) and doubtless her father had known George Boldt at the Philadelphia Club. This was when Boldt's decision to take the demotion from hotel manager to headwaiter began to pay off. 'Willie' Astor probably was introduced to the Bellevue by Mary's father and so may have become acquainted with the Boldts when he was courting Mary, visiting Philadelphia every weekend. Perhaps Mary as well as Willie became acquainted with George and Louise at the time, for one of the socially innovative features of the Bellevue was its unquestioned suitability as a place to dine with wives and lady friends.

"The Astors were pleased with the Boldts' hospitality during Mary's confinement. Shortly, Waldorf became annoyed by his aunt's new designation of herself simply as "Mrs. Astor," as if she were "*The* Mrs. Astor"—as indeed she became known, eclipsing Waldorf's wife. He struck back. His Fifth Avenue town house shared a block frontage, between 33rd and 34th Streets with his brother's mansion. He told Bartlett to demolish the house and build a commercial hotel that would put *The* Mrs. Astor in its shade. And so it came about—so they say.

"But historic fact is rarely so storybook-like. Bartlett told the tale differently. He maintained that Astor had never considered building a commercial hotel on his house site in order to offend his aunt, but had in fact first rejected Bartlett's proposal to building a hotel there as an investment—objected to 'owning a tavern.'

"Bartlett said that he persuaded a reluctant Astor, but they needed a proprietor for a new hotel, and both thought of the Boldts in Philadelphia, who were of course now known to the Astors as well as to Bartlett. Nevertheless Bartlett recalled that only 'after much persuasion' did he induce Astor actually to meet Boldt regarding this business. By this time George Boldt 'had climbed to comparative fortune and fame in Philadelphia,' so he wasn't an unknown quantity. Indeed, Boldt had acquired 'the name for superlative excellence' with the little Bellevue. But he was something of a gamble, as the Boldts had operated only an intimate, little hotel, and this was to be a major, urban facility.

"Bartlett didn't surprise the Boldts for George's eye had been on the New York City prize for some time and probably he planted the seed in Bartlett's mind. They had been discussing a New York hotel project for several years, but hadn't found the right site until Waldorf decided to give up his house. Boldt had told Bartlett that he would like to take over operation of the new Holland House hotel then being built. That may have forced Bartlett's hand.

"Although it was Abner Bartlett who most probably was the real key to the Boldt success story, the New York hotel proposition didn't come on a silver platter as a gift to Boldt. He drove a hard bargain, insisting 'on a profit-sharing arrangement which should yield him an income, in case he made good, such as no hotel manager in this country had even known before.' Bartlett agreed to an incredibly opportune deal for Boldt. Waldorf Astor would build a big facility to Boldt's specifications. Boldt would have to furnish the hotel and would run the place as his own, merely paying a fixed rent on a twenty-five year lease. The profits, if any, would be his.

"The question of the cost of the building to Astor, and its name were related. It may have been Astor's own notion to call the hotel by his middle name, "Waldorf." Although Bartlett wrote Astor: 'Mr. Boldt, who is . . . here today, desires me to thank you for your concession in giving the name he so much desires to have. . ,' this may have been mere courtesy. Bartlett went on to say that 'your wishes as to the exposure of the name upon the building and flag shall be fully carried out.' This suggests that Astor already identified the project with his name. Because 'Waldorf' was to be the name of the hotel, it had to be first class. Perhaps this was mere luck for Boldt, or possibly he and Bartlett had shrewdly suggested this name to Astor. Apparently there was no budget for the building, as Waldorf wanted it to be the finest hotel in New York City. With such a facility Boldt could, as he foresaw, 'revolutionize hotel keeping on this continent.' He could create a seductively glamorous place, using Astor money to attract trade, merely paying a fixed rental. It turned out to be a very lucrative proposition."

"But Boldt had to buy all the furnishings and equipment for the large hotel. He didn't sell the Bellevue, but borrowed capital to enrich the elaborate building with costly contents. Louise decorated the rooms, even to pincushions on the dressers. Period photographs reveal her taste in décor—rather excessively rich for our taste today, but this was the early 'nineties. Boldt, who never advertised his hotels in any way, was a genius at public relations. The grand opening of the Waldorf was gala Manhattan event, a charity function attended by the very sort of trade he hoped to attract. But disaster struck. The nation plunged into a depression. Boldt thought he was ruined. That was when he and Louise first came to the River, where our local chapter of the story begins."

"Boldt recovered financially, obviously?"

"In short order. He managed to attract a class of trade that could maintain a privileged life style amid the depression. In fact, the excessive indulgence of costly entertainments at the Waldorf became something of a national scandal. But as Boldt

Waldorf interior of the 1890s, probably decorated by Louise Boldt

no doubt shrewdly knew, any press is good press, and the Waldorf was becoming a national icon."

"What happened to Mrs. Astor, next door?"

"Naturally, she wouldn't enter the new hotel, supposedly intended to humiliate her—which explains George's reference to wanting to see her come in, more than any other person. Her star was rising socially, and she was becoming dominant in New York and Newport high society. She could not abide living next to the vulgar commercial facility, however, and built a larger mansion farther up Fifth Avenue. Her indignant husband, when he learned of his cousin's affront, threatened to build New York's biggest (and I suppose smelliest) stables on their property, next to the Waldorf. Very shortly, however, their son, John Jacob Astor IV, saw the success and growing prestige of the neighboring hotel. Jack, who knew the Boldts personally, was amenable to Boldt's persuasion. Nevertheless, he and his cousin Waldorf were at odds. 'It was Boldt himself who did much to pave the way for a reconciliation.... Using all of his powers of persuasion' he got the alienated cousins to consider what would be virtually a jointly owned hotel. Abner Bartlett was again helpful as liaison.

'Jack' Astor told Boldt that he would build an even larger, grander hotel on his half of the block. He wanted, alas, to name it after his mother, Caroline Schermerhorn Astor ('*The* Mrs. Astor')—so it might have become the Waldorf-Schermerhorn. Wiser heads prevailed, and Jack agreed that his portion would be called the Astoria."

"Thank God."

"Yes. And just as there was the story about his cousin, so there's an anecdote about how Jack Astor came to build the huge addition. You see, the Astors (after giving up the stable idea) decided to abandon their Fifth Avenue mansion on the site of the Astoria after they found a tramp sleeping in a guest bedroom. The house was contaminated, became *déclassé*.

   "Another popular story about these Astors has to do with Boldt's innovating the radical policy of registering single women as guests. At the time it was supposed that any single woman taking a hotel room would have dubious intentions. As Boldt reportedly told his house detective, 'You tell dem, Joe, that ve don't vant our place to be used as *rendez-vous* by ladies wid so many friends!' One night Jack Astor's wife Ava (pronounced with the broad 'A,' 'Ah-vah") who was a rather imperious patrician, insensitive and not too bright, was bored at a party and walked out alone. On passing the Astoria (that her husband owned) she decided not to go further, but stepped in and demanded a room. Ava (who of course supposed everyone in New York should recognize her, but perhaps hoped they didn't on that occasion) disdained even to give her name. The desk clerk, as a matter of policy, politely refused to give the lady a room. When another clerk recognized the indignant beauty, he wisely overruled the hotel's established policy. Learning about the breech of rules the next morning, Boldt didn't fire that clerk for turning away Ava Astor, but changed the regulation, deciding thereafter to admit single women as guests, setting aside a floor for them.

   "When it came to building an addition on land belonging to the other Astors, again Boldt already was familiar to them. John Jacob Astor, like his cousin Waldorf, had courted and wed a Philadelphia girl, the Ava of that story, Ava Willing. Fortuitously, the historic 'Yellow House' of the Willings was directly across the street from the Boldts' little Bellevue Hotel. Unlike 'Willie' Astor, who rarely went to the Boldts' Bellevue, 'Jack" Astor was a regular visitor—a vocal fan who 'often acclaimed the virtues of Oysters Bellevue and the Terrapin.' By the time of Jack's wedding, Boldt was also operating an annex, the Stratford Hotel, another small place across the street from the Bellevue. The Astor family and servants booked the Stratford for the occasion, filling eighteen rooms, while other wedding guests stayed at the Bellevue. The Boldts served the Astor-Willing wedding breakfast.

There's another story, too: the bride's mother, Mrs. Edward Willing invited her son-in-law's mother, *the* Mrs. Astor, to the Assembly, a ball that was the most ultra-exclusive Philadelphia event. When the governors of the Assembly refused admission to the New Yorkers, Mrs. Willing hastily arranged her own ball at the Boldt's Bellevue, across the street from her house, on the same night as the Assembly. A private railroad car full of Astors, Vanderbilts and the like attended it. The surprise event was said to be a 'bomb' dropped socially in Philadelphia, requiring Mrs. Willing's friends at the last minute to choose between her ball and the Assembly.

"Considering the usual antipathy of patricians to commercial hotels, these events were momentous. Remember that Jack's mother was *the* Mrs. Astor, the social queen of New York and Newport society, and that she and her husband were at that very time so affronted by the new Waldorf Hotel being planned as their immediate neighbor.

"Even while planning the Waldorf, Boldt was worried about competition for premier status. When Jack Astor (or his business advisors) suggested following Waldorf Astor's example, to build a new hotel next to the proposed Waldorf, Boldt 'busied himself,' as we may imagine. Boldt's involvement in cousin Willie's objectionable Waldorf Hotel was less a recommendation than was Jack Astor's family familiarity with the Boldts' Philadelphia operation. Jack agreed to build the great Astoria hotel addition for Boldt to operate. Originally, he wanted a totally different, competitive hotel, even though Boldt would be proprietor of both hotels. Although Jack's would rival the Waldorf, it should have the same elegant cachet. Boldt cleverly negotiated concessions, like making the floor levels the same, and then providing access doors between the buildings that could be sealed, if required. In the end, he got what he wanted, the integrated grand hotel, the hyphenated Waldorf-Astoria. It was completed just as the great Bull Market took off, at the end of the 'nineties, so was perfectly timed to cash in on the financial euphoria over the turn of the century.

Boldt was awash in a tidal wave of money, some of which funded the extravagant building campaign at the Thousand Islands."

"It's hard to see how renting hotel rooms could provide that sort of revenue."

"Boldt didn't merely rent hotel rooms; he sold prestige and self-esteem. The new rich, coming east to the sophisticated Big City to spend new fortunes, were insecure. They wanted to buy acceptance, and Boldt was able to sell them the illusion of having arrived. He learned, back in Philadelphia, I think, with their little Bellevue, that if you charge far more than what's reasonable for anything, there's a certain class of patronage that will beat at the doors, trying to buy their way in with fistfuls of money. You asked if Boldt was a snob; he made his fortune from calculated snobbery."

"That's not too attractive an aspect."

"No. It's not. One might focus instead on his indulgence of patrons, creating the sense of luxury, the aura of privilege. Another eminent hotel man said, 'Mr. Boldt invented the theory that the patron was right.' Indeed, his Rule # 3 was: 'The guest is always right. Be as courteous to the man in a five-dollar room as to the occupant of the royal suite. It is an old rule but it never changes'."

He rose and went to his bookcases. "That reminds me: have you ever read Willa Cather's short story, 'Paul's Case'?"

"No."

He pulled a volume from a high shelf. "Here it is. Read it. It's about the Waldorf-Astoria. What a shock it must have been to the Boldts. Surely they read it—unless George managed to shield his family from it. How horrifying it must have been!"

"How so?"

He opened the dusty book to a yellowed bookmark. "Here it is. Let me read a passage:

> When Paul went down to dinner the music of the orchestra came floating up the elevator shaft to greet him. His head whirled as he stepped into the thronged corridor, and he sank back into one of the chairs against the wall to get his breath. The lights, the chatter, the perfumes, the bewildering medley of color—he had, for a moment, the feeling of not being able to stand it. . . . The flowers, the white linen, the many-colored wineglasses, the gay toilettes of the women, the low popping of corks, the undulating repetitions of the Blue Danube from the orchestra, all flooded Paul's dream with bewildering radiance. When the roseate tinge of his champagne was added—that cold, precious, bubbling stuff that creamed and foamed in his

glass—Paul wondered that there were honest men in the world at all. This was what all the world was fighting for, he reflected; this was what all the struggle was about."

"But what's so bad about that? Sound's pretty attractive to me, in fact."

"Ah, but did you catch the phrase, when he "wondered that there were honest men in the world at all"? The story is about temptation of illusory values—or at least values that may be real, but ephemeral. Nothing wrong with good champagne, but its effervescence doesn't last. It goes flat."

"How does the story come out?"

"Paul kills himself, rather than leave the fantastic if shallow life of the Waldorf."

32. Islands are illusory. Disengaged from the larger world, they float as fragments from some different realm of existence. Out across the water, nearby chunks of green landscape recede to gray mounds farther off, becoming mere specs in the hazy distance. When one enters this floating world, pieces of substance move, appearing and disappearing. What seemed a land mass now breaks into pieces, and then the pieces float away. A world of islands is a surreal place.

The magical quality of the Thousand Islands was recognized long ago, attracting romantic escapists who savor the quality of unreality—some of whom built fantasy castles on these islands. Faded photographs portray an even more enchanting place, where tall-masted white yachts, seductively curvaceous, regally plied the waters, while great paddlewheel steamboats carrying throngs of sightseers chugged among the islands. Suave, polished wooden launches, enclosed cabins at the rear, with chauffeurs behind the windshields of open forward cockpits, served as nautical limousines, carrying islanders to and from their islands. Professional guides towed Thousand Islands skiffs, now admired as classic craft, in tandem to fishing grounds, or rowed great distances. Tall grand hotels became landmarks visible for miles. Teams of gardeners tended vast banks of flowers; women dressed in buoyant yards of filmy organdy, supplementing broad-brimmed hats with ruffled parasols. It was gorgeous, *grand luxe*.

Courtney wanted to capture something of this quality in the play. Costumes might be recreated, but it would be difficult to convey the unique quality of place. Painted scenery would be hokey, but possibly some old picture post-cards could be reproduced, projected on a scrim. But how might the book itself—the spoken word, which is what a play is about—convey the heady atmosphere of unreality and privilege?

"We can't stop the forward movement to have characters standing about, admiring the scene," Courtney cautioned. "Everything will have to be suggested by a few props. Lots of real, cut flowers, for instance. Big, big bouquets. The sound of offstage steam and motor boats. That sort of thing. We'll have uniformed servants, opening doors and lighting cigars, et cetera. The aura of privilege. They'll get it."

For some reason I recalled "Paul's Case." Maybe that was what was bothering me—I was groping for what Willa Cather had said. And what was that? On reading the book that Pete lent, I put down the story still wondering what it meant. Cather didn't write it as a tract about social justice, to pillory the rich collectively, or to plea for the suffering of the poor; it was more about Paul individually, a young man alienated from the real world who sought to realize fantasy as a substitute. What was the connection I sensed? '. . . The cold, precious, bubbling stuff that creamed and foamed in his glass' was 'what all the world was fighting for; . . . this was what all the struggle was about.' But the effervescence is ephemeral, and the wine goes flat.

33. Courtney showed me a photograph of teatime on the verandah of the Yacht Club, looking like a florist's showroom, where elaborately dressed ladies appeared somewhat bemused and overwhelmed by the encroaching verdure.

"Boldt brought up the decorator from the Waldorf, along with all that ferny stuff and splendid food for gala events at the Yacht Club. He had a refrigerated railroad car carry meat, fowl and produce from his farm to the hotel, and brought back provisions for the club, as well as his several establishments here. Boldt had vast cutting gardens on his estate. They transformed the clubhouse into a floral bower—looking somewhat like a float in the Rose Bowel Parade, I'm afraid, but they thought it lovely. There was always a big bash at the end of the season—coinciding with the Gold Cup races during the halcyon seasons. Boldt's reception to introduce his new daughter-in-law, Estelle, to Thousand Island society was a particularly grand affair."

"Estelle and George, Jr. had children?"

"Yes, two lovely girls, Manuelita and Louise. George Boldt was devoted to his grandchildren as long as he was alive. Built a playhouse for them with a 'Dutch kitchen.' Estelle became 'a prominent figure in Bay society.' After his father's death, Estelle and Cricket divorced. Estelle and the charming little girls continued to come to the River for some time. Cricket never cared as much for the River as his sister, who came back the rest of her life. Clover was more athletic, more the sporting type. Her lively interests, and those of her first husband, in particular, may have been sufficient to overcome any unpleasant memories. Clover was never one to look back anyway. Cricket probably was the more sensitive of the two, hating the association of the place with his mother, her unfulfilled dream, and tragic death. I recall hearing that George Boldt commented that Clover should have been the boy. After his death, she seemed to be the principle executrix —'she [was] in full charge of the Boldt estate'—a role sufficiently unusual to be newsworthy, as was her getting half of the Boldt fortune in her own right. Shortly after her father's funeral she became a vice-president of the hotel, occupying an office there and assuming much responsibility. Her brother was nominally the president, but he 'had no taste' of the job—although he stuck it out for three years. My sense is that Clover had more of her father's acumen."

"There must be Boldt descendents of George, Junior."

"Yes, but being girls, the Boldt name died out with them. That branch of the family hasn't been around here often, so I don't know much. I think that they gravitated to the West Coast, where George, Senior was building a retirement home when he died. Estelle was Mexican, you know."

"You've seen the Boldt place at Montecito?"

"Never been there myself, but a friend of Meg's, out in Santa Barbara, looked up the place and visited it. Meg has snapshots."

"Was it as grand as we would expect?"

"Not grandiose, certainly. Montecito is still upscale, and the house is commodious, predictably in a sort of California Mission style. But Boldt seemed to have spent most of his heroic building ambition on the Heart Island project. He summered more simply at Wellesley House, you know—although it was still a large country house, requiring a staff to operate. And the entire Wellesley Island estate with its farm continued to be a major operation. One writer said, 'Wellesley Farm is one of the finest farms in the entire east'."

"Do you suppose Boldt planned to winter in California, and continue to summer here?"

"Who knows? For a while he came less frequently, then became involved in local projects for a while, such as the uncompleted big hotel begun at the golf course, but in later years came less again. He thought that dampness at Wellesley House, built right on the canal, worsened his sciatica, which almost disabled him at times."

"What did he do up here, fish?"

"I never heard of him fishing—too busy building things. But, of course, he was keenly interested in the farm. And hunting—ducks, in the fall. He was one of a group of hunters who formed a club, down at Chippewa Buy. Clubhouse is still there."

"So in some ways he was one of the guys?"

"More so on the River than in the City. He wrote in a letter, shortly before he died, 'I shall particularly love to have you visit me some time next summer at Alexandria Bay. It is there where I am more like myself, and it is there in that beautiful spot where I think you will see more of the real man'."

"Did he ever return to Heart Island?"

"No—at least, not for a long time. We have these comments." He pushed the glasses up his nose. 'Not since the day of his wife's death . . . has George C. Boldt . . . put a foot upon Heart Island.' That was five years after Louise died. Two years later Boldt said, 'I have not gone through the house, nor have I definitely decided to finish it . . . .' Probably Boldt didn't care to go back to Heart Island, to see its worsening condition. The buildings over there were vandalized, even during his lifetime, although a caretaker lived on the island with his family, on the upper level of the Power House. Dobbins couldn't be all over the island at one time, however, and curious sightseers found it irresistible, landing on all shores. Boldt could look at the Castle from Wellesley House, of course. My parents remembered seeing the small, gray-bearded man with his odd pince-nez spectacles on a black silk cord, in his cape, cane, and yachting cap, strolling in the evening through the big flower garden on Tennis Island, where he could gaze at Heart Island."

34.   Clifford Dobbins was now an old man, living alone in Alexandria Bay. He had lived with his parents on the upper level of the Power House, in a comfortable apartment there. It was destroyed in 1938 when fireworks, set off from Heart Island, ignited the wooden roof of the building (now reconstructed). Clifford had been a child when George Boldt was alive, so his recollections were dim, colored by years of hearing stories about the man and the place. What did he remember? He told me again about his dad's troubles in keeping tourists off the island. He never saw Boldt there, that he recollected, but did see him on Wellesley Island. Boldt was at the Yacht House often, since that's where the boats were and where the estate superintendent lived, in a house attached to the boat building. Everyone was in awe of the great man, he remembered. What stuck in Clifford's childish imagination was a story

Overgrown Heart Island as seen by George Boldt in his last summer visits to Wellesley House. Perhaps the saplings along the shore have been planted to block the view.

he heard, that Boldt had a secret lookout on the interior of the Yacht House, so that he could watch from the higher reaches of the big space to spy on workers below. "He was everywhere," Clifford said, "and saw everything."

35. What made George Boldt so successful? As Clifford had observed, Boldt was a keen observer. Boldt believed that "a good executive must be naturally observant." Then Boldt had to follow through, at his hotel as at his River home, "keeping at the servants in his nervous, energetic way." Pete agreed with this, but first recalled Boldt's "unflagging enthusiasm," then his attention to detail and organizational skill, then observed that he was imaginative, inventive and exacting, devising ingenious new ways of doing things. The scale of the huge Waldorf-Astoria required efficiency of operation, particularly if Boldt were to reap a profit while maintaining an extraordinary level of service to guests, and while retaining the compelling allure of personal attention. The novel logistic system of the world's largest hotel provided the subject of articles in national journals. A series of commercial lanternslides, apparently made for public lectures, showed behind-the-scenes operations of the Waldorf. Boldt initiated a training school for employees, the first in any hotel. It not merely

instructed them in prescribed tasks, but broadened their abilities in other areas, making them more versatile.

"He wasn't one to coast—or to rest on those laurels that surrounded the 'W A' logo," Pete observed from his note-strewn desk. "No, he was a compulsively creative person, obsessed with unattainable perfection." He rummaged through the papers. "Here are some more comments: Boldt 'became the foremost hotel expert in the United States, if not in the world. . . . Few appreciate the triumph of generalship that the successful running of a hotel like the Waldorf means.' Boldt established many new operational arrangements, such as 'branch service,' which treated each floor of the hotel as a unit with its own receptionist or room clerk, services and management. He developed the 'assistant manager system,' which gave more personal responsibility to young men who showed skill in public relations—generally college graduates who were intelligent conversationalists. He made cashing of personal checks a policy, calculating that benefits outweigh losses.

"Boldt introduced to America what now is known as 'room service': delivering hot meals to guestrooms. He was the first to install telephones in every guestroom and shoeboxes for guests to deposit shoes in the corridor to be shined. He loved new gadgets, like pneumatic tubes to deliver paper messages. Two of the very earliest wireless stations in the United States were on the roofs of Boldt's hotels. Innovation combined with attention to detail made the Waldorf-Astoria 'one of the most perfect machines in existence'."

"So keeping one step ahead in technology, as well as in awareness of social attitudes, was part of the success story."

"Certainly. In fact, the first of George Boldt's Five Rules: 'Always have plenty of hot water on tap to supply every faucet in the hotel simultaneously.' That came ahead of everything else. No doubt his experience proved, as he said, 'There are more hot-water cranks than any other kind.'

"Boldt regarded even the smallest details as contributing to his larger vision of the character of the hotel. His controversial prohibition against employee beards and moustaches was a case in point. Ever concerned with image, Boldt forbid male employees to have facial hair—at a time when beards and moustaches were common (and he himself wore a beard). And, it was said, 'above all he abhorred "vistling."' Any employee who "vistled" in his presence was earmarked for early discharge.' Once he instantly discharged a valued employee spotted chewing gum. Boldt—or more likely Louise, who decorated the guestrooms of the original Waldorf—was the first to hang pictures in them. The lavish use of fresh flowers may have been her

The Water Castle (Power House) with modern lower bridge and railings

contribution as well, but George himself was passionately fond of flowers. The original Waldorf provided a margin in front of the building for a flower garden, 'and a brilliant show it made with its scarlet geraniums, timid violets and yellow tulips with the brilliant colored awnings above it.'

"Here's a quiz question for you: what two things that you find on restaurant tables were introduced by the Boldts?"

"Flowers, I suppose."

"No, in addition: candles and sugar cubes wrapped in paper. The Boldts' dining tables and their table settings were famous and 'changed the look of America's dinner tables.' More importantly, Boldt shaped new attitudes with major social implications. His hotel, 'more than any other in history, managed to influence the manners, even the pattern of life, of a goodly proportion of an entire people'."

"Isn't that a bit much? How could a single Manhattan hotel have such impact?"

"Ah, let me count the ways: Perhaps most importantly, Boldt (or we should say, 'the Boldts,' plural) changed customary attitudes regarding appropriate behavior, especially of men regarding women. When the Waldorf-Astoria admitted single women as guests it was considered 'shocking! Unheard of!' Boldt was the first to open all the public rooms (except the Men's Café) to women, abandoning the segregated Ladies' Parlor. He was the first to serve single women in a prestigious dining room (previously no respectable lady was supposed to enter a public restaurant unaccompanied). When he abolished the detested 'Ladies' Entrance' to the hotel, it was regarded as a landmark event. Boldt initiated daytime musicales at the hotel to attract both women and prominent men such as Morgan, Gould, and Belmont. He created the Waldorf Garden as a venue for afternoon tea, introducing the teacart. 'The ladies were tremendously enthusiastic. They could have a cocktail poured into a teacup and sip it as if it were plain Orange Pekoe.' Soon it became 'socially correct' for ladies to give teas and afternoon receptions at the Waldorf. Eventually even *The* Mrs. Astor, who had been so outraged at construction of a hotel next-door, 'was pleased to transfer many of her smaller affairs' to the Waldorf-Astoria. The Boldts had learned from the Bellevue that providing a venue for wives (and in time single women as well) was a key to success. It was said, 'thus the crafty innkeeper "got women going" from the start. And women . . . played a big part in making the reputation of his establishment.' Boldt's Rule #2: 'Never speak abruptly to a women guest nor be indifferent to her complaints. A woman's attitude in a hotel is based on two assumptions: That she is there to have things done for her without any trouble to herself, and that she can leave when she wants, on five minutes' notice.'

"Boldt transformed the functional businessmen's lobby into a luxurious lounge where an orchestra played after dinner—and created there the famous 'Peacock Alley' where women were not merely in their element, but were framed in a gorgeous setting. And men came, and stayed, to see them. His was the first hotel where men could smoke in the presence of ladies. Special ventilation averted offensive odor. Boldt would suggest to businessmen, accustomed to sending their wives up to their rooms after dinner, that they 'bring Mrs. ___' to join them in the lobby, where 'a Turk and his son, costumed, with a little perambulator, made and served coffee.' Boldt trained waiters to serve 'dainty little glasses' of liquor in the lobby—no highballs, of course. He knew that the ladies wanted to 'get an eyeful' of Peacock Alley and of each other—and perhaps to strut a bit themselves, showing off their gowns.

"As observers commented, the Waldorf 'sent the old-fashioned "Ladies' Parlor" into the limbo wherein it really deserved to go.' Boldt was said to have 'destroyed at one stoke the fine old English custom of the ladies leaving the gentlemen immediately after dinner.' He was 'one of the first to capitalize on New York's growing desire for "night life."' As many as thirteen orchestras played at one time in the Waldorf-Astoria—'we play checkers with pianos here,' a staff wit observed (they had fifty-four pianos). The flowers, the music, the glamour, *le tout ensemble*, were devised with the ladies in mind. In [Boldt's] houses womankind was to have the full fling ... except for ... smoking or drinking in public.'

"Boldt wasn't that progressive?"

"No—say, you're having Fay Templeton appear in your play? Here's a great tie-in. Oscar seated Fay, who was of course a Broadway stage celebrity, prominently in the Palm Court (or one of the other restaurants—I don't recall). While all eyes were still on her, Fay pulled out a cigarette and asked Oscar to light it for her. It was a sensation. Politely but firmly he reminded her of the rule about women smoking. When Fay, equally politely but firmly insisted on smoking, Oscar asked her to leave,

Drawn by C. D. Gibson

Waiting for tables at the Waldorf; Thirty-fourth Street

and again, politely but firmly escorted her from the room."

"A publicity stunt?"

"Of course. Boldt never paid for advertising, but didn't regret this sort of incident that would keep the hotel on the front page. Fay certainly benefited as well."

"The incident doesn't gibe well with the notion of him as a women's liberator."

"No, he was conservative culturally, but nevertheless was a ground-breaker when it came to accommodating women. Boldt installed the first women's billiard table and women's shoeshine service. He introduced fine shops on the ground floor, including a florist, candy and luggage retailers, a hairdresser, and a theater ticket office. The Waldorf 'launched the new custom of [ladies] "lunching out" and became a popular venue for afternoon bridge.' It was said, 'The Waldorf-Astoria is for the women, when all is said and done!' 'Mr. Boldt caught the idea [that] men do anything to gratify women's yearning to be exclusive and autocratic [and] minted it into millions'."

"So it was only the women who wanted to be 'exclusive and autocratic'?"

"You sound like Meg. Regardless, the Boldts understood human psychology, and I expect that Louise taught George much about 'what a woman wants.' It was observed that he brought the ladies out of the Ladies Parlor and put them on display in Peacock Alley, the Palm Garden, and other glamorous venues. Surely the men didn't object to that. The Waldorf-Astoria became 'a theater, offering a continuous performance in which the actors and actresses also constituted the audience, . . . the greatest show in the city. . . .'

"The Boldts had learned the better-mousetrap lesson—if you do something better, being distinctive, success will follow. If you make a challenge sufficiently difficult, some ambitious patrons will appear. As commented, 'the intrepid Boldt . . . precipitated a fresh crisis of good taste when he decreed that no gentleman would be admitted to the Waldorf's dining rooms at the dinner hour unless he was wearing evening dress.' The Boldts learned at their *recherché* little Bellevue hotel that if you charge enough for anything, some people will stand in line to prove they can afford it. It was a useful and profitable lesson.

"Boldt found at the Waldorf, when he introduced room service of meals, that the service became so popular to be impractical. He then attempted to discourage request for room service by adding a hefty surcharge. The result? Of course: more, not fewer, guests wanted to show they could afford room service, which then became an important money-maker for the hotel.

"Boldt's insight was like Disney's a century later, that if you spend enough money to create the biggest and best of anything, the world will come. Boldt was 'the originator of hotel magnificence.' He and Louise had built the reputation of their Bellevue on its cuisine, and he made the new hotel more than a place to sleep, but famous for its fine restaurants and aura of luxury. As I may have mentioned previously, most hotels had operated on the American Plan, where meals were included in the cost of a guestroom, so hotel dining rooms served mostly resident guests. Like the Bellevue, Waldorf operated exclusively on the European plan and abandoned the usual hotel *table d'hôte* menu in favor of *à la carte*. Boldt intended his restaurants to vie with the finest in the city, such as Delmonico's—which the Waldorf 'outshined.' Old 'Del's' seeming 'tawdry' by comparison. Boldt paid his head chef $10,000 a year, at a time when the average worker was earning little more than $500 a year."

"Was the menu innovative?"

"Not radical—Boldt was conservative and knew that his newly rich clientele wanted to buy into a conservative, patrician culture. There were innovations, of course, but fairly tame. The Waldorf-Astoria created dishes that have become popular mainstays, such as Waldorf Salad. The Waldorf's chicken à la king became an American staple, as did other inventions such as deviled eggs and fruit salad that we suppose Americans have eaten forever. The Waldorf introduced wild rice served with game, but was especially noted for classic dishes more highly regarded among epicures, such as *Ris de veau financiers*.

"Service (preferably by Oscar himself) from a novel, flame-warmed chafing dishing became a hallmark, with Lobster Newburg the hotel's most popular supper item, with 800 portions often prepared during the after-theater service. Boldt's was the first hotel in New York City to offer fine vintage wines. 'The Waldorf-Astoria transformed the art of gastronomy from a pursuit of patricians into a popular recreation.'

Gradually the place became for New York City what the Bellevue had become for Philadelphia, 'less hotel [than] institution for . . . urban life,'—'the club of all clubs.' 'Its very coming seemed to mark a distinctive change in the urban civilization of America.' Indeed, it was said, "It seems unlikely that any center of hospitality on this continent will ever again achieve, as certainly none did before it, the concentration of prestige which has made the Waldorf-Astoria a great national institution.' As you may imagine, the list of such accolades is a mile long. There have been many books written about the Waldorf-Astoria, and hundreds—probably thousands—of magazine articles and newspaper items. The place represented *la dolce vita* for generations of Americans.

"And Boldt's institution became world-class: 'Not merely the sheer magnificence of the house itself, but the distinctively international tone which Mr. Boldt succeeded in implanting within it from the beginning, has made it a magnet which has reached far across the sea.' Indeed, a proud moment for George Boldt was entertaining Prince Henry, Kaiser Wilhelm's brother, who gave his German-American host a medal on departing. Indeed, as Albert Crockett observed, it's difficult to convey how, 'for one brief period [the Waldorf Astoria] filled a unique and important rôle in American life and cultural history.'

"As they say, 'nothing succeeds like success,' and the prestige of the Waldorf snowballed, until it was popularly said that eventually everyone in America walks through the lobby of the Waldorf-Astoria, the 'crossroads of America'—everyone that mattered, that is. Since its construction, every President of the United States visited the hotel. By actual count, about twenty-thousand people entered the hotel every day. A society editor called the long promenade between the dual entrances on 33rd and 34th 'Peacock Alley,' a name that stuck—although it was sometimes called 'Rubberneck Lane.' It was the place to see and be seen in New York City. Called, 'the Vanity Fair of America,' it had more than four million visitors a year.

"And now Boldt Castle itself is drawing about a quarter-million a year."

"True—now, as then, because of the Boldts' creative imagination. Much of the hotel's phenomenal success derived from Boldt's personal qualities—his inspiring leadership of employees as well as his engaging magnetism for guests. One writer said, 'Boldt was known for charming qualities that earned loyalty of hard-driven staff and made him famous as a host. He said, simply, 'I tried always to be courteous. I tried to please.' He also said of courtesy, 'It's the cheapest thing in the world, if you provide it yourself, but the most expensive thing to buy'—and he was selling it. It was more than mere politeness, however. He had a genius for making people want to do things the 'better' way—a trait that would be annoying in less psychologically adroit hosts."

"Folks didn't mind being told how to dress for dinner?"

"That's what they were buying—Boldt's continental *savoir faire*. That's what New Money was for, you see, to acquire status. As said in 1898, 'Every chappie from Maine to Texas . . . has a personal interest in Herr George Boldt [who] makes chappies drink cocktails from crockery coffee cups. Herr Boldt is indeed a wonder and soothes the ruffled feelings of an offended chappie with the same grace that he fires the offending waiter. He is all things to all men.'

"The Waldorf-Astoria was a social blender and a social school. Boldt wouldn't turn away the likes of Bet-a-Million Gates, who made his home in a lavish Waldorf suite, but who ate peas with his knife and belched his way through Peacock Alley. Perhaps Boldt prevailed by the principle that people will rise to the occasion. If you create a stage that requires a certain act, most people may play the role. Those less naturally sensitive to cultural and social cues, like Bet-a-Million Gates, might be influenced by peer pressure.

"The contrast of the rough-mannered new arrivals from the frontier with the urbane cosmopolitanism of the Waldorf-Astoria was comical, and jokes traveling around the country on the vaudeville circuit did much to spare Boldt the cost of paid advertising. To wit: a westerner, new to the City, served a steak, asks Oscar, "You call this done? I've seen critters worse hurt than this get well." Or the stand-up comedian might tell about the preacher, served milk punch (spiked of course), who exclaims, "Oh Lord, what a cow!" Boldt didn't object to these jokes, any more than he did to Fay Templeton's publicity stunt. He had an instinct for public relations, a keen perception of social values, and a shrewd sense of psychology. As a contemporary observed, 'Never grander was his tone than when he dealt with a thrifty soul who complained that his bill was too high. Boldt tore the bill in two and told the complainant he need bother neither to pay nor to return, since the Waldorf was only for those who could afford the best.' No doubt his 'grand tone' was intended for the gallery, and the fact that this anecdote was published is evidence of his instinct for publicity. Boldt's personal courtesies were, of course, self-serving in part—like his *bon voyage* presents to guests sailing to Europe. He realized that travelers would show the enclosed card, signed 'Mr. George C. Boldt', to the whole liner of affluent travelers, who would be eager to show off the attention of the Waldorf-Astoria host.

"Boldt was a 'crony' to regular patrons and flattered shamelessly, trying to please. For instance, he appeared at small dinner in a private Waldorf-Astoria dining room to tell the single table of guests that although he had recently 'entertained Li Hung Chang, the Duke of Marlborough [and others] he would rather get up a dinner for fifteen rubber men than for anybody else in the world.' That was his way. It didn't matter that the huge hotel had served five-thousand meals that day, and the host probably made much the same presentation in several private dining rooms, and possibly at a great banquet in the ballroom. George Boldt, regardless of his eventual wealth and prominence, was never too important or busy for this sort of personal attention, even to a small dinner party of 'rubber men.'

"As Oscar recalled, his 'interest and enthusiasm' for guest's welfare never flagged, and was offered 'at every hour of the day.' Whenever he had a free moment, he devoted it to being 'on the floor' to meet guests. A popular ditty of the day went:

> At the Waldorf 'Hyphen' Astoria,
> No matter who or what you are,
> Should Mr. Boldt pass through and not 'How do you do,'
> Don't pay the check—There's something better yet,
> Let everybody know that your name with him will go,
> And then they'll think you're in the smartest set.

"Boldt had an incredible memory, and by acquiring mnemonic tricks was able to recall names of people met only casually years before. In fact, his Rule #5 was: 'Know the name of every guest, remember it when he comes the next time.' They said, Boldt always 'took infinite pains' to know who was a guest in the hotel, sometimes sending a bottle of rare vintage wine to a visitor's room. Boldt conveyed the impression to whomever he spoke that the person was important to him, hence to the world. But he was demanding of employees. His Rule #4: 'See that every order is obeyed with military discipline.' And he meant that. He was Prussian, remember—and an effective leader. But he wasn't overbearing. Essential to his exceptional leadership quality was the way he treated employees, even errand boys, with the same respect he gave patrons. To a little bellhop he would preface an order with, 'Son, . . . if you have the time . . . .' Of course, he had been an errand boy in a hotel once himself. Everyone was enormously flattered, and loved him for his personal attention."

"Was he an imposing figure—in appearance, I mean?"

"He was short and 'slight of build,' but was very dignified in appearance and bearing. He dressed with extreme conservatism, almost invariably appearing in a black suit and tie, and no jewelry whatsoever except the signet ring he wore, bearing the Boldt crest. Those pince-nez spectacles on a black cord were a sort of trademark. As an old friend of his commented, 'everything about him is immaculate.' He was noted for his taste."

"Did Boldt retain a German accent?"

"Probably, all his life, to some degree, but being meticulous, he took great pain to overcome it. In his late years he had 'acquired a command of almost unaccented English that . . . became a source of some pride'—although the Continental flavor of his early speech wouldn't have been detrimental to his public persona. We're told that 'when he got excited, his tongue would lose control of the English syllables.' He rarely lost control, however. Boldt's care in presenting himself may have seemed a courtly manner. Impeccably dressed, he was well spoken, articulate —an avid reader as well as a confident conversationalist, the former by inclination, the latter by profession. He conveyed the impression of being polished and well educated. But don't get the impression that he was a reserved, reflective type. As Oscar said, he had 'the energy of a dynamo'.

"After Boldt's art came his science. Much of his great success derived from his organizational skill. As a technician, Boldt is generally credited with 'invention of the modern hotel.' But that's another whole aspect of his achievement. Of more interest to you, I think, is the Boldt touch."

"Yes. We sense that with all of his work."

"They say Boldt could have been an artist, or pursued other vocations. Boldt had vision, and could imagine the unseen. His images were concrete and particular to the smallest detail. He used only fresh, clean new bills to make change. Boldt not only put candles on dining tables, but rose-colored silk shades on the candles, because he foresaw that they would flatter a woman's complexion. Women appreciated the touch.

"Boldt installed a trout pond in the Grill Room, where an attendant baited hooks for gentlemen who quaffed cocktails as they fished for their dinner—or pushed each other into the pond. He installed a skating rink on the roof. He had a steam yacht that took guests on cruises around Manhattan. Coaching, employing teams of fine horses was socially in favor at the turn of the century, and coaches took passengers up to a country inn up in the suburbs. Boldt introduced sun parlors. And 'royal suites.' And put an early Ping-Pong table in the men's bar, before any patrons knew the game. One of Boldt's most effective inventions was the red velvet rope, strung across the entrance to Palm Garden—another innovation. The threat of denial challenged those sufficiently distinguished (or affluent) to stand in line trying to get in. The Palm Garden 'made the Waldorf famous.' 'Scores more people than the restaurants could hold swarmed in at every mealtime. They tried to gain entrance with lavishly magnificent tips.' Price was no object. Profits soared.

"One can trace the progression of Boldt's cultural influences, particularly related to hotels, from the Graf's small spa on Rügen through the elite Philadelphia Club, then the creation of the Boldts' intimate Bellevue, finally culminating in the colossal but magnificent Waldorf-Astoria. His deftness was in retaining the illusion of classy privilege in the world's largest hotel. Oscar, standing guard at the 'famous red plush' rope to the Palm Garden, gave the impression that the humble applicant was privileged to be admitted—despite the fact that the Waldorf-Astoria served those eight-hundred lobster Newburgs in an evening. Amazing.

"Boldt understood psychology. Someone wrote, 'He had a real knowledge of psychology and of men, and of the workings of their minds.' He knew how to create the ambiance of privilege, that 'gorgeous golden blur, a paradise (where) ... ingenuous joy and ... consummate management . . . melted together.' 'The Waldorf-Astoria was the court that fed America its fantasies of the good life' . . . 'Paul's Case.'"

36.   Many an hour was wasted, wrestling with writer's block. When my imagination followed George to Philadelphia, there to meet Louise, my narrative faltered. How could I write a biography, when the subjects were so unknowable? Louise was a mere fourteen years old when they met; George was twenty-five—eleven years older. Louise was only fifteen the next year, when they wed, and George was twenty-six. What to make of that? Young people may have matured earlier in those days, and surely George, thrust out on his own, became an adult young, of necessity. But Louise? Wasn't a marriage between the mere teenager and the older man a bit odd? Louise's father was Boldt's boss, so the courtship must have been under his watchful eye. But would most fathers want to see a fifteen-year old daughter marry a man eleven years older? Was it a shotgun wedding? Their first child wasn't born for twenty months, suggesting no urgency. But why did they not have a longer courtship? Here again, the most important aspects of the story were unknowable, and the prospect of a Boldt biography receded further.

A photograph of Louise on horseback, with George on another horse and their two youngsters in the foreground, was startling. Louise hardly looked plausibly the mother of the two youngsters, both of whom appeared to be school age already. Louise was still a thin girl, still appearing to be the teenager. In contrast, full-bearded George might be taken for her father, an uncle, or a much older brother—but surely not as her husband. Rather, a high-school boy might seem a more appropriate date for this youngster.

Although Louise had no more children, she didn't retain her girlish figure. Weight soon became a continual problem. At the Waldorf, she was required to preside regularly over multi-course dinners that lasted for hours. These trials of endurance were conventional among the affluent at the time, but the time also required fashionable women to have wasp waists. Corsets tried to conceal Louise's expanding girth, and she tried diets and turned to reducing treatments at spas.

George was concerned about Louise's public appearance, I would learn from Mrs. Baird, and he became critical of her increasing heft. It wasn't easy for Louise, surely. George had become entranced with a slight wisp of a girl—a youngster who had disappeared, who had been left behind in Philadelphia, when they made the big move to New York City. Louise Boldt, then although only thirty-one yeas old, already was becoming matronly.

37. The move to Manhattan wasn't merely a huge gamble, financially, but meant leaving their Philadelphia home, uprooting the children, who would leave behind schools and young friends, and of course meant that the parents would leave behind adult friends as well. Philadelphia had been Louise's lifelong hometown. Living in a midtown Manhattan hotel, for a family, wasn't an attractive prospect. Furthermore, the move meant leaving behind the little Bellevue Hotel that George and Louise had created together, that they had made so successful and renowned, and where Louise had a role and a recognized presence. Manhattan wouldn't be the same. There would be a huge staff to assist George. And George hired Oscar, to do pretty much what Louise had done at the Bellevue. After furnishing the place, Louise would have no real function at the Waldorf, beyond serving as hostess in their large private dining room. She would have all the help she needed to run the family quarters, have abundant and elaborate food from the hotel kitchen, and have constantly changing hotel guests as company. It was at this point, shortly after moving to New York, when George was despondent, that they first came to the Islands. Probably Louise wasn't elated with their recent change of fortune, either. Given this situation, despite their financial plight at the time, the prospect of buying an island summer home was irresistible.

"It was an afternoon much like this," Pete observed, his voice raised over the whirring fan. "Clover Boldt Baird, in her little booklet, recalled the first visit of George and Louise to Alexandria Bay. They returned to their hot room at the Thousand Islands House, intending a siesta after a large noonday repast. According to family lore, they looked out on a stifling afternoon to see the water glassy and island trees motionless, except for one small island directly across from them, where leaves rustled. It was an omen, they thought. The Boldts were attuned to omens. Whether this in fact was how the Boldts came to Heart Island may be less relevant than the way the family retained the tradition of the Boldts' reading of signs to determine significance."

"They were superstitious?"

"George particularly—but how seriously he took his observances, or whether they merely amused him, we can't say. Surely he paid attention to such things, but I suspect he was more attuned to the intellectual game than genuinely concerned about misfortune. Symbolism was significant to him. Let me tell you about the complex meaning of the Boldt crest, which I suppose George invented." He produced a photograph of a stained-glass window showing the device. "First of all came the main figure, here, the heart—a symbol related to Louise's birthday on Valentine's Day as well as to Heart Island. The coincidence of the birthday with the island name had been a favorable omen, as was the heart-stag coincidence. As the heart was Louise's sign, so the antlered stag might represent George. Not only was the stag associated with the sport of hunting, but as St. George had slayed the dragon, so the stag by tradition was enemy of the evil serpent. The name 'Boldt,' means 'bold.' The linguistic accident had possibilities.

The Boldt Hart

"So as you see it, the Boldts devised a family crest employing the heart together with the hart. In heraldry the heart when shown surmounted by another device, as we see the Boldts' heart crest topped by a stag, signifies that the appended element is but a dependency of the central heart. The stag is reliant on the heart; George was dependent on Louise. Furthermore, in European tradition the stag was recognized as a representation of the Tree of Life, its branching horns representing the limbs of trees reaching heavenward. This is precisely how we see it at Heart Island, the bronze sculpture silhouetted against the sky. An enemy of the serpent, the stag is associated with heaven and light —just as we see it atop the Castle. In classical mythology, the stag had mystical powers, for he was the messenger of the gods." The professor, glasses sliding down his nose, was waxing professorial, warming to his subject. "The stag is also a symbol of resilience and regeneration, for its horns regrow when broken off. As the stag is dependent on the heart, the regenerative quality of the stag's horns again after damage in battle derives from his mate. Remember, the Boldts came when George was trying to recover from a breakdown. George Boldt's resilience to disappointment, his protection from discouragement, was strength given him by his wife, Louise. In truth, he never recovered fully from her death."

He pointed to the heart. "What's within the heart? The letter 'B,' for Boldt, of course, but fashioned organically so that it becomes transformed into an entwined stem, terminated with two sprigs of clover. Now you might think that the clover symbol has something to do with luck, the Boldts being superstitious, but that isn't a heraldic, and certainly not a Germanic notion." The professor seemed pleased with his perspicacity. "And these are three, not four-leafed clovers. The trefoil historically symbolizes the Trinity, but here the reference is less religious. George and Louise named their daughter Louise Clover Boldt. The two clovers represent their two children, their stems intertwined as brother and sister.

"The symbols taken together convey more meaning. Within the main element, the heart, representing Louise, secondary symbols indicate that her husband (the letter "B") and two children, growing organically from him, are within her heart. Atop the heart, the stag represents George, dependent upon Louise, but aspiring heavenward."

"The heart isn't red."

"Right. The heart isn't red, the color of blood and passion, but blue, the color of sky, connoting spirit, devotion and innocence, qualities ascribed to Louise. The letter 'B' and its entwined clover leaves are rendered in gold, and gold also bands the heart. Gold here signifies not mere wealth, but superior quality. A wreath of green laurel leaves encircles the whole, as it did for the Waldorf-Astoria logo, representing not merely achievement, the crown of the victor, but in the fuller classical tradition, difficulty surmounted, quality of character prevailing." The professor smiled, satisfied with his lecture, then had another thought.

The Boldt crest

"A further omen, or so it may have seemed to the Boldts: Hart Island had been unoccupied for some time. The deceased Congressman's family declined several offers. The place seemed to be waiting for the Boldts. No doubt the Islanders who guided the Boldts on a yacht tour knew full well that Hart Island was available for the right price, and made sure the Boldts became aware of its availability. Probably the guides had arranged for George and Louise to land at Hart Island."

38. Meg was less interested in arcane interpretations. "Omens aside," she said, "in selecting an island the Boldts didn't seek isolation. They didn't care to withdraw to idyllic wilderness, but preferred the exposure of a stage, viewed by the grandstand of hotel verandas, and from village docks where excursion boats converged and thousands of excursionists assembled daily. On such a public stage they could construct a colossal stage set."

"What was the island like?" Meg produced an old photograph, showing a close-up portion of the house, somewhat obscured by trees, backdrop to a man (probably Hart) sitting on a rock.

"A. J. Warner, the prominent Rochester architect, designed it—but his records were burned in a fire, so we have only photographs, mostly taken from a distance, with the building largely hidden by foliage. This view tells us more." The building seemed large, for a summer cottage, but not overwhelming. "It appears that the house was stuccoed, since the walls seem so smooth. There was careful detail—notice all the little brackets, carrying what appears to be decorative trim at the second story line, or perhaps a slight overhang."

The surroundings appeared natural, grass unmowed, retaining clumps of wild trees. Was that common, to savor the unspoiled character of one's island? Meg thought not, as most Islanders felt compelled to tidy things up, usually planting lawns and flower beds—very labor intensive, so as to evidence one's fiscal capability, perhaps. Castle Rest probably had been innovative and influential locally, not merely in adopting a rustic character of building, but of carefully retaining the natural character of its surroundings. Did the Boldts find the natural quality attractive?

"Well, they bought the property—but George Boldt (and perhaps Louise as well) was a compulsive improver. They couldn't leave well enough alone. The Hart House would have suited me, but not the Boldts. But it's interesting," Meg continued, "that from the beginning they didn't wipe the slate clean, to start over with a new plan. Instead, they progressively adapted what they found, little by little, until we wound up with Boldt Castle. That's one reason it's such an eccentric form, which makes it fascinating. It's slightly irrational."

"You see here, even before the Boldts came to the Thousand Islands, some features of the future Boldt Castle. The building isn't compact, but fairly large, eighty-four by seventy-six feet, broken into several elements, projecting in all directions. On the right is the base of the tower, which rises eighty-five feet above the water. That will become the tallest tower of the Castle. On the left is a curved porch, which will become the curved verandah that we see on the west side of the Castle. Of course, only the ideas were retained on the site. The building itself apparently was moved over to Wellesley Island. You see the tower and curved porch still there."

"But the Hart House over there isn't stucco."

"No, but I expect you would find evidence of the old material under the shingle cladding. Boldt was into shingle siding for his buildings—those that weren't stone, of course. Wood shingles were an appropriate material, left to weather naturally.

Heart Island before demolition of the frame house. The original Hart cottage appears with lower roof to the right of the flag pole, its tower gazebo partially obscured by the higher roofs of the Boldt addition. The new kitchen wing was built of masonry for fire protection and was connected to the service dock by an enclosed passage. The basic arrangement presaged the plan of the future castle.

Probably the stucco cracked and required constant repair, and would always look unsightly where patched. Cladding the whole building with new wood shingles probably seemed a good refurbishing tactic.

"The windows have been changed, of course. Larger panes of glass became more readily available in the 1870s, and so most cottages here have two-over-two sash, whereas those of the original Hart House were four-over-four. Boldt liked large panes of glass, and the Castle had single-paned, double-hung sash, one-over-one. Architecturally, this wasn't as satisfactory as smaller paned windows would have been—not merely for historical character, but to give scale to the building. With such large windows and big panes of glass, the structure doesn't appear so monumental as it would have, had they used more traditional fenestration. Probably William Hewitt knew this, but the Boldts were demanding clients. We know, from surviving drawings, that they often sent their architects back to the drawing board. "

"The old and new portions of the building didn't go together very well, did they?"

"No, it doesn't take an architect to see that. They're radically different in height; the roof slopes differ; the towers likewise have divergent forms. The architect, if there was one, must have cringed, and even the Boldts probably recognized the problem. They occupied this huge villa, which was one of the largest on the River, for only four seasons, before removing it and starting over."

"You mentioned an architect."

"We don't know for a fact that it was Hewitt. Boldt used different architects from time to time, and the Hewitt firm had the commission for his new Bellevue-Stratford Hotel in Philadelphia, so Boldt may have engaged them at the same time, when beginning the Castle project. We know that they did the Power House, built while the old structures were being removed, but don't know that they were involved in the earlier work, such as the Alster Tower. The firm's records are lost, and no one in Philadelphia seems to recall much about the Hewitt organization."

"Why do you suppose they made the addition and its tower so tall?"

"Boldt was a man of vision, and I expect he wanted to see his roof and tower rising above the treetops, to crown the island. There was no need to go up so high, which only meant a lot of stairs to climb. There was plenty of room to expand outward, if so many rooms were required. I think that the decision was aesthetic. And it

Hopewell Hall Today

Although shorn of its landmark tower, many roof dormers, and two boat houses, (shown on page 13) Hopewell Hall remains a showplace pointed out on the Thousand Islands boat tours.

worked—then, as it does today. The building became a landmark, visible for great distances across the water."

"But what a lot of stairs to climb."

"I suppose the two top floors provided servant quarters. There probably was no elevator in the old house. The Castle would also have these four main stories—plus another lower level where the ground sloped away, and addition to higher tower levels. But the Castle provided an elevator, allowing family and guests to go from the lowest level indoor pool to the high entertainment and reading rooms, enhanced by fine views.

"So, you see, we know the old frame house evidenced some important aspects of the future form, so Hewitt didn't invent the major arrangement. The Power House was his alone, however, and it shows us what he might have done with the castle notion, given free reign. It was quite different in character from the frame house addition—more deft in its touches, such as the slight curvature of the conical tower roofs—and, of course, the notion of clustering many towers—round towers. This doesn't seem to be by the same hand as the rather cubic and clunky frame addition. Possibly when the Boldts saw what they got with the addition, they decided to engage a good architect. They probably were delighted with the Power House. Quite a charmer."

"What do you think of the Power House restoration?"

"They got it right, in the main. The Authority thought it necessary to add the lower connection to the building from the island, I suppose, to satisfy requirements for handicapped access. This was unfortunate, since it undercuts the effectiveness of the flying stone bridge. But in time, perhaps, that heavy-handed piece of reinforced-concrete engineering, with its high iron railings, may be removed. I surely hope so."

39.   The summer was slipping away, so I had to focus on what I was supposed to be here for: the play. It now had a working title, "Heart's Desire." Courtney's position, seated at the keyboard but turned to me, one elbow on the paper-covered music rack, by now had become familiar, as had the large central hall of his house, where Courtney's Steinway grand resonated effectively—all those wood surfaces and lofty stairwell, with big stained glass window at the landing. Family, guests, and even help vanished during the hours when we worked—where they went, I don't know, but probably that's what all the boats were for.

"I think I got the pivot," I ventured. "Casting Ben as our hero's old buddy will pay off at the Alster Tower scene."

"Ben's going to be there? At Clover Boldt's party—you mean as a waiter, I suppose. The Frontenac could have catered the affair, sending some black waiters."

"No. That's the surprise. May brings him along as a guest."

"A black fellow as a guest? Oh, come on."

"Well, actually he's appearing as a performer, you see. The Boldts and all their guests hope that May will entertain, and she includes Ben as part of her act."

"So? What's the point?"

"Here's the setup: none of the guests suspect that Bart is an imposter, a local fellow in borrowed finery. Bart is really a buddy of Ben, the black waiter, of course, but they don't let on. Scheming May has devised our plot twist for us. First, she shocks the sedate assemblage with her raucous act: a black dance routine with Ben. The perplexed guests applaud politely. Ben doesn't exit though. As May has directed, he stays to enjoy the party. Ben is snubbed—insulted by Mary's purported 'fiancé' who fancies he's speaking for Clover, the hostess, whom he imagines to be embarrassed by the incident. Bart reacts with his testosterone, casting off his phony role to side with Ben, to the astonishment of all. May breaks the stunned silence by signaling the band to reprise the number. She grabs hands of Ben and Bart and all three lurch into the dance. Mary's 'fiancé'—the 'good provider' that she hoped to catch—is aghast, his suspicions about Mary and Bart confirmed, when to everyone's surprise she leaves the ranks of the stunned onlookers to join May, Ben, and Bart in an even wilder dance. Got it?"

"That's the moment of decision, I take it, when Bart and Mary both give up their notion of making it in this league."

"Yes, and decide on each other. They go back with May and Ben to the real world. The final twisteroo is the revelation that May, Bart's fairy godmother, actually sent our hero on this mission to rescue Mary from her mistake in hooking the effete 'good provider'.'

"Well, at least it's a musical climax. I'll say that much for it. I don't know about the racial business, though. This is supposed to be a light comedy. Why burden it with a heavy subtext?"

"It's another layer. You know, I was casting about for something May and Ben could present that would be calculated to get the rise they wanted. You know what clicked? Langston Hughes' "Advertisement for the Waldorf-Astoria.' Of course, being written in1931 it's not about the institution of Boldt's day, but maybe we could use it. Imagine May and Ben delivering this at the Alster Tower:

> Oh, Lawd, I done forgot Harlem!
> Say, you colored folks, hungry a long time in 35th Street, they got swell music at the Waldorf-Astoria. It sure is a mighty nice place to shake hips in, too.
> . . . . . .
> Drop in at the Waldorf this afternoon for tea. Stay to dinner. Give Park Avenue a lot of darkie color—free for nothing! Ask the Junior Leaguers to sing a spiritual for you. They probably know 'em better than you do—and their lips won't be so chapped with cold after they step out of their closed cars in the undercover driveways.
> *Hallelujah! Undercover driveways!*
> *Ma soul's a witness for de Waldorf-Astoria!*

"You devil!"

"Not me—Langston Hughes. Think you could put that to music?"

"Doesn't scan—prose, you know. And I'd have to change 'Park Avenue' to 'Fifth Avenue'—but Hughes might forgive that."

"Want to give it a try?"

"We'll have to see how it plays."

As we strolled from the house down to the dock, I mentioned to Courtney that the old photograph of the Hart House showed the island then looking more like Heron Island, retaining wild ground cover and clumps of saplings, whereas now Heart Island looked like a city park, with paved walks, mowed lawns, and flower beds. "They can't resist fixing it up," he commented.

"Of course, with a quarter-million visitors each summer, it would be difficult to retain a wild, unspoiled character."

"But it was that way, for decades. It was so much better—which knee high grass, billowing in the breeze, and dirt paths, eroded by the traffic and rain. The unkempt grounds made the Castle seem more remote, more mysterious. It was more romantic, but more authentic. It's not authentic any more."

"You're opposed to making it attractive, aren't you?"

"Attraction is in the eye of the beholder, I suppose, but all the mystery is gone now. It's synthetic entertainment. Big business. We lost the haunting ruin that was so much more compelling. The real thing. Boldt Castle, as Nanette Lincoln put it so aptly many years ago, was forever 'complete in its incompletion'."

Heart Island in the 1940s, before development by the Thousand Islands Bridge Authority

"They've spent more than fourteen million, and you think it all has been a mistake?"

"No. Of course, not—not entirely. The place had to be stabilized and made safe for visitors. Vince Dee saved a treasure for us. Without Vince and the Bridge Authority, all might have been lost, forever. I don't fault what they did, so much as how they did it. Too much do-it-yourself, with too little professionalism. It's all well intended, but much of it wrong headed."

"How would you have done it differently?"

"Ask Pete. He might have steered them in a better direction, if they had wanted any direction from anyone." I was stepping into my little aluminum boat when Courtney added, "You know, your Hughes bit reminds me: we could use Fats Waller's number, written about the same time, "Loungin' at the Waldorf." Know it? I have the recording of the 1978 musical, 'Ain't Misbehavin'.' Play it for you next time."

"Is it the right tone for May and Ben's climactic dance number?"

"Right on. Sassy, sly, snide—in-your-face." William Elliott's snazzy arrangement is

a duet—perfect, absolutely perfect, for May and Ben (singing Fats Waller's part).
The black waiter's puttin' on airs as George Boldt himself! The sarcastic parody will
leave 'em startled, stunned, speechless when the devilish duo pulls this stunt at the
Alster Tower."

I was surprised that Courtney had fallen in line so readily. Either I had mis-
judged his sense of patrician solidarity or his creative urge proved the stronger inclination. The latter was especially surprising since it entailed forgoing composing
music for the climactic scene himself.

40.   "Vince wasn't insensitive, I think, to history," Pete observed about the Chairman of
the Thousand Islands Bridge Authority when it acquired the Boldt property and
began a campaign of improvement. "But he was a realist—a doer, more than a
thinker—and he knew that getting things done required compromise. He got a lot
done, with a lot of compromises.

"Vince realized that investment in the Boldt property would have to produce
quick results, if there was to be momentum to a restoration program. In short, pri-
ority had to be an immediate payback, as recognized by visitors. The purpose of the
project, from that point of view, was provision of a major regional attraction to
tourists. If we now find a sort of public park over there, with commercial franchises,
that result followed from the basic intention.

"More specifically, the initial strategy wasn't to bury large sums in authentic
restoration that might not be seen or appreciated by the average visitor. Hence, the
decision to use a substitute material for the roofing project. From their perspective,
the average visitor doesn't know the difference, and the money saved was used for
other things that do make a difference to the casual viewer."

"Like flower beds and lawns."

"Exactly."

"Or 'finishing' rooms."

"They don't seem to have made any distinction between restoration and fabrication.
Again, the intent is merely to satisfy and please the ordinary visitor. One keeps
hearing over there, 'Isn't it sad they didn't finish it,' and "Will they ever finish it?'
Day after day, this is what one hears from visitors. Naturally, after a while, they
think about satisfying the visitors. They may be trying to do the right thing, but I'm
afraid they're really going to 'finish it'—which of course means the place will be totally destroyed as an authentic experience, becoming mere fakery, of dubious stylistic
accuracy and questionable visual taste."

"Did you suggest a different sort of direction to them?"

"Yes. I've always thought the place should be left as George Boldt intended it, an unfinished work. I remember seeing plaster molds lying around, and crated wood-work. The story has it that when the famous telegram arrived, the workmen 'dropped their tools.' Wouldn't it be great to see the tools still lying there?"

"But visitors complained, didn't they, when they found nothing inside but empty rooms full of graffiti?"

"Much of that graffiti itself had become historic. They painted over dates going back to the 1920s, or earlier, I think."

"But most people were disappointed to find the place a vandalized ruin."

"Disappointed? Saddened, perhaps. But that's the true message of the place. It's supposed to be sad. It's tragic, telling us about human folly, human loss, and hu-man values. It has a profound meaning, if recognized—but it's being trivialized. Pots of geraniums!"

"But still, vacationers don't want a downer." Imagining the Authority's view, I heard myself giving Courtney's argument—that one should follow, rather lead, the audience. My collaborator had insisted that our scenario should have the hero win the Gold Cup race, because he supposed the audience would demand the hero to be a winner. "Maybe you're right, Pete. What would you have done at Heart Island, if they had asked your advice? You mentioned leaving tools and building materials lying about . . . ."

"There needs to be an interpretive program, for sure. I did one for them, remem-ber? There may be different modes of presentation, but they should add up to a clear, compelling idea, a thematic message, not mixed signals. Now they're going off in all directions—talking about a human drama, about the poignant incomple-tion of the dream that almost become a reality—at the same time they're trying to complete the dream and make it a reality. Can't have it both ways. The audience comes away unmoved or even confused: 'What was that all about?' Shiny new brass lighting fixtures and marble treads don't gibe with purposeful abandonment, trans-forming the monument into a testament of love lost. It doesn't work. You under-stand that, as a dramatist."

"Of course, it doesn't work. But what would have worked?"

"Less 'fixing up' of the building fabric, and more interpretation—the *son et lumière* sort of presentation, using sound and light. The walls of all those rooms, left with white plaster surfaces, instead of getting mock historical finishes, might become screens for projected images. The story might be told by recorded sound as one walked from empty room to empty, seeing only phantom images projected on the walls."

"That's theater."

"Of course. What the place needs now, especially after so much of the heavy-duty work has been done, is less a construction crew than a theatrical company. Do you know what they do over at Beechwood—the Astor place, at Newport? The butler opens the door, greeting you as a guest of Caroline Astor—who is supposed to be in the house, about to receive her visitors, but she never actually appears. Costumed actors portray staff and guests of the period. I recall that they did this sort of reenactment at 'The Mount,' Edith Wharton's lovely place in the Berkshires, until the work on its major restoration intervened. The theatrical device is clever—but Boldt Castle, unlike these other properties, was never finished and used, of course. It might have been left as it was, in its poignant incompletion. The Alster Tower was, however, and could be restored and refurnished to reconstruct period life, using interpretive actors, perhaps. The Alster Tower is a unique, fascinating place."

"What about 'restoration' of the Italian gardens and other features?"

"Well, gardens are reversible and quickly vanish, so less harm is done, I suppose, by planting some flowers. But if they invent a particular design, that's something else. You know (but I'm not sure that they know) that the Palm House was completed, and the original drawings are extant. If they want to recreate something that actually existed on Heart Island, this would be more appropriate. It could become an attractive addition to the complex.

"Sooner or later, they'll run out of ways to spend the huge revenue they generate over there. Rather than continuing to invent things that never were, it might be better to recreate things that disappeared—perhaps moving on to other islands. The Thousand Islands Yacht Club casino, for instance, could be rebuilt as a major public facility. Castle Rest was one of the key landmarks. It could be rebuilt with a fraction of what has gone into Heart Island in recent decades."

41. Boldt Castle's rotunda, rising through five stories, now is dominated by a restored freestanding staircase, combining massive wooden railing with white marble treads, the combination to which Meg objected. Perhaps most assertive, however, is all that polished brass—of the central hand rail that became the focus of the broad marble stairway (where there never would have been a freestanding railing but only a cas-

cading carpet) and the brass glitter of many decorative lighting fixtures. They have
frosted glass globes and bell-shaped drop shades and, yes, they do suggest gas lights,
and do look Victorian. I could see what Meg meant. This great hall surely would
have looked much different, had it been completed during the first decade of the
twentieth century.

"Yes," Meg agreed. "Look at this similar staircase at Eastman House in Rochester. It may be as broad as the one at the Castle, but how much lighter in feeling,
so much more elegant! Of course the period style of the McKim-Mead-White
building is different, but more importantly the taste of the time had moved away
from the massive Victorian. The same architects' neo-classical Vanderbilt mansion
on the Hudson was built before Boldt Castle was designed. And on Long Island
Mrs. Mackay had insisted on a 'severe' stone house, built concurrent with the Castle,
and likewise in the French chateau manner."

"At Rochester they haven't installed a utilitarian metal railing in the middle of the
broad staircase, as they've done at the Castle."

""No," Meg agreed, "so the argument that the New York State Code requires this
addition seems debatable. And isn't it more effective, merely with the cascading
carpet?" Most important houses of the period would have had such an oriental run-
ner on the stairs.

"They should have looked around at other buildings contemporary with Boldt
Castle," Meg said, "—like the great hall of the Breakers in Newport, which has the
right sort of electric light fixtures." She pulled up a web site image. "See, they're
larger, simpler—and bronze, not polished brass. Quality. Thomas A. Edison designed electric lighting fixtures for Boldt's Philadelphia Hotel, built at the same time
as the Castle. Those lights are still there, in the ballroom. Boldt might well have
acquired identical fixtures for the Castle. We have photo albums that show interiors
of other Island houses at the time, such as nearby Belle Isle, built by Boldt. And we
have pictures of rooms in his Wellesley House—and of course, other summer homes
of the time are still extant here on the River. There are plenty of models."

But what did it look like then, on the day when the terminal telegram arrived? I
tried to visualize the plasterers at work, vats of wet plaster being mixed on the rough
wood subfloor, white plaster dust everywhere, plasterers on scaffolding and younger
fellows carrying hods of wet plaster up ladders. The huge space would be alive,
noisy . . . and then the holler from below: "Hey, guys. Knock it off. We got bad
news here . . . ." Then silence. Years of silence, with plaster hardened in the vats,
molds thrown down on the floor, plaster dust now ground into the rough wood
subfloor, tracked about by sporadic visitors who had broken into the abandoned

The Castle from the Alster Tower as the scene appeared in the 1940s.
The gazebo recently has been reconstructed, as seen in the photograph, p. 113.

Castle. It wasn't a pretty sight. It was melancholy, but compelling. The mute monument was eloquent.

Pete was correct. The ersatz "completion" of the ruin had been a mistake. Regardless of historic accuracy, it couldn't be authentic and couldn't work. The shiny new hardwood floors didn't convey the same message as the dirty, rough subflooring had. He was right: they were pulling to two directions, trying to tell the tragic story of deliberate abandonment, while at the same time trying to deny that abandonment, which was the point of the whole story. Even if one weren't a historian or architect, it simply didn't work. One went away with no clear sense of what the place meant, or what the interpretation was trying to say. It was just a very big building, sort of unfinished, sort of finished, dressed up a bit. The grass was nice, and the flowers pretty. People took a lot of photographs.

An exhibition mounted on freestanding panels on the main level was informative about the Thousand Islands, and about the Boldts. The installation was well designed, but the presentation tried to be so comprehensive about the history of the resort as well as of Heart Island that it didn't focus on the main story to be told here—the personal drama of George and Louise Boldt. Rather, one got the implied message, "Of course, we all know that the place was abandoned . . ." as if its abandonment was something to be passed over lightly or corrected. No doubt the Bridge Authority was proud of what it had done to remedy seventy years of neglect, and perhaps naturally focused instead on what was being done, and what would be done in the future. This is why a consultant would have been helpful, but of course they didn't know enough to know that they needed help. Now the Authority has ordered the huge dome to be filled with stained glass. Doubtless this will be quite an imposing feature, bowling visitors over, but it will be a total fraud. The glass dome was never completed, or probably never even designed. There's no way of doing it right, but so many opportunities for making the sort of mistakes made in the past—costly mistakes.

What might have been more effective in the rotunda than a general exhibition devoted to the Boldts and the Thousand Islands, would have been an explanation of what this place was like the day the telegram arrived—how much had been completed, what was stored in crates in the lower levels, how many men were working on the site, who delivered the wire and told the workers, how they left this very room. More relevant than pictures of the Thousand Islands in different eras, and of the Boldts at different ages, might be images of construction workers at the very time—like a remarkable photograph of some sixty men at the Oak Island granite quarry, cutting stone for the Castle. Authentic reality would be more compelling than synthetic ambiance.

42.   I sensed a need to get closer to the Boldts' family life. Courtney's own recollections went back as far as the 1930s, when only Clover continued to come to the river, and she was middle-aged. Jean Hammond, however, was a generation older. I imposed on her generosity once again.

"I didn't know George Boldt, Junior and his wife," she explained, "nearly so well as the first Clover and her husbands—and as the present Clover and her's, of course. At this distance, my impressions of the old days may be mostly what I picked up from others—the common gossip, you know."

"My sense is that Clover was brighter than her brother."

"Oh? Well, Clover was a sort of take-charge person, an organizer. She held things together here for decades, when everything seemed about to fall apart."

"How do you mean?"

"A community leader, you might say—especially as a sponsor of sporting events. She was a prominent hostess, particularly in conjunction with tournaments and races."

"Such as?"

"Oh, the polo matches, you know. Those dashing young men would arrive and Clover knew that all of us (who were youngsters then) were dying to meet them."

"But her brother wasn't so active?"

"We didn't see so much of him. He had a place over by the Club—not so expansive as Clover's, but it seemed to suit him. His wife Estelle—she was Estelle Savin, who was Mexican—preferred Wellesley House. She and the girls stayed at the Tennis House nearby."

"With Cricket?"

"Who? You mean George, Junior? We never called him that, but now that you mention it, I do remember that as some sort of college nickname he acquired. He and Estelle divorced. She was *so* attractive—I suppose that was part of the problem."

"And he was, maybe, a bit slow?"

"Not so swift as Estelle, I'd guess—at least she made a dazzling impression on everyone."

"I suspect," I ventured, "that George, Junior probably was something of a disappointment to his father."

"I would hardly be aware of that."

"I've heard that the father seemed more partial to Clover. From what I discovered, she seemed to 'take charge,' as you put it, when their father died."

"That wouldn't surprise me."

"Cricket was a lightweight, it seems. He was said to be 'a quiet, rather retiring man.' Although 'a great worker,' he had difficulty qualifying for university admission, but following (I quote now) 'eight years of vain effort,' he managed to get into Cornell."

"His father was a benefactor, you know. Clover gave Cornell the Boldt Tower in his memory."

"A tower! That figures—as does his son's eventual admission to Cornell. As an older student, and 'after supporting an army of tutors,' Cricket graduated with an AB degree, but he left blank in his yearbook the space for 'future occupation.'

"I don't think he ever had one, really. It must have been a strange life. When young, we used to imagine how marvelous to have those gorgeous horses and fast cars to enjoy all summer. The reality, I was surprised to learn, was that George, Junior wasn't even here, but at Cornell or Columbia, attending summer school."

"Given the Boldts' extravagance, you might think that Junior was spoiled by an excessive allowance from his father; to the contrary, he was 'considered the tightest proposition in his class'."

"I'm sure he never had to go on welfare; I suppose he clipped coupons all his life."

"A brief taste of hotel business, after his father died, was sufficient. They said that Cricket 'was frank enough to admit that he was not a born innkeeper, and he resigned'."

"Knowing the boy's limitations, his father probably tied up his inheritance in a trust fund. George, Junior must have been bored to death. I recall that he traveled a lot in later years. He wintered mostly at Miami Beach."

George C. Boldt, Jr. ("Cricket"),
about the time of his mother's death,
when he was a student at Cornell University

"He looks pleasant, charming in fact, in his photographs, and probably was good company."

"Yes, it does seem generally folks were pleasant here. I suppose we like to remember the appealing things, and we were all here to have a good time. Clover and her husbands were a lot of fun—I'm talking about the first Clover now."

"Her first husband was quite a sportsman, I understand."

"Do you mean 'playboy'? That's how he was widely regarded. George Boldt must have been disappointed by Clover's marriage to 'Gus'

Miles. Alfred Graham Miles had spent his summers on the River, where he met Clover. The Miles family wasn't in the same league financially as the Boldts, but had been wealthy longer. The William A. Miles Company was the oldest ale brewer in New York City, and the family had been on the River—at Lotus Land—before the Boldts arrived. Gus was a happy-go-lucky sort of guy, a 'crazy loon,' I think Grant Peacock called him. Like George, Junior, Gus went to Cornell, but Junior at least graduated. Gus didn't. He played football and was on the track team at college."

"He was the father of the present Clover?"

"Yes. But Gus disappeared around here after the breakup. He was a happy fellow when young, but the sort of man who never grows up. He became more difficult as the years passed."

"Clover sounds like an interesting person. I imagine that living at the Waldorf-Astoria as a teenager, dining regularly with dignitaries there, and later becoming familiar with celebrities like George M. Cohan, made her an urbane sophisticate."

"Clover?" Mrs. Hammond laughed. "I suppose I don't know what you mean by that. She was a rugged, outdoor type. But everyone regarded her as 'a very clever girl,' and she was poised, of course. She had been 'finished' by Miss Spence (like many young women of her generation and class here on the River) and so had acquired proper social graces. She spoke perfect German and fluent French. Clover was at ease in all kinds of company—she traveled in Europe with Cornell President A. D. White and his family. Clover was slightly deaf, but didn't want to admit it, so she often missed what was said, but faked it with a noncommittal smile or nod. This sometimes gave her a rather distant quality, but never unpleasant."

"Her mother's death must have been a great blow. She was still a teenager."

"Just when she was 'coming out', as debutantes used to do so importantly, her mother's death forced her back into seclusion. Even before Mrs. Boldt's death, Clover was pressed into service as the Boldt hostess. Mrs. Boldt went to European spas and during her mother's absence, Clover served as hostess at the Waldorf 'captain's table.' After her mother's death she was obliged to continue this role, even up here, at Wellesley House."

"Pete tells me that Clover had taken an interest in her father's business during his lifetime, making suggestions, and it was she (not her brother) who was the one to take charge of the Boldt family affairs, after her father's death."

"Yes, she was a woman of many parts—very capable woman. And a mother, of course. Clover was determined not to spoil her daughter (as Grandpa George did his granddaughters) but made our present Clover work for treats.

"What caused the breakup of the marriage—her first, I mean?

"Now, how would I know about that? . . . We all did know, of course, that Gus became a problem for Clover, and she divorced him, setting up a trust fund to provide him income. It was a messy business, press reports of his forcible eviction from his New York hotel suit being an acute embarrassment. She then married Nils R. Johaneson—'Sunny Jim,' we all called him—but after twenty years the second marriage also ended in divorce. Clover's only child, her daughter, our present Clover, also has remarried, to Alec Baird of Toronto. That's Alexander Gordon Baird."

"Is the present Clover like her mother?"

"Oh, no, not at all. Our Clover is rather shy and retiring and, of course, being disabled by an early bout of polio, she has never been so active as her mother. Clover now seems to have found some measure of serenity in later years. She's a poet, you know, and loves her flower garden."

"Like her grandfather."

43.   Seen through the open door, gleaming stripes of rolling swells came across the smooth water from a freighter recently past and nudged boats in the slips below. Under our wicker chairs the lapping of water accompanied the eerie creak of wood against rubber bumper. Otherwise, this seemed the quietest moment of my summer. Pete's boathouse workroom seemed more solitary than my lonely hotel room. There had I worked alone, focussed on my computer screen, while here Pete was sitting behind me as I stood at his balcony door, watching the big ship silently grow smaller. Pete might not have been here, however, except of an occasional "hmm" as he read the first piece of my writing that I shared with him. The remoteness of his island, like the heat in this loft, now seemed oppressive, and time was slowing to a standstill. I should have simply left the manuscript with him, it occurred to me, rather than endure this wait for his reaction.

The draft was a depiction of what life might have been like at Boldt Castle, had it been completed and if the Boldts had lived there. I prepared the piece for Clover Boldt and asked Pete's well-informed reaction, explaining that I had drawn upon novels and short stories by Henry James, William Dean Howells, Edith Wharton and personal recollections of Jean Hammond and others. This was a composite portrayal of the sort of people who populated these summer homes during the

Gilded Age, conveying the daily lives that they led at places like Newport, the Berkshires and Thousand Islands.

I had to explain to modern readers how a "country house" differed from the sort of summer cottage we may know better. First of all, in this class there was much moving about, much coming and going. Very wealthy families had multiple residences, often several seasonal homes, each of which might be occupied only occasionally, for short intervals. Dark Island Castle, for instance, Jean Hammond told

"The Towers," Dark Island, Ernest Flagg, architect

me, wasn't built as a summer home, to be used for a half year; rather, Commodore Bourne ("Born," as she had corrected my pronunciation) told his family he was building a little shooting box for fall duck hunting. He enjoyed the party's surprise when their boat emerged from the clustered islands of Chippewa Bay. All aboard saw the startling vision: a lone island farther out, crowned with that a shining granite structure, tile roofs glistening in the sun. Jean had laughed. "Some shooting box, eh? It's for sale. Price reduced from four to two million, or something like that. They say that Michael Jackson and some other celebrities have looked at the place, but no takers yet."

"That's a lot of money for an occasional party house."

"Nothing compared to what it cost, or would cost to build today—they figure about forty million."

In a sense the great country house was less a family summer home than a party house—the venue for special events, house parties when groups of friends and acquaintances gathered. After entertaining, the owners of one country house might move on to join the party at another country house. Staff, of course, stayed on to maintain the property, kept at the ready, should the owners return at any moment. This mobility of the upper classes explains the tenuous social community of resort colonies, where all of the owners of properties were rarely together at the same time.

Families usually were larger at the turn-of-the-century than now. Often they were extended with relatives as members of the household. Each person in a large family would have his or her own circle of friends and acquaintances. Children of-

The Arch of Triumph, Colonnades, and Temples of Love

A water gate opened into an artificial lagoon, a protected basin that provided
sheltered dockage for visitors' boats. Carved in high relief from the granite
heart above the arch on the island side is the date 1900. Round stones for the
flanking colonnades had been piled on the embankment in January 1904,
when work at Heart Island was terminated, but the flanking colonnades and
round, domed Temple of Love pavilions were never completed. The
monumental arch of triumph stands, however. Above the granite heart at the
apex of the composition the stag, or "hart," would have raised its antlers to
recall the Boldt crest, as a similar bronze sculpture does on the main-channel
façade of the Castle. This author's reconstruction derives from a design
sketch that the architect William Hewitt prepared for approval of the Boldts.

ten went to different private schools, connecting into several social networks of peers
and their parents. Their elders had more leisure, at a time when servants provided
household support, than do most adults today. Many adults and young people at
one of these summer homes might each develop a different, large social network.
Guests abounded.

To envision life at a Thousand Island country house—as distinct from a mere
summer cottage—first of all one should bear in mind that the coming and going
entailed family as well as guests. Not only did each member of the family entertain
his or her friends; each was obligated to visit elsewhere in return. It would have
been unusual to find all of the family at home on any particular day or weekend
during the summer. Various members might be at the mountains or the shore,
rather than on the River. The island house, however, might usually be full with one
person's friends or another's —sometimes in fact with all the family's guests, but
none of the family.

Unless coming from Montréal or from Great Lakes ports by steamer, a visitor would arrive by train. The very rich, like John Jacob Astor, coming to Heart Island, might arrive in a private railroad car. Those families on the River, like the Packers, Wilburs and Pullmans, that maintained their own cars might put them at a guest's disposal. Some visitors rented private railroad cars. Otherwise, if coming from New York City, as most guests probably did, one might book a Pullman compartment on the regular night train from Grand Central Station, awaking Saturday morning on the Clayton station dock.

"There's no train station at Clayton now," I had commented to Jean.

"No, only that small park at the lower end of Riverside Drive—across from the A&P supermarket, you know. That's where the terminal used to be. Hard to image a dozen or more trains daily arriving there, and large steamboats and yachts off shore, waiting a turn to tie up at the dock."

Your host or hostess might not be on hand at Clayton to greet you, if you had been invited to an island house party—nor even any member of their family. There would have been many other houseguests to entertain, and an hour or so might be required for a boat ride to and from Clayton. Imagine yourself emerging, one sunny Saturday morning, from your railroad car at the Clayton waterfront. Likely you would look in vain for a familiar face. Rather, a strange person, the Captain of the host's boat, perhaps, or possibly the host's or hostess' private secretary, might discretely inquire if anyone was destined for, say, Heart Island.

If bound for a nearby island, certainly a great yacht like the Emery's "Calumet" wouldn't be fired up and brought from the distant yacht house on Picton Island for the short run across the channel. A smaller but faster launch would be sent. If destined farther, however, even though the faster boat would expedite the trip, a big yacht like the Boldts' "Louise" might be sent to assure a more comfortable cruise. You might be welcomed with a salute from the cannon aboard the splendid, tall-masted ship off shore.

"A cannon?" I had asked, incredulously.

"Oh, yes," Jean had explained. "This was the drill. Nautical tradition." A sailor in spotless whites awaited in the yacht's tender at the dock to carry you and your escort to the yacht. Other sailors would be attending to your luggage, which by now has mysteriously disappeared.

Because you would not have had proper breakfast at the early hour, a morning repast would be served on the yacht's afterdeck, to be enjoyed while cruising among the Thousand Islands. Naturally, Boldt provided the elegant fare of the Waldorf-Astoria, and the same deferential service, provided on the yacht by a white-jacketed steward.

Imagine your first sight of Heart Island: the skyline of towers, steep roofs and gables, one surmounted with the Boldt stag, rising above the tree tops; below, the Alster Tower at the water's edge, and the great Arch of Triumph, crowned by antlered stags and flanked by colonnades, terminating in domed pavilions.

The yacht idles off shore, as you are assisted again into a smaller tender, one of the many launches in the Boldt fleet, then carried through the great arch, into the boat basin, there to disembark at the foot of an *allé* , flanked by sculpture, that ascends to the Castle.

Possibly some member of the family greets the visitor on disembarking, if the occasion warrants such special attention. More likely, if the visitor is insufficiently distinguished, a senior staff person, possibly Mr. Boldt's 'man' or Mrs. Boldt's secretary, might be on hand, to do the honors, as probably the butler would be too busy, some distance away, within the Castle.

As one enters the lagoon, the Arch of Triumph frames the Castle. The plan provided for the visitor to ascend an axial *allé*, flanked by symmetrical statues or other garden features. At the top of the slope, the design indicated a principal feature—possibly Boldts' Bensoni sculpture, "Flight from Pompeii." The formal plan, suggested here by the author's drawing, may strike us as contrary to the more natural, wooded character of the island as it became known during a century after abandonment of the project. The Boldts similarly intended to develop a formal Italian garden on the other side of the Castle, re-moving the extant Dovecote. Life at Heart Island would not have been casual or rustic.

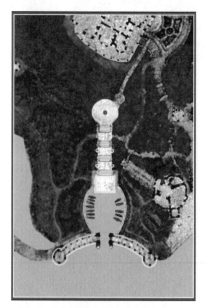

Detail of architects' original plan showing Arch of Triumph and flanking colonnades, boat basin, and *allé* approach. The Alster Tower is the circular form at right; causeway and lagoon are at left.

Disembarking from the launch, Heart Island reveals itself quite differently: to the left, black swans glide across the lagoon. Young ladies in white organdy who feed the Boldts' rare ducks from a rustic bridge look up, smile and wave. To the right, the Alster tower rises above the Roman plunge, in which young men splash and beyond, in a shady grove, a pavilion is dappled with sunlight. Ahead, terminating the vista, rises a cliff of granite, culminating in clustered towers, terra cotta roofs and stone chimneys. So this is Boldt Castle!

Escorted by your guide, you stroll up the *allé*, between hedges that provide dark ground for white sculptural figures. At the summit, in a central place of honor, is (as your escort explains) "The Flight from Pompeii" by Bensoni. As the new visitor traverses a walk along the main front, from between stone columns of a long veranda people glance down at the newcomer. Ahead, others converse under the trees and sky on an open, projecting terrace. As one approaches broad granite steps that ascend to the building, one hears from below echoing laughter and splashing from the indoor pool.

Your guide escorts you across the corner of the great hall, its full dimensions still obscured by columns and mezzanine overhead, into a formal reception room. Rather than sitting on one of the Louis XVI gilded chairs, you gaze into a tall mirror above the carved white marble fireplace, at the reflection of paneled walls, embellished with classical arabesques, and of the lofty ceiling and crystal chandelier. From beyond curved plate glass tower windows comes conversation and laughter of other guests, entering through raised sash where a breeze billows heavy lace curtains.

Muffled by the heavy velour of the *portière* in the doorway, voices are barely discernable: "Perhaps Mrs. Boldt is receiving today," and a reply, "I am sorry, Madam, Mrs. Boldt is not receiving today." The lady sighs, concluding, "Please give Mrs. Boldt my card." After a moment, another voice: "Mrs. Boldt is not in?" is followed by the same reply, "Mrs. Boldt is not receiving today." Votive cards would be placed by the butler on a silver tray, beneath the glowing stained-glass portrait of Louise Boldt. This might be as close as many a supplicant might get.

Reception Room as restored. Furnishings are not original.

Hearing someone approach, you turn to greet your host or hostess as the portière is drawn, only to see another unfamiliar man in formal attire enter. No, he is not one of the Boldts, either, but introduces himself as Hughey, the Butler. Suavely, he apologizes for the Boldts, who are otherwise occupied: Mr. Boldt is detained in

the City on business. Mrs. Boldt is required to attend a committee meeting and
luncheon at the Yacht Club. Miss Clover is hosting a tennis match with luncheon
at the Tennis House (or a golfing party, with luncheon at the Golf House, or a polo
practice with luncheon at Wellesley House). Mr. Boldt, Junior is not cavorting with
his young friends at the Alster Tower, as one surmised. "The Junior," as his father's
friends call him, no outstanding student, is required to attend Summer School at
Cornell.

Reception Room, original detail when the room was initially opened to the public

Hughey then asks you to accompany him, diagonally across the Rotunda.
Emerging from the low side aisle into the central space, one's gaze is drawn upwards,
taking one's breath away. Up through several stories, surrounded by tiers of galleries, the central well of the castle soars upward to a great dome of stained glass. Light
pours down on a broad, freestanding marble staircase within the hall, polished like a
mirror on both sides of the rich, cascading carpet.

Under the mezzanine at the opposite side of the Rotunda, Hughey presses a
button and an elevator door opens. The wood paneled interior is not large, but
Hughey carries no baggage. You comment, "But I left my luggage aboard the boat,"
to which Hughey, smiling, replies, "It will await you in your suite." An underground railroad has whisked it unseen from a service dock to the Castle, where por-
ters have delivered it to your room.

Flowers greet you in your quarters. Flowers are everywhere, indoors and out.
Louise is fond of them, particularly roses, the scent of which mingles with that of

furniture polish in many rooms. Ice water seems to be always at one's elbow, in silver pitchers, glistening with condensation, reflected in silver trays. Hughey spreads apart heavy lace curtains at the windows. The glass shines, polished like the table tops. Making sure the windows are adjusted to suit one's preference, Hughey explains the mechanics of the up-to-date plumbing, including a marble stall entwined with silver pipes, looking like an instrument of torture: it is a "rain bath," he explains. Hughey then demonstrates controls for novel heating and electric lighting, turning on and cautioning one about another novelty, the electric fan, and showing the location of buttons that one should press to call one's maid.

Demonstrating, an Upstairs Maid promptly appears. Hughey introduces a pleasant Irish girl as Maureen. You ask yourself, "Is this place a summer cottage, or a hotel?" If Boldt Castle is run like the finest hotel in the world, the Waldorf-Astoria, it is no coincidence.

Before leaving you Hughey explains that an al fresco luncheon is to be served at noon on the north terrace for those in sporting attire; formal luncheon to be served at one o'clock in the dining room. You must appear puzzled, for Hughey explains that chilled food would be available outdoors, warm food indoors. He even produces a handwritten menu for the more formal luncheon. A cold buffet will be available on the terrace. He confides, in a more intimate tone, that guests coming in from fishing or other outdoor activities might feel uncomfortable mingling with others indoors, dressed less casually. What one wears is serious business.

Maureen again asks if one cares for a cup of tea. Then she inquires, not if you will have a bath, but if it should be hot or cold. After pouring your bath she wants to know exactly what you wish to wear on dressing after the bath, before she unpacks the pile of awaiting luggage. Upstairs maids are far more important in this leagues than some might imagine. Here one bathes and changes costumes several times a day. One is always assisted by a servant who finds and lays out one's clothes, and assists a lady with dressing. Those corsets have to be tied. The guest isn't supposed to lift a finger, even to opening a drawer or closet door. To do so would be to deprive some young Irish girl her livelihood.

After emerging from the bath in one's robe (the lace dressing gown or silk kimono are favored by ladies, worn with embroidered slippers), assuring the maid that the clothes laid out are acceptable, and bidding her off, you finally sigh, relieved to be alone and unencumbered with ritual.

Hughey has encouraged you to feel at home, to explore the island, to use any of the facilities, and to introduce one's self to other guests. Left alone in your room, uncertain of protocol and a bit overwhelmed by the grandeur of it all, you may hesitate to venture forth. Instead, you may deliberate about the proper attire, you may test the down-filled mattress, or perhaps jot first impressions on heavy station-ary embossed with the Boldt crest. Eventually, however, you must decide what to wear and venture forth.

Opting for the early meal on the terrace, wearing your more casual clothes, you descend by elevator, uncertain of the route to the north terrace—but no concern, for every need has been anticipated. The elevator door is opened by a man, likewise in formal attire, but younger that Hughey. Introducing himself as the Assistant Butler,

he escorts you across the Ro-tunda, through the Billiard Room and onto the veranda. Ahead is a vista down through a shady grove to the lagoon, reflecting the great Arch of Triumph, flanked by its colon-nades. Here, the young guide points to the right, in the di-rection of laughter and conver-sation. Around the corner, where the veranda expands into a large room without walls, are perhaps twenty fellow guests, mostly standing, milling about among the potted palms, chat-ting.

The assemblage is gor-geous, mostly because of the extravagant display of flora and plumage atop the broad, plat-ter-like hats that the ladies bal-ance atop their mounds of carefully coifed hair secured only by giant, pearl-tipped hat-pins. Gowns are vaporous but elaborate, layered with gauzy silk and lace, ruffled and sashed. Every dress is white. Necklines are high at midday; it would be gauche to wear jewels at midday, except for pearls and modest broach. The ladies carry furled parasols in white-gloved hands, or artfully manipulate fans. The adventurous among the younger women might appear at luncheon in the shorter, ankle-length "rainy day" or "golf" skirt that they were permitted to wear for sports or walking, worn with a simple shirtwaist. For such modest costume (favored by daughters, in deference to more lavishly costumed matrons) a flat-brimmed hat, with no plumage and but a simple ribbon, is considered appropriate.

"Sporting attire," it turns out, still entails hats for all, regardless of gender or age (since the terrace, although largely undercover and even provided with a fireplace) is theoretically out-of-doors. Gentlemen seem uncertain whether one's hat should be on one's head or in one's hand, as one is under cover but in open air, or whether to favor a straw skimmer, a tweed golfing cap, a leather yachting cap. or even a plaid tam; certainly the derby is not worn in the summer. Particularly elegant and expensive is a fine, fedora-shaped Panama. Every gentleman wears a jacket, generally of blue serge or tweed, but as this is sporting attire, it may be of eccentric cut, long and loose, mismatched with one's tweed golfing knickers or white flannel trousers. The young, or fashionably venturous, wear their trousers cut full, with large cuffs on pegged legs, worn short to reveal plaid or monogrammed socks, filling the gap above massive brown oxford shoes. More sedate gentlemen wear pearl gray spats to cover black, high shoes. In concession to summer heat, vests are not required at a summer resort. Ties at the neck are as essential as hats or caps. Out of doors, however, cravats may be more of the order of loosely flowing scarves; by this device, during the summer one may evade the high, stiff collar, worn with one's tie on the outside. Spectacles are worn *pince-nez*, or sometimes dangle from a black ribbon. Men may wear jeweled cuff links and, like their ladies, wear white gloves, but carry walking sticks rather than parasols. This is sporting attire, for a casual lunch at Heart Island.

The Head Butler, Hughey, greets you as an old acquaintance. Playing host in the absence of the family, Hughey makes introductions and endeavors to start conversations with a word or two about the most recent arrival. The new visitor may at first feel the outsider, but quickly learns that everyone else here seems to be equally unfamiliar with the place or even with each other, having become only recently acquainted.

Socially insecure guests and even those more secure who are conservative address one another as "Mr." and "Mrs.," or "sir" and "madam." Humor is rarely volunteered, lest it be regarded as being "low." George Boldt's taste is very conservative, so the Boldts retain genteel social forms—though manners are becoming somewhat less formal during the 'nineties. Nevertheless, it is "bad form for women to be intellectual" so social conversation is largely "forced and dull," comprised of polite, conventional exchanges. Life in these great country houses is odd. A gentlemen of the old school, dismayed with the fast ways of the smart set, observes, "The party is in a ceaseless state of metabolic flux. You come down to breakfast to find that your

charming neighbor at dinner the night before has gone off . . . to some other country house. . . . Somebody else—probably a complete stranger—arrives during
breakfast and introduces a discordant note that doesn't, perhaps, even begin to blend
in with the general harmony for two or three days. It is upsetting." Another veteran
of country house life says that the dining room "till noon, looked like the coffee
room at a . . . hotel." Another comments: "At breakfast . . . the guests plan something among themselves and the host and hostess are free to join them as they please
. . . It is only at dinner that all are brought together and conversation kept up."

The Boldt table is legendary. "Nothing interest[s] him more than cuisine," they
say. In this, "his stickling for detail became almost a passion." His waiters have to
be tri-lingual and provide perfect service after attending the hotels training program.
Aa Oscar observes, these are "the halcyon days when dining [is] an art . . . the menu,
the wines, everything perfect!" With all of the talent and resources of the Waldorf-
Astoria at their disposal, as well as the provisions of the vast Boldt farm on Wellesley
Island, the Boldts maintain a high standard of cuisine, beautifully presented. Again,
roses adorn the buffet, where cold food is arrayed on beds of crushed ice. Among
other options, the diner may choose, say, cold Vichyssoise, followed by cold lobster
with the chef's fresh Mayonnaise, served with Asparagus bathed in herb butter, together with fresh, hot bread, direct from the Castle's own ovens, washed down with
an ample supply of Boldt's favored German white wine. How did the Boldts find
fresh lobster at the Thousand Islands? A refrigerated railroad car has brought provisions directly from New York City.

As this purports to be more or less a picnic, guests find places for themselves at
small linen-covered tables for four, each with a nosegay of American Beauty rose
buds in the center and decanters of wine at each corner, one at each guest's elbow.
The wine steward circulates to ascertain that sparkling crystal glasses do not remain
full, lest his choice of vintage displease. Desert and coffee, served with European
porcelain marked with Boldt crest, extend the repast until voices come from the adjoining Dining Room, where other guests have opted for more serious dining. The
Wine Steward dutifully disappears, together with most of the staff, and guests are
left to their own devices, attended only by a single waitress at the buffet, who tends
the tea pot and coffee urn and again passes the silver tray of petit fours.

Diners converse overlooking the water that extends to Wellesley House and its
gardens, where the huge houseboat, La Duchesse, is moored, and to the great Yacht
House, where the tall-masted yacht, "Louise," rests outside tall doors built to allow
her to enter her berth. This piece of water, visible from the most-used terrace of the
Castle, bustles with many passenger and service boats arriving and departing from
piers at the several Boldt facilities.

Since this is supposed to be camping informality, with permission of the ladies at the table, cigars are drawn. Magically, the Assistant Butler appears with lighted match. If daring, perhaps an actress like May Irwin or Fay Templeton, a woman may produce a cigarette from a silver case. A mellow fellowship prevails until it is too late in the afternoon to think about the sport for which one presumably is dressed; it is almost time to think about another bath, and dressing again for another event, tea at five o'clock.

If not a round of golf, tennis or a fishing expedition, one's table companions urge a few hands of bridge. The initiate is well advised to be cautious: cards are played for high stakes at grand country houses. The interval of an hour or two allows the new arrival to tour the island, however, or even to go by launch to nearby Wellesley Island, to see more of the vast Boldt estate. A boat ride through the gorgeously floriated canals is highly recommended, as is a tour of the great Yacht House complex, with its shop where Gold Cup racing boats are being built. Surely one should inspect the huge houseboat, "La Duchesse." A climb to the observation platform atop the Yacht House tower is advised, for an unforgettable view of Heart Island. The new visitor is referred to the Assistant Butler, generally to be found in the Lobby, off the Main Hall, who arranges transport and guide for the estate tour.

The "Lobby," you discover, is the command post of the sprawling Boldt domain. The entering visitor was unaware of it, for it is not an entry vestibule, but is located between the public and service portions of the Castle. Mr. Boldt's private office is nearby, where he meets regularly with the Estate Superintendent, and has his ticker tape machine, to be always abreast of the stock and commodities markets. The Lobby is Hughey the butler's cockpit. He serves as a sort of concierge. Here guests may consult him about railroad connections, or ask him to book steamboat passage to their next destination. Here guests' luggage arrives from the railroad tunnel, here visitors' golf clubs, tennis rackets, fishing rods, polo mallets, photography equipment and other gear is stowed in lockers, to be produced on demand by guests. Here their luggage also is stored during the visit, and here the staff assembles for Hughey's inspection to begin each shift, and the servants return from errands to await further orders from the Butler or Assistant Butler. The term, "lobby," of course, like the service that it provided, derived from Boldt's hotel management background.

There is a state of the art in hotel service, attained by a few of the world's *ne plus ultra* hostelries—like the Villa d'Este at Cernobbio—where service not merely is impeccable, but totally inconspicuous. It is said of Boldt, "The supreme thing . . . upon which he had set his heart and soul, was the perfection of his service." Heart Island is the sort of Nirvana that is rare in the world. No effort is spared, but the effect appears effortless. Separation of circulation of staff from that of guests is essential; separation even of guests in different attire is desired, less the proper ambiance be disrupted.

An afternoon stroll around Heart Island, with walking stick or parasol, reveals many marvels, not the least of which is the Water Castle, a miniature stone château located offshore, connected by a flying stone bridge. On the highest tower are clock faces, oriented in several directions. Within the tower are fifteen chimes, ranging in size from twelve and fourteen feet long. Philadelphians objected that they were too loud for the Wanamaker Department Store. When they began to drive business away, Wanamaker gave them to his friend, Boldt, for Heart Island. They are heard distinctly four miles away, sounding every quarter hour.

Terra cotta fountain

The quaint Water Castle in reality is a modern powerhouse. Heart Island's engineer proudly shows visitors the electrical generating plant, with 'three dynamic dynamos, . . . each having a power equal to that of thirty horses,' driven by three Otto steam engines.' A barge, towed by Boldt's tug, brings coal for the power plant, as well as for the kitchen stoves and ovens, and for domestic hot water and hot water heating systems. An impressive array of levers and dials arrayed on white marble slabs suggests the complexity of Heart Island's infrastructure, requiring a full-time engineer to operate and maintain.

The walk around the island is ever eventful, every turn revealing a new delight: a swinging bridge spanning a natural cove, a Japanese stone lantern atop a granite outcrop, a giant terra cotta shell forming a niche, within which a gargoyle's grotesque head spurted water into a basin. Although Heart Island is not large, it is so intensely developed that it seemed much larger, for at every few steps there appears another surprise.

Beds of flowers bloom everywhere. A spot of sun warms the thin soil over the native granite, especially along the shore; deeper in the island tall trees create cool recesses of shady lawn, the oaks framing varied views of the Castle's many towers. Central to the view outward on the south side is the village of Alexandria Bay, where two grand hotels, the Crossmon House and the Thousand Islands House, vie for prominence. At almost any daylight hour, giant steamboats converge on the channel-side dock of the village, while many smaller yachts and fishing skiffs enter and depart from upper and lower bay docks.

The Alster Tower, the visitor discovers, is another miniature castle itself, perhaps even more intriguing and enchanting than the main house, which really is too huge to comprehend properly. Situated at the very water's edge, the Alster Tower serves well as a playhouse (a "casino," as such recreation buildings were then called on these Thousand Islands estates). Many small, fast launches are tied to the dock here, and much noise comes from within: bowling balls dropping on hardwood lanes, followed by the striking of flying pins, ragtime dance tunes resonating within the Shell Room, much laughter and calling back and forth, from atop the tower to passing boats and to swimmers in the Roman Plunge below.

Returning to the lagoon, with the Arch of Triumph and Peristyle beyond, the visitor retraces his path to the Castle entrance, hastening his pace, for it is time to dress again for the next event, tea at five o'clock.

The late afternoon tea ceremony may be conducted at any number of delightful places on Heart Island, for gazebos, balconies, terraces and gardens abound. Today, the Assistant Butler has advised those passing through the Rotunda that tea is to be served at the Roof Garden. When suitably attired in less sporty, but not yet formal regalia, you find your way to the top of the Castle. The elevator carries you to a gallery, which surrounds the stained-glass dome, its upper surface visible through openings along the corridor that rings it. You are directed by the volume of noise, echoing throughout the corridors. A cluster of houseguests and other visitors awaits in the gallery, at the entrance to the Roof Garden. It seems that every other Islander's houseguests want to see Boldt Castle, and that five o'clock is a popular hour for an uninvited "call." Off the gallery is a room full of palms, where a half flight of steps leads upwards to an upper level, where a wall of glass opens onto a roof terrace. Hughey, the Butler, announces one's name on entering, in a loud voice, as the chatter of guests reverberates under high, sloping ceilings—the underside of the Castle's steep roofs. Again, hats are worn by ladies. This being nominally a "garden," gentlemen however seem a bit uncertain about whether to wear or carry their hat. As the hostess is absent, there is no tea table where she presides over the teapot, but instead a buffet, so profusely embellished with sprays of roses as to suggest a casket in an undertaker's parlor, and resplendent with Boldt Silver and porcelain, emblazoned with the Boldt crest.

The victuals are tastefully restrained, however. Dainty sandwiches and French pastries are arrayed on silver salvers. Guests do not help themselves to the buffet, but await servants who pass among them bearing trays. Lemonade is offered, as an alternative to tea, as well as decanters of wine and cordials.

Every visitor eventually makes his way through the assemblage onto the balcony, again to view Alexandria Bay and the busy main channel of the St. Lawrence, seen even more spectacularly from above the treetops. Many guests watch the big, side-wheel steamboats docking at Alexandria Bay and passing close to the shore of the island below. From their top decks, throngs of tourists gaze upwards and wave. Informed guests then point out other showplace summer homes on nearby islands; some visitors turn away from the view to look upwards. Following their gaze, you see overhead the gilded bronze stag, emblem of the Boldts. Having almost forgotten about one's missing hosts by this time, you are startled to hear a friendly voice. "Hello, there. I'm Clover Boldt." The rather plain but attractively athletic young woman, dressed more simply than any of her guests, is back from her golf, tennis, polo or whatever. Her work shift has begun. She is on duty, to serve as Boldt host-ess, and is sure to repeat Hughey's apologies, promising that her mother will join the guests for dinner. After chatting briefly, Clover turns to Hughey, at her side, who escorts her to meet other members of the weekend party.

New acquaintances made at luncheon and tea linger on the balcony, perhaps warming their tea with a bit of rum, or even asking Hughey to refill the delicate cup with a Manhattan cocktail. Although wine was served at the table, it would be *gauche* to stroll about with a wineglass in hand at other times. The principle topic of conversation among visitors at luncheon had been the Boldt family, and one's con-nection to one member or another—an anecdote or two verifying one's degree on intimacy. Now, at tea, the guests compare impressions of Heart Island and the Wellesley Island estate, suggesting other sights to see—the stables, with the Boldts' fine horses, or the elaborate farm, where gaggles of geese numbering in the hun-dreds.

On departing, at the steps of the Roof Garden, Hughey or his Assistant informs guests that dinner will be served at eight, the party gathering in the Rotunda at seven-thirty. He requests, "Please descend by the staircases, reserving the elevator for other visitors returning to their suites." It would be awkward for those in swimming or riding attire to encounter others dressed for dinner emerging from the elevator. A previous visitor to Heart Island might whisper, "Do be there before Mrs. Boldt's entrance. She emerges precisely at seven-thirty."

Strolling around the fifth floor gallery, a companion points out the Reading Room at that level, which supplemented the main Library being off the Grand Hall. This high retreat, favored by guests who wished a less public lounge, opens onto

Roof Terrace view looking towards Sunken Rock Light House

a balcony that overlooks the lagoon and Triumphal Arch. With only about an hour remaining before once again changing costume, the new visitor visits the Palm House, a glass structure high enough to accommodate tall Palms trees, and its adjoining conservatory, filled with orchids and other tropical blooms. It adjoins the "Hennery," as it is called, with its collection of exotic fowl in the base of a stone tower, topped by a dovecote.

Many others are exploring the island, some carrying the new Kodak cameras. Suspecting that it might be regarded as gauche for Boldt houseguests to take pictures, one gradually realizes that all of these people are not proper guests at all. Small boats tie up at various places along the shore and curious sightseers disembark.

The Italian Garden terrace provides a promenade above and a long service tunnel below.

Apparently total strangers are allowed to wander about the grounds. The Power House chimes sound six-thirty. This is a reminder that it is time to go back to one's suite, to discuss with Maureen the proper dress for dinner at Boldt Castle.

Depending upon one's status, the guest's suite may be luxurious or even lavish. Most accommodations provide a sitting room with fireplace, some with a private balcony, plus a bedchamber and bath, walled with hand-painted tiles. If one does not care to descend for breakfast, Maureen advises the guest, a steward will deliver and serve it on the table in one's private parlor.

"How do guests dress for dinner at Boldt Castle"? the visitor asks. Maureen de-murs that she never ate anywhere except in the Servant's Hall, but occasionally she did peek over a gallery railing, to look down at the assemblage in the Rotunda before dinner. And how were the guests dressed? Very grandly, Maureen was sure, but she is unable, or hesitates, to be very specific. Most importantly, how would Mrs. Boldt be dressed? That was critical for the lady, lest a guest outshine the hostess.

It would be rash for a lady to put on her most resplendent garb for the first eve-ning's dinner. A lady's jewels should be left behind, other than a modest string of pearls or two, perhaps. Ball gowns would be inappropriate, one might suppose. "Oh, but no," Maureen corrected, "sure there will be dancin' tonight in the Ball Room, for the orchestra is comin'." Nevertheless, a lady would not select her finest ball gown for the first evening, in deference to her hostess.

After seven, a splendid procession assembles on the galleries of the upper floors, which encircle the rotunda. Gentlemen, dressed in black dinner attire, cutaway coats or tuxedo jackets with white gloves, escort their white-gloved ladies in rustling gowns, proceeding in stately tread down the several flights of stairs to gather on the marble floor under the glass dome. A fire glows in the fireplace there, except in the very hottest weather, for Louise does not care to see a fireplace unlit, and likes an aroma of wood smoke throughout the house, mingled with the ever-present scent of roses.

Guests, transformed by formal dress, mingle in a brilliant scene, where dia-monds (worn by initiates who knew that the hostess would wear hers) sparkle among the ladies' pearls. Gowns are all décolleté, providing expanses of white shoulders and bosoms, ample for the display of Tiffany's most ambitious creations. Earrings glint and gems glitter in elaborate coiffeurs. Most couples move about, a few settling into the deep lounge chairs of the adjoining library, where another fire glowed beneath the elaborate carved Flemish Oak mantelpiece, and a few guests even step out onto the terrace off the library. Clover Boldt circulates busily, Hughey, in black tie and swallowtail black coat, at her side. Miss Boldt, with Hughey's prompting, greets everyone once again with cordial familiarity. Hughey carries a silver tray bearing boutonnières for the gentlemen, the lapel flowers matching the dinner floral pieces, and envelopes, one addressed to each gentleman, which he delivers. Within is a card, on which Mrs. Boldt's secretary has written the gentleman's name, together with that of the lady whom he is to escort into the din-ing room. No refreshment is served before dinner, but the high volume of guest's conversation and laughter suggests than many had ordered Scotch or Manhattans in their suites before descending.

Clover inquires of each guest whether he or she hasn't met any of the others present, making introductions where required, particularly of gentlemen to the ladies who will be their partners. When the distant Power House chimes sound seven-thirty, conversations pause as guests follow one another's glance upwards, to the head of the stairs. From her suite on the second floor, Louise Boldt has emerged, pausing to smile at the assemblage before descending regally, her satin train cascading behind her down the carpeted stairs.

If one had not met her previously, the visitor might be surprised to see such a small, gentle looking woman—hardly the image of an imperious grand dame. Slightly plump, she has a round face with upturned nose and a friendly expression. The tavern-keeper's daughter, as everyone knows she is, appears slightly displaced in this grandeur, like an actress miscast, but surely she seems at ease in this role. Louise Boldt has spent virtually her entire life entertaining guests, and is so accustomed to the part as to appear almost habitual in conducting the proceedings. State dinners, after all, have been almost nightly events in the Boldts' enormous private dining room in New York, created from the old Waldorf ballroom after the new Astoria was constructed. If the newly arrived guest at Heart Island has been slightly ill at ease in such surroundings, Louise, even more than her daughter, makes them feel comfortably at home. Unlike Clover, Louise has not attended the best schools, has not cultivated the accent and polished demeanor of the younger generation. Belied by her diamonds and pearl-studded Worth gowns, Louise Boldt is open, accessible and genuine.

After Louise has circulated among her guests, accompanied by Clover and Hughey, chatting casually with each, Hughey withdraws to the dining room doors, which he swings open, announcing in a loud voice, "Madam, dinner is served." A procession is formed in the Rotunda, each gentleman giving his arm to the lady who is to be his dinner partner (all of which has been carefully arranged by Louise during the afternoon, on her return from the Yacht Club). Tonight a Senator escorts Louise, leading the other couples to the Dining Room.

Many candles, shielded by rose-colored fabric shades, glow upon glittering silver and sparkling crystal. Epergnes and flat baskets of flowers line the center of the long table. Waiters stand against the wood-paneled walls; Hughey glides inconspicuously about, overseeing everything.

The diners find their twenty-four places marked by cards. A waiter draws back the chair at each place. Louise sits at the head tonight, since her husband is absent; Clover sits at the foot. Louise is framed in the great plate glass bay window, with the Yacht House seen through trees across the water in the distance. At her right is the most honored guest, who has escorted her into the dining room—frequently a

Boldt Castle Rotunda

The author's reconstruction of the hall as it might have appeared, had it been completed
with marble staircase, bronze railing, and stained-glass dome, viewed from the ball room.

Washington visitor, sometimes a Cabinet Member, the Vice President or even the President himself. Mere millionaires, a dime a dozen in this set, go to the foot of the table, to converse with her daughter, Clover.

On finding their places, gentlemen remove their white gloves; ladies do likewise, laying them with their fans on their laps. Diners find awaiting at each place an incongruously plain dinner roll, inside a folded napkin. The experienced diner is wary neither to be surprised nor to allow the hard roll to fall on the floor. A sophisticated guest knows that the roll is to be promptly removed, not to be placed on the china, but laid on the tablecloth. It is never to be cut with a knife, but broken by hand. At each place is centered a porcelain charger, carrying the Boldt crest. A feature of the silver arrayed around each charger is a charming saltcellar, with a miniature spoon. At each place one finds a small bottle of Apollinaris Water, opened and covered with a chilled glass tumbler, as well as a wineglass for the first course.

Servants moving simultaneously down both sides of the table then deliver little neck clams, arranged in crushed ice on silver trays with red and black pepper in little silver pepper pots—the conventional prelude to a lengthy summer dinner. The guest should recognize the special seafood fork next to his plate. There is no formality about beginning —not even waiting for host or hostess to proceed.

A handwritten menu at each place, next to the card with the diner's name, indicates the fare. The guest may choose between two or more offerings for some of the ten or so courses, allowing one to pace one's self, considering the formidable task ahead. Hughey hovers between the sideboard and an attentive position behind his mistress, supervising the several waiters (or "footmen," in parlance of the time). The servers do not inquire regarding one's preference, but mutely with white-gloved hands offer each dish to the diner, who is expected to nod without interrupting conversation. One has to be mindful of the menu and be prepared to decline offerings, lest he or she be overwhelmed with food. A guest does not serve one's self from the container, but allows the waiter to do so. All of the ladies are served before the gentlemen, so the waiters with their containers circulate around the table twice, for each of the ten or so courses.

One begins to eat when served, rather that waiting for others to be served. Otherwise the lengthy circuit of serving would cause food to cool on the plate. Hughey pours wines from the Castle's wine cellar, representing the vast cellars of the Waldorf-Astoria. Wines vary from one course after another, while the imbibers' fluent conversation becomes gayer as the evening progresses. The butler does not interrupt to inquire if a glass should be filled, but does so uninstructed. A lady who does not care for more wine should touch the rim of her glass as a signal. As an intermission, a fruit ice is served about midpoint.

Menu

Huitres
Gumbo do Volailles Printamer
Filet do Sole Anglaise à la Marguery
Salade do concombres
Couronne de Rise de Veau
avec champignon frais à la crême
Côtelettes d'Agneau
À la Robinson
Pommes de terre sufflées
Salsifis à la crême
Pigeonneaus rôtis
Salade turqoise
Plombière aus marrons
Petits fours

Apollinaris   *Café*

Mrs. Boldt served this dinner for thirty-eight in the Boldts' private dining room at the Waldorf-Astoria at 7:45 PM on Friday, January 2, 1903. The cost was $95. The repast was washed down with:

		Courses were:
18 gallons of champagne punch	liquor 2.— [dollars?]	Oysters
6 gallons of Lemonade	6 B… [illegible]	Chicken soup
4 [bottles of] Pommery [wine]	50 Garcia Pant. (cigars)	Cucumber salad
2 [bottles of] Rye	170 Cigarettes	Sweetbreads
78 [bottles of] Apollinaris[water]		Veal cutlets
2 [bottles of] Ginger Ale	Misspellings of the original	Soufléed potatoes
4 [bottles of] Bramberger	menu have been retained	Roasted pigeons
2 [bottles of] Julienne	(the steward's handwritten	Turkish salad
	copy, not the guests' copy).	Chestnut ice cream
		Fancy cakes

At intervals, the tablecloth is removed, one servant on each side of the table rolling it up, while others remove the centerpieces. Another tablecloth has been laid beneath —several, in fact, for the different services. All are of white damask, ironed on rollers so as to avert creases, except for the final dessert cloth, which is delicately tinted to match the floral pieces. Finally, small dessert napkins, embellished with colored embroidery, are placed on decorated china desert plates, and finger bowls are set on the table, within them small glasses filled with perfumed water, fresh flower petals floating on the surface. The cognoscenti are aware that, on concluding, one may raise the glass to the lips to rinse them, but should not drink. Instead, the guest pours the liquid into the finger bowl, in order to rinse the fingers before wiping them with the napkin.

After the disappearance of several table cloths, and appearance of many species of silver and glassware, together with an ample sampling of the extensive Boldt cellar, the visitor clearly realizes that dinner is the feature event at Heart Island, lasting hours. This is the one time during the day when the host family and all of its guests come together, when conversation is expected to be at its most stimulating—as vivacious as considered genteel, of course—or possible for the conversationalists.

Men and women alternate in the seating arrangement but women are not supposed to be informed about current events or be savvy about anything the men do. They may ask questions and be good listeners. Otherwise the exchange is largely of pleasantries. There are certain taboos—anything even suggesting sex, of course, or politics, or religion—or the servant problem. One never should comment on the food, even to compliment the host or hostess, since to mention it would suggest that one didn't expect the best food available.

Dinner partners (husbands never sit with wives) change nightly which allows those with limited repartee (new millionaires and their spouses are not noted for being socially adroit) to tell the same stories over and over again to new audiences. If not exactly sophisticated, the dinner party is at least adult—visiting children dine with their governesses, who come along, housed on the fifth floor of the Castle, under the eaves; young adults have a much better time than their parents, they suppose. Not being required to be so mannered, the junior set dines together at the Alster Tower, or aboard the "Louise" or "La Duchesse," at Wellesley House, or at a shore dinner on some island. Clover surely would rather be with them, than with her seniors, but *noblesse oblige*. When her "Papá" comes to the island, he takes over the head of the table, "Mamá" the foot, freeing Clover to join her friends. Her brother, "Cricket," is not much help. Clover wonders whether his Summer School at Cornell is not merely a ruse, to free him from the tedious ritual of Heart Island.

Among these diners, moving upwards socially is taken very seriously. It is said that Boldt is 'conservative in his ideas; as modern ideas go, extremely conservative.' That should be qualified, for according to another writer, 'There [is] nothing too new in all the world for George C. Boldt.' The latter referred to modern technology, however, and Boldt is very old-fashioned in what he considers respectable behavior. Although the Waldorf-Astoria has been the first to allow men to smoke in the presence of women, it will be one of the last to allow women to smoke. As Oscar puts it, "Our innovations [are] startling and sensational, but they [are] always genteel."

Boldt's manners are impeccable. 'He [will] bow and kiss a lady's hand [and] 'greet his guests with that delightful formality that completely [wins] the hearts of all that ever met him. . . . [He] would have shone as an international diplomat.' Boldt himself refers to his '*savoir faire*.' The Boldt children are expected to acquire proper manners—to dress for dinner, to rise whenever an older person entered the room, to address elders, including their parents, as 'Madam' and 'Sir.' They may cut up a bit with their peers at the Alster Tower, the Tennis House, or some other venue. But life in the Castle is very ritualized.

Now the sun sets beyond the great glass windows while they dine, and when dessert finally comes, hundreds of electric lights glitter outside among the trees. Strains of music enter the room, echoing in the heights of the domed Rotunda, where the orchestra plays. This is the signal for the ladies to excuse themselves. The hostess does not ask, but comments, 'I suppose that you gentlemen will have your coffee here.' As Louise Boldt rises, all of the gentlemen do likewise, elaborately protesting the ladies' departure. They nevertheless offer their arms to their partners, whom they escort in another stately procession, under the illuminated stained-glass dome, glowing overhead, to the wood-paneled Library that adjoins the Ball Room. There tea and coffee (and Mirabelle liquor) await the ladies in front of the glowing fire. Through the open French doors the ladies wander onto circling veranda and terraces, there to exclaim at the spectacular illumination of the grand hotels at Alexandria Bay, from whence came more distant strains of mingled music. They savor the ambiance as they await their gentlemen, who have returned to the Dining Room to partake of Havana cigars (Boldt's own brand) and decanters now on the table.

None of the ragtime music heard at the Alster Tower sounds in the Castle; George Boldt frowns on modern dancing, preferring the more courtly waltz and other traditional forms of the dance. The older generation, after such a meal, is not inclined to much physical activity. The gentlemen eventually join the ladies in the library and on its terrace. Tea now is offered as the music ceases while Louise Boldt chats briefly with everyone, before suggesting that they adjourn to the adjoining Ball

Room. The orchestra resumes; the guests dutifully perform a few perfunctory steps in the ballroom, before most of them drift out through its wide bay window, onto the terrace overlooking the Italian Garden.

As a continuation of the promenade around the Castle, provided by its long verandas, a belvedere extends atop a high granite wall (which encloses the service tunnel below, with its railroad). This long terrace overlooks the main channel, where the lights of many boats flit about like fireflies. Distant islands are ringed with lamps, cottage verandas with paper lanterns, and towers outlined with electric lights. The grand hotels of Alexandria Bay glitter with colored bulbs on porch and roof, and the tall central tower of the Thousand Islands House is a great lantern, its huge stained glass windows aglow. All of this brilliance is reflected in the black water of the St. Lawrence. Within the Italian Garden itself, illuminated fountains sparkle among beds of flowers. The spicy, pungent aroma of miniature, clipped boxwood hedges mingles with the perfume of Rubrum Lilies.

Behind the lighted clock faces of the Power House, the great chimes peal. The orchestra ceases, and from within the ballroom comes the thunder of its pipe organ, filling the whole castle and its gardens with music. Then, to the astonishment of all, the Power House carillon, far at the opposite extremity of the garden, begins playing, accompanying the organ!

The music diminishes to a distant murmur. Louise Boldt, diamonds sparkling like the stars overhead, circulates among her guests, bidding them goodnight, and urging them to continue without her. Then she retires to her Castle, satin train following behind as she strolls slowly through the garden, up the granite steps into the Ball Room, then to the elevator, and so to bed.

Whenever I dip back, in fond memory, none the less, into the vision I have here attempted once more to call up, I see the whole thing overswept as by the colossal extended arms, waving the magical bâton, of some high-stationed orchestral leader, the absolute presiding power, conscious of every note of every instrument, controlling and commanding the whole volume of sound, keeping the whole effect together and making it what it is. What may one say of such a spirit if not that he understands, so to speak, the forces he sways, understands his boundless American material and plays with it like a master indeed? . . . Such was my impression of the perfection of the concert that, for fear of its being spoiled by some chance false note, I never went into the place again."

Henry James, speaking of George Boldt and his Waldorf-Astoria, 1904

Louise Boldt

*   *   *

"What do you think?" I asked nervously, like a schoolboy inquiring about his exam. Pete simply grinned, putting the papers down. The teacher's smile told me my grade. "Do you think Clover will like it?"

"She'll love it."

44. When it came, I wasn't surprised. Pleased, yes, and gratified that my work in preparing preliminary sketches of a Boldt book had borne fruit, but in truth I had anticipated the invitation to Hopewell Hall. It had taken several draft segments sent for her comments, sketches of key incidents in her grandfather's life, to persuade Clover Boldt Baird that I was not merely competent, but indeed was going to do the book.

Vast drifts of pastel impatiens covered the ground, dappled by sun beneath tall trees; high banks of white and pink phlox perfumed the air with an aroma of spice. Like her grandfather, Clover loved flowers. Hopewell Hall reminded me of one of those heady affairs at the Waldorf today, when the dramatically lit scene is inundated with sumptuous floral arrangements.

Alec Baird descended the stone steps of the large house to greet me, escorting me along the porch to its end, where Clover sat smiling in her wheelchair. We relaxed on thick, chintz-covered cushions in rattan chairs and chatted under the main tower, where the verandah expanded into a circular space, contained by stone balustrade and massive columns. The rough granite rock reminded me of Heart Island, which was not visible from here. That was one reason the first Clover had preferred this house to others on the estate.

Clover was pleasant, but obviously uncomfortable talking about the past. "I really don't know anything," she complained. "Mother never discussed family affairs with me, and didn't want to talk about family with other people either. There has always been so much curiosity. There have been those dreadful stories. Mother wisely refrained from even commenting. She was above that."

After talking in a general way about my approach to a Boldt biography, I came to the point: "You know, the question I hear most often, from visitors at Heart Island and from other people here, is, 'How did she die?'"

Silence. Clover seemed startled, expressionless. Then Alec piped up, in cheery voice: "But we know that, don't we, dear?" That brought an expression to Clover's face—was it merely annoyance, or alarm? From her wheelchair, Clover was unable to give him a kick under the table, probably didn't want to grimace as a signal, and didn't think fast enough to interject. Alec went on: "She died by taking an overdose of something, didn't she?" He looked at Clover.

After all my difficulty, it was that simple.

Resigned to the cat being out of the bag, Clover sighed and opened up. "That's what has come down in the family. She took too many pills, or whatever she was taking. Mother faulted her father. I suppose it was because George Boldt was such a Prussian autocrat, always giving orders and expecting to be obeyed. He demanded that his wife lose weight so as not to embarrass him in public. My grandmother had been ruining her health in her last years, with all sorts of treatments at spas and quack medicines—trying to satisfy her husband. He was a perfectionist, you know."

"I learned that Louise left the River for the last time to go to a German spa—Carlsbad, a particularly aristocratic resort."

"Probably for a crash diet program, so she could get back into her gowns for the New York season."

"Yes, Carlsbad was noted for its crash reducing programs. The Boldts had been there before."

"It may have been there that she got the medicine that killed her."

"The death certificate says she died of heart failure."

"The medicine could have done that," Alec ventured. "Junior's secretary—George, Junior, that is, Clover's uncle—recalled that Louise had died of the overdose in Carlsbad, where she went from here."

"Oh? But apparently Louse died in New York. Probably she came back for the opening of the new Manhattan town house and was in it over Christmas. Wasn't it another tragic irony that they would have just moved into the new townhouse—a place of her own, finally, after so many years at the hotel?"

"I don't remember that," Clover commented. "Is the house still standing?"

"Yes, it was next to the old Tiffany's, a gorgeous building on the corner of Fifth and 37th, marred now by a fast-food joint. The Boldt house also has gone downhill. To see it today, you'd never believe the Boldts lived there. It's been cut up into apartments. Of course, we know that Louise went to Carlsbad in August, and surmise that she returned to New York, from press accounts when she died, and from the death certificate."

"Mother never mentioned the New York house, only a few blocks away from where we lived, on Park Avenue. She was that way. I've always supposed that she didn't want to entertain any questions about an unpleasant topic. Mother was only eighteen when her mother died. She had to serve as grandfather's hostess—a role she disliked. Mother was never a socialite, really, and surely she was relieved to marry, to move over here from Wellesley House, and to escape from so many obligations to grandfather. He was very demanding, but not unkind. I remember only loving attention to us grandchildren. We adored him as a doting grandfather, but of course really didn't know him in his other roles."

"You presented George Boldt very favorably in your book."

"I believe in that adage, 'don't say anything, if you can't say something good.' What's the point of criticizing those who are gone? They've done wonderful things over at Heart Island, I understand, and all those people who visit there ought to see my grandfather in his best light. He was a remarkable man."

"Yes, indeed."

45. What went unasked was why Louise took the overdose—whether it was accidental or not (the later speculation best left unsaid). Clearly, Clover Boldt Baird didn't

have a sense that Louise Boldt had been a deliriously happy woman, suddenly cut down at an early age by an unforeseen illness or accident. Contemporary accounts shortly before she died refer to her unspecified health problems, a condition perhaps supposed because of visits to German spas for health "cures." Many of the treatments at those institutions were for substance abuse and addiction, but Louise's problem apparently was merely a tendency to put on weight. Whatever substances she was taking, and perhaps killed her, may have been taken merely to appear as her husband wanted.

Appearances were very important to George Boldt, who was an artful illusionist. That was evidenced by his ability to convey a sense of luxurious privilege and exclusivity in a colossal hotel. In this sense, the Boldts lived in a realm of fantasy—and the extravagance and opulence of the Waldorf-Astoria was fantastic. They played roles in an unreal world of sudden wealth and limitless means, a world of privilege envied and finally attained, if only briefly, by Paul, the youth of Willa Cather's "Paul's Case." He satisfied a compelling dream by finally going to the Waldorf, and to kill himself, rather than coming back to reality.

For Louise, the incredible fantasy was over at age forty-one.

46.   I found Courtney carrying rubbish out to be burned in a smoking metal drum. In faded shirt and worn jeans, he looked like a caretaker for the big house—which, indeed, he was. "So you got to talk to Clover, finally?"

"It was worth the wait. You probably know what I learned, about Louise's death."

"You understand why it's not something that fits very well with the public legend."

"Not with the image of the happy lovers, their rapture suddenly interrupted by cruel fate. My hunch seems right, that there was more to the story."

"Life is more complicated, often more mysterious than fiction, isn't it? But we want simple myths. Legends serve a purpose. They simplify and idealize our confusing existence."

"Isn't truth more important?"

"Do you intend to destroy the Boldt myth now?"

"The Boldts were real people, with real problems. Will it hurt the Castle enterprise to have visitors understand what the historic monument really means, and to have a better sense of George and Louise Boldt as three-dimensional individuals, not stock, story-book characters?"

"But you don't understand: the management is still in the fantasy business over there. Just like Boldt himself, they're purveyors of illusion. They know it, and don't want pleasant images marred by ugly facts. Nix to *momento mori*."

"Come again?"

"You don't know the Martinelli painting, 'Memento Mori'? It's frequently called 'Death Comes to the Banquet Table'. A hideous skeleton enters to disrupt the festive banquet. The producers of the Boldt Castle show don't want visitors to be disturbed by the apparition."

"That's simple minded. Boldt Castle will mean much more, if we know and begin to understand the reality that it represents. It's a tragedy. An American Tragedy."

"They don't want tragedy over there."

"No, potted geraniums. . . . You know, it's like that question we left hanging—how to end our play. Should Bart win the race?"

Visitors arrive at Heart Island, Power House in distance.

"What's the connection?"

"Don't you see—it's the same thing? You don't want to challenge the audience with anything that isn't sugar-coated."

"I know what works. To end a comedy with the hero losing the race sends cross signals to the audience—confuses them. They wouldn't know whether to laugh or cry. You gotta tell 'em, you know."

"Life is full of cross signals. "

"Well, you're a writer." He smiled wanly. "Maybe you've got some sense of drama yourself."

"Thanks."

"OK, let's try it your way. Run me through it again."

"Well, after the big break-up scene, the climax at the Alster Tower party, comes the morning after, the Gold Cup Races. Although now fallen from favor, after the falling out of the night before, Bart still has had to go off to drive the Yacht Club's boat. Mary, on reflection, questions her impulsive behavior and wonders if she has done the right thing in alienating her prospective 'good provider"—or, now recognizing her concern for Bart, whether he has wrecked his chances. Maybe if he wins the race, he'll be the hero of his patrons, and will return both of them to favor."

"Yes, I got that. The racing is going on offstage. The drone of distant motors becomes a roaring crescendo. Then Bart reenters, alone, I suppose. Not carried on the shoulders of admirers. He has lost the race. That's the way you want it?"

"Yes. But he wins the girl, naturally. Instead of being welcomed into privileged society, they return from the enchanted islands to the mainland. On the dock, where the play began, they're greeted by May and Ben."

"We have a concluding quartet. What was that tune of May's that you found—something about the simple life?"

"'Live Humble.' . . . Are you thinking what I'm thinking? Maybe we should have May and Ben sing that song, May's 'Negro Hymn,' to Bart and Mary when they return to the mainland from the enchanted islands. Can't you see it? Bart and Mary hand in hand—he back in his mechanic's coveralls on the Clayton railroad dock, and flanking them our portly, middle-aged white comedienne and our lithe, young black waiter. How's that for a finale?"

"See if you can get May's music from the Library of Congress. May was a great entertainer, but I don't know how she was as a composer. But I doubt that the tune would work as a finale—not a 'Negro hymn,' please. Maybe we can use it someplace, but for the last word I think we might complete the mirroring of the opening, with a reprise of May's 'Frog Song.'

"Yeah, that works with the final twisteroo: we realized that May has sent our lowly Clayton car-washer—a knight in spite of himself—to rescue Mary from Louise Boldt's fate. May has planned the whole thing.

"Aha! . . . Yes, the fairy godmother tipped us off at the outset, before she waved her wand." Courtney waved his pencil, a wand and his conductor's baton, as he croaked,

> Dere's some frogs I know is powerful fond
> Uf spendin' time in 'nother's pond.

"Have you thought about the parallel between May's life and Louise's?"

"Can't say that I have. Why?"

"Oh, not that it's important to the play, but here was old May, slogging around her farm in her rubber boots, living a rich, full life long after Louise was gone, her Worth gowns discarded, her Castle abandoned. What made the difference?"

"It could have been simply Louise's poor health."

"Yes, but what else? May divorced her husband and became her own woman—not merely succeeding in the very competitive entertainment business, but succeeding as her own business manager. She invested shrewdly in real estate and raised two sons as a single mother. You ought to see the article she wrote, syndicated nationally in newspapers, on how she told her boys about sex! That's our May, for you!"

"Yeah, quite a gal. But what's that to do with Louise?"

"Louise knew as well as George how to create and operate a hotel. May, you know, turned her lavish island home (the place she never really enjoyed) into an inn. Louise might have done that, finding something to do, something constructive—fulfilling."

"But George would never have allowed that."

"You got it."

Courtney was intrigued. "She might have had to leave him—as May did her husband."

"Yes. But of course, she couldn't do that. 'Love is Forever,' eh?"

His eyes widened. "You're suggesting that she was a prisoner of love, that her Castle would have been like a fairytale prison—Louise as Rapunzel in her tower?"

"Yeah. As Meg put it, Boldt had this thing about towers."

Louise Boldt

47.   Pete looked up, over his foggy glasses. "You got what you wanted over at Hopewell Hall?"

"Enough, I expect. It was a surprise, even though I had suspicions."

"Nothing is verifiable, you know. It's just more hearsay, more folklore."

"But the family's folklore ought to have more credence."

"Perhaps. It's interesting, about oral history, how events become garbled in transit. Although accuracy of detail is always suspect, there may be reason to suppose some original basis in reality. The local lore about Louise running off with the chauffeur, while probably far from what happened, still may have had such durability because folks at the time didn't see the Boldts as the devoted couple presented subsequently by the official legend. That was largely perpetuated by Nanette Lincoln, you know."

"Who?"

"She was the *New York Times* correspondent on the River, back in the days when the resort was of sufficient interest to warrant regular social reporting. When Ed Noble bought most of the Boldt estate, he decided to get some payback from that white elephant, Heart Island, which in fact he had tried to exclude from the package. He really wanted only the golf course and other Wellesley Island property. Tourists had been invading Heart Island, uninvited, for decades, vandalizing it. Noble charged admission, and, *voilà*, he turned the sow's ear into the proverbial silk purse, financially. I remember an article in *Fortune* magazine that noted how it was characteristic of his lucky touch. Noble commissioned Nanette Lincoln to write a booklet, a sort of capsule history and guide about the island. It was really well done, as writing, if not as careful history. Nanette, like Clover's journalist friend years later, in another booklet, accepted romantic clichés about star-crossed lovers. Local folks around here were merely amused, but generations of tourists were fed the myth. Anything, repeated often enough, becomes accepted as truth."

"Tell me, Pete, what do you suppose really happened?"

"Oh, I can suppose, if that's what you want—mere supposition. What are the key factors? Look at it this way: George and Louise had a home and family life in Philadelphia, where Louise was also his genuine partner, working along side him in creating that jewel of an elite establishment, their little Bellevue Hotel. Then comes 'the big break'—put that in quotes, for irony: Astor builds the Waldorf for Boldt, who moves his family to midtown Manhattan. After all the excitement of building the great facility—and Louise decorated all the guestrooms—came the sudden letdown. Os-car supplanted Louise as Boldt's right

George Boldt, 1894,
when the Boldts first visited Hart Island

hand at the hotel and she was out of the business, isolated from her husband's work by echelons of management—but she wasn't out of the building, alas, for they lived at the hotel (in a townhouse appendage, actually). As hotel authorities noted, 'twenty-four hours of residence [at the hotel] suggest a twenty-four hour workday. Guests expect to call on the manager at any time. . . . The resident wife becomes an informal manager operating in a gray area of responsibility and authority.' So here are Louise and the kids living in that dense midtown sector, between the Waldorf and, a block or so away, Macy's, with few neighbors, few friends in the new city—like many 'hotel widows and fatherless families' of hotelmen. The kids go away to school, so Louise was left alone most of the time—George was a workaholic, remember, and they lived on the job, except Louise no longer was part of the job. George 'was on the job twenty four hours a day,' they said. Picture that. Was Louise happy? Then the depression of the 'nineties struck. Disaster. George collapsed with a nervous breakdown. His doctor and acquaintances urged him to get away from his problems. So they came to the River.

"Then the skies brighten, for the Waldorf becomes accepted by fashionable society. But success means only more preoccupation by George with his work. Within twelve months of opening the Waldorf, Boldt begins to think about expanding onto Mrs. Astor's property next door and persuades her son Jack to demolish the house she vacated. Less than two years after the Waldorf opens, Boldt persuades John Jacob Astor to outdo his cousin by building an even grander portion of the hotel, the Astoria, only. Ground is broken in 1895, the year they buy Hart Island. This may be more than coincidental, as we shall see, for Louise is to be shut out of the Astoria planning, which consumes George, while Hart Island gives her a project. With the opening of the Astoria in 1897, the hyphenated hotel, the largest and tallest hotel in the world, becomes a sensation. The huge enterprise generates fantastic profits. In 1899 the Boldts, suddenly millionaires, decide to build their castle. Again, perhaps more than coincidentally, George is moving on to build the huge new Bellevue-Stratford Hotel in Philadelphia. The Castle is another project for Louise.

"Euphoria is in the air in 1899. The deep depression of the 'nineties had been stubborn, but is finally past. 'After two or three years of false alarms . . . when the improvement really came, there were few to recognize its tremendous extent and significance.' The arrival of prosperity was unexpected; the boom came with 'astonishing suddenness.' The year was 'a turning point in our history.'

"Now George Boldt became a player on the stock and commodities markets, and became a banker. He had become a multi-millionaire, a 'capitalist,' in a matter of five years or so."

"Heady stuff. But what of Louise?"

"There had to be a sense of unreality to sudden wealth. One might imagine affluence affording a sense of security, but in truth easy-come implies easy-go, and a new fortune could have seemed ephemeral and transitory, especially when George became involved in high-flying financial speculations. Possibly the Castle venture was in part a matter of cashing in some chips, to have salvaged something tangible should the bubble burst.

"Cricket went off the Cornell, and Clover to Miss Spence's finishing school, and here was Louise left at the Waldorf-Astoria, hotel staff attending to her every need, but expected to be on stage, to serve as hostess at the captain's table, in that enormous private dining room, the original Waldorf ball room. How jolly. Did the jewels and Worth gowns compensate adequately? Was she more than a mobile exhibit, equivalent to the ornate clock in the lobby?

"When the Boldts became socially ambitious, their identity with the commercial hotel had to be a liability. Would proper Fifth Avenue matrons call on Louise Boldt, at the hotel? No, she required a place of her own. True, the Boldts had resided in a townhouse appendage to the Waldorf, #13 (naturally) 33rd Street, but after two years it was torn down to expand the hotel. The Boldts moved into new quarters, which had a separate street entrance but functioned integrally with the hotel. At the famous—or infamous—Bradley-Martin Ball, a national scandal of wonton extravagance during the depression of the 'nineties when real hardship was being felt on the cold, winter streets outside, absurdly costumed guests used the Boldts' private entrance and took over the family's quarters for the evening. After this sort of public exposure, Louise could never maintain the fiction that this hotel annex was her private home, where she might expect proper society matrons to come to call. Louise wanted a place of her own. She got it, briefly—a large town house several blocks away, assembled from two town houses, next to Tiffany's.

"But when she moved in, where was George? Still keeping those interminable hours at the hotel, seeing his wife 'for only fleeting minutes.' During the years before Louise died, his workweek sometimes was eighty-four hours—more than double our notion of a full-time job. Imagine Louise, spending lonely evenings in her new town house—the place of her own that she wanted. And what might George be doing, all those evenings when he was absent? She might have wondered, even become suspicious, don't you think? But not for long. Within thirty days of moving in, she was dead."

Pete's pause was a void, except for the faint cry of gulls on a distant rocky islet. He stroked a gray temple reflectively. "Would life have been different for George and Louise at Boldt Castle?" He peered at me quizzically over the top of his glasses. "Did she really look forward to moving into that vast structure, being alone so much of the time? Or had the grandiose Castle really been George's project, really *his* trophy house?

As I had no answer to venture, he continued. "While the Castle was rising, Louise was developing her health problems, requiring periodic 'cures' at distant spas. What was that all about? The family thought it was about her weight problem. I think it may have been more."

He waited for my question: "What?"

"Such a dramatic change of life had to be disorienting. Willa Cather observed, in 'Paul's Case,' that 'he doubted the reality of his past [but] he had no especial desire to meet or to know any of these people.'"

Pete's notion began to dawn on me. "You're thinking of mental problems?"

"Stress, at least. I've collected a few relevant observations." He pulled out a folder from the pile on his disk. "One late nineteenth century commentator said, 'There are few persons who know the excitement and the fear that exists among capitalists today.' And Jay Gould, that market manipulator, added, 'Capital is scary.' And then the mega-tycoon, John D. Rockefeller, confided, 'All the fortune I have made has not served to compensate for the anxiety.' Remember that George himself had a breakdown a decade before Louise died. Perhaps it was her turn."

"And you said there was a financial crisis shortly before she died."

"Right. The 'Rich Man's Panic,' as they called it, began during the summer of 1903, the last year of construction at Heart Island, only months before Louise Boldt died. U.S. Steel stock plunged from $58 to $8 a share, taking most of the market down with it. Boldt may have held substantial USS stock. Regardless, he was heavily interested in the Trust Company of the Republic, which was about to fail during that year, when Boldt, a member of the Executive Committee of its Board, stepped in to run the bank. Summer of 1903 was a difficult, stressful time, and the future must have looked uncertain, or ominous."

"It's ironic—we think of great wealth as sparing people of problems."

"No, as they say, real financial success isn't making lots of money; rather, it's not needing to worry about your money. Boldt, however, was always venturing at the edge. I think he was addicted to the thrill of gambling."

"Do you suspect that in addition to financial concerns there may have been personal problems, between Louise and George, as well as the children?"

"That has to be more conjectural, doesn't it? Stress generally results in tense relations among those concerned. Basically, I think we may characterize George, for better or for worse, as a 'self-actualizing' type of person. The psychologist Maslow viewed personality as developing through progressive levels. The "self-actualizing" person, having satisfied other, more basic human needs, has advanced to a certain level of maturity where one no longer is preoccupied with the sort of psychic security afforded by personal relationships. In a word, the self-actualizing person is, in a real sense, 'selfish.' The 'genius' type—say Einstein, Picasso, or Frank Lloyd Wright—is often a poor mate or family man. Louise, however, may not have advanced to George's personality stage, but may have remained at the level where love and intimate personal interaction were her foremost needs. With the kids leaving the nest, and George consumed by his projects, you may imagine her plight."

"When she last left the River, she may have gone to Europe to some sort of clinic . . . ."

"You recall that the Boldt's big break—into the big time, that is—came when Mrs. Waldorf Astor was confined in one of their Philadelphia hotel rooms for one of Dr. Wier Mitchell's 'cures.' What was the complaint? Mitchell, the famous Philadelphia physician and novelist (no doubt known to the Boldts), was regarded as an international specialist in neurasthenia."

"What's that?"

"A neurosis, generally emotional in origin, entailing fatigue, depression, worry and sometimes real physical pains. Dr. Mitchell had many clients who were women, often privileged women constrained by their position from engaging in any sort of useful activity. In short, they were often the Noras of the 'Doll's House,' wives enshrined by devoted but often distracted husbands."

"You're suggesting the Boldts?"

"Only suggesting. My wife, also an historian, is interested in women's history. She referred me to a sensational account by Charlotte Perkins Gillman of her own illness and treatment—probably by the same Dr. Mitchell who treated Mrs. Astor at the Bellevue. Gillman's story, "The Yellow Wall-Paper," conveys the experience of treatment of this malady and has become a minor literary classic as well as a staple of Women's History courses." Pete pulled a file from his desk drawer. "Asked about why she had written it, Gillman responded:

> For many years I suffered from a severe and continuous nervous breakdown tending to melancholia—and beyond. During about the third year of this trouble I went ... to a noted specialist in nervous diseases, the best known in the country. This wise man put me to bed and applied the rest cure . . . and sent me home with solemn advice to . . . "have but two hours' intellectual life a day," and "never to touch pen, brush, or pencil again" as long as I lived. . . .
>
> I went home and obeyed those directions for some three months, and came . . . near the borderline of utter mental ruin. . . .

"Fortunately a friend helped Gillman regain contact with the real world, to go back to work, and to find some life for herself other than being 'a parasite,' as she put it. Louise may never have had this good fortune—if indeed she suffered from the same complaint, fairly common at the time among women in her class and social position.

"Depression—clinical depression, that is—is more than sadness or chronic melancholy. It's more than debilitating. It's a progressive illness, a downward spiral, where one ceases to care, even about recovery. Again, Willa Cather described Paul's suicidal depression, 'He had the old feeling that the orchestra had suddenly stopped, the sinking sensation that the play was over'."

"And the pills that Louise overdosed, may have been given for her depression?"

"The family believed an overdose was the cause of her death. Perhaps the reaction to an overdose was the heart failure indicated on the death certificate. But some medications prescribed for depression have disastrous consequences if one suddenly stops taking them. I know personally of an instance where suicide resulted. Possibly in Louise's case the withdrawal anxiety was so great that the overdose was taken as an intended antidote. Who knows?"

"Louise's death was unexpected?"

"Yes, death came as a shock, although Louise had health problems for years, reportedly entailing indigestion—which actually might have been angina. Her doctor had seen her during the day; she died about 10 PM. Up here folks were aware that she hadn't been well for about a year, but her death was totally unexpected. George, Jr., twenty-two years old, was at Cornell, and was called by telephone. Clover was eighteen years old, so she may have been still at the Spence School. But as that was in New York City, Clover might have been at home. Chances are that George was not. He was gone most of the time."

"Do you suppose that the physician who signed the death certificate was the same as the one who prescribed the medication she took?"

"That seems immaterial now. What may be more relevant is how little comment there was at the time about the untimely death of Mrs. Boldt. She was only forty-one years old, you know."

"How did George Boldt react?"

"No question about that. He was devastated. He never recovered fully. No doubt he was plagued by regrets—not merely for what might have been, but for what had happened in the last decade of their lives—of her short life. He lived on for thirteen more years, alone."

"Thirteen was his 'lucky' number."

"Those last thirteen years were difficult. The Arch of Triumph, erected as the twentieth century opened, marked the peak of his career. The later years were

George Boldt, widower

downhill. Possibly Louis's death coincided with a major stock loss, for as I suggested, U.S. Steel plunged at the time—which could have contributed to Louise's
despondency. Perhaps Boldt had even determined to suspend the Castle project
before she died, which might have been a factor. Regardless, he did run into financial turbulence thereafter. The Great Bull Market was over, and financial panic hit
in 1907. Boldt encountered one of the greatest crises of his life. A probable run on
his bank threatened disaster. Boldt was one of those summoned by J. P. Morgan to
the famous all-night session in his library, and the financier ordered Boldt to keep
his doors open and to contribute to a fund to assist other threatened institutions.
Boldt's bank went into bankruptcy, but he earned Morgan's enduring respect.
Boldt evidenced his sense of honor and his responsible diligence in salvaging assets
of the failed financial institutions for depositors, stockholders and creditors.
Morgan valued character in a man, at a time when there were many swashbuckling
pirates in finance. Boldt became a personal friend of J. P. Morgan, who was said to
have strolled often from his residence and library to have morning coffee with the
Waldorf-Astoria proprietor."

"What do you suppose they talked about?"

"Not about finance, to be sure. More likely music, a recent concert—both liked
singing and were fans of the Mendelssohn Glee Club, and both loved animals, including cattle—and especially birds."

"Boldt must have valued that friendship."

"Indeed, but his own health began to wane shortly after Louise's death, and then
came another great shock. Tommy Hilliard, Boldt's 'beloved assistant' and real hotel operations manager, one day suggested that the chief pick a guest room number
at random to visit. They took the elevator to the floor. Opening the door, Boldt
was aghast. 'They're not all like this?' Hilliard replied, 'Sir, this hotel is rotten.'
Boldt suddenly realized that the Waldorf, after a decade, was going downhill.

   "Distracted by Louise's death, the Bellevue-Stratford opening, the financial
panic and the failed Trust Company of the Republic, Boldt by his own account had
neglected the Waldorf-Astoria. Now he had to pour money into renovations. He
himself had astutely observed, however, that the successful life of a New York City
hotel was forty years, and ten years had passed. The Waldorf-Astoria was no common hotel, of course, and remains prestigious to this day, after more than a century.
But New York City was evolving rapidly as the twentieth century opened and newer
hotels, such as the Plaza, attracted attention farther uptown. The Waldorf would
remain an old friend, but new acquaintances were entrancing.

"And times were changing otherwise, to Boldt's displeasure. 'Lounge lizards' now danced the erotic tango during the afternoon at the Waldorf. Women drank cocktails openly, and smoked. We shouldn't think of Boldt as a prude—hardly, in his business, where he had a 'loyal following' among the 'fast set,' the hard-drinking high rollers of the time. But Boldt was a man of taste and consummate style—and new styles were alien to him. Boldt tried to adapt the staid image of the Waldorf with frequent remodeling and novel new features, such as the first hotel roof garden. The grand hotel survived, for its reputation was now international. But the original Waldorf-Astoria was in the last phase of its life cycle. In 1911, a year after the 'rotten' revelation by Tommy Hilliard, his 'beloved assistant's' resignation was another personal blow. Hilliard had joined Boldt as a boy at the little Bellevue, but now advanced his career at a newer hotel. During the last year before his death the Waldorf-Astoria lost money—substantially. The 'situation was very serious.'

"Most distressing, surely, to George Boldt was worsening tension as the First World War approached. He was, of course, German-born, and still conversed in German with his children and many friends. Another of his life's great tragedies occurred shortly before he died. On May 7, 1915, off the coast of England a torpedo from a German submarine struck the American trans-Atlantic ocean liner, the Lusitania. Many of Boldt's personal friends and longtime patrons were killed. When survivors were brought back to New York, he opened the Waldorf as an emergency relief center. He consoled survivors personally. Probably he never spoke German again."

"So he died a broken, disappointed man—completing the tragedy."

"You writers like the broad brush, don't you? George Boldt didn't decline so dramatically. He was resilient—to a degree. Although he never recovered from the loss of his wife, he poured himself totally into his work—which had always been his way. He said, 'I have learned not to give disappointment a second thought.' He tried not to look back, as he was 'never a man to live in the past.' One of Boldt's critical qualities was courage. Remember, he was the boy who came alone to a New World at the age of thirteen. His life was a series of leaps into the unknown. There were episodes not even mentioned yet, like his early sojourn in Texas, where he tried farming. Boldt was conservative in matters of taste, but bold (as his name indicated) in trying the untried. He was never one to rest on his laurels. Instead of retiring to enjoy the rewards of his great success, he worked incessantly to the very end. As said, he 'conducted the multitudinous details of his business with a personal zest that unquestionably hastened his end.' During a busy fall weekend at the hotel he put guest beds in the library and dining room of his own suite and insisted on making a speech, against his physician's advice. He didn't spend much time on the River at the end, since the dampness of Wellesley House, built right on the water, disagreed with his sciatica. Nevertheless, although finishing a new winter home in California, he had planned to spend several weeks during the winter at the Thousand Islands—he never made that. One of his close associates recalled his tense grip, as he grabbed an arm for support, to avert falling when he insisted on standing for some business appearance. Most consuming of his interests in his later years was construction of a system of residence halls for Cornell University, where he served as Chairman of the Board of Trustees. Boldt was the major fund-raiser. He persuaded his friend George F. Baker to build a magnificent dormitory complex there. Plagued by 'worry and overwork,' Boldt nevertheless went on 'working and planning, despite advice' of his doctor and his friend, Baker. The strain began to tell. On the New Year's Eve preceding his final year, after saying that fatigue compelled him to retire early to his hotel suite, he (who 'saw everything') returned unexpectedly to spot the late night manager on the dance floor (and Boldt never liked public dancing, but now had to tolerate it)—and the manager was dancing with a guest! Enraged, Boldt went out on the dance floor and slapped the fellow across the face. They said, 'that

Wellesley House

affected the old man so that he didn't last.' He wasn't able to greet President Wilson when he arrived at the Waldorf—a sure indication that something was gravely wrong. 'What Boldt was attempting to do in his establishment—to keep his personal oversight over everything, to introduce innovation—sometimes years too late—found a man of his age unequal to the effort. He couldn't run his big hotel single-handed. An illness that did not at first seem of a serious nature found a system worn out by worry and strain. . . .' He continued living in the hotel, where he died with his boots on—that was December 5, 1916. His physician said 'overwork and a general breakdown' contributed to his death. There was a huge model of the lower campus as eventually built—'his idea for a great dormitory system for Cornell'—in his suite when he went. It was as he wanted it."

"How did he die?"

"Why, it was his heart. Of course, his heart. He had worn it out—his 'great heart,' as Oscar put it. What else?"

"During those last summer visits he never went back to Heart Island—which was where everything turned around for him."

"So they say. And (I quote) 'there are those who said that Boldt had begun to die when he lost his wife.'"

"What do you suppose he thought about Heart Island during those last thirteen years?"

"Probably he didn't want to think about it, any more than necessary. Not merely did he identify the Castle with Louise, but the great pile may have seemed a monument to his mistake."

"You mean spending so much money on the monumental structure?"

"No, more than that. He had the money, if he thought it prudent to spend on the Castle project. I think it was more complex. You see, I expect that Louise fell in love with the original place they first bought, with its wooden cottage. This was within her grasp. George bought if for her. They might have been happy together there.

"But what happened? George lurched into his creative, improving mode. It was simply his nature—a tropism. He couldn't leave well enough alone. Probably Louise was enchanted with the first projects, erecting garden walls, little gazebos and other delights. I suspect that George then decided the cottage was too small, and that they required the big frame addition to accommodate more guests and staff. Louise may have gone along—her husband wasn't one to accept disagreement, at any rate. He himself said that *his* (note the 'his') intention was to have the finest house on the River. But Charles Emery, up at Clayton, had a ballroom—so they must have a ballroom. Emery had a model farm, so Boldt would have one of those, too. Emery's chateau was built of stone. Their frame house, even after being more than doubled in size, wouldn't do. They would have to remove it and rebuild, in fireproof, masonry construction. Boldt was in high gear in his building mode, having constructed the Waldorf and its even larger Astoria addition, and then the Bellevue-Stratford in Philadelphia. Suddenly the Castle project took on the colossal dimensions of these major campaigns.

"And Louise? Was she thrilled, or bemused, or alarmed? Probably all of these, at different times. Perhaps the initial thrill became alarm as she saw what was happening to her little cottage.

"George probably knew this, since they were so close, but like most of us, he probably went into denial, allowing his own enthusiasm for the heroic campaign to supplant his concern for Louise's real preference."

"So, in a sense, you see the Heart Island project as initially Louise's thing, which George, deciding to 'help' her, took over and made his own?"

"Yes. He was mad about building, and taking over (particularly from a woman and wife) was probably his Prussian, paternalistic way. Remember that she had been his child bride. Louise, having finally found this place of her own, may have felt brushed aside, left out again—just as she felt cast off when she wasn't allowed to be part of the team for the Astoria campaign, after George has made Oscar his successor to Louise in the hotel operation. This. . . ," Pete paused, as if to draw a conclusion, . . . searching for the definitive words, "not 'alienation,' certainly, but rather 'disengagement,' we might say, may have been the central issue of their later relationship, monumentalized in the Castle."

"It's a gender issue, isn't it?—and that's a paradox. After all, Boldt was innovative about admitting and catering to women in his hotel."

"Yes, and his canny way with women was attributable to a wife who had worked along side him to create the Bellevue and Waldorf mystiques. Her instinctive empathy for what women wanted was essential to his rise. But then she was pushed out of his creative world, to be enshrined in her Castle."

"So we ought to understand it as more than a sentimental Valentine, a token of 'Love Forever'."

"Much more, surely," Pete agreed, "but Boldt may not have sensed that himself—probably not."

"Don't you think that, after Louise died, when the stimulus of the creative building project had vanished, when adrenaline-withdrawal had set in, Boldt may have realized that he had preempted Louise's project and made it his own? Do you suppose that Louise may have realized that she was never going to get *her* place, and that George later suspected as much?"

"I doubt that Boldt was so introspective. He was too busy being a doer to be that much of a thinker. Compulsive work was his therapy. It averted too much brooding of that sort. 'I never look back,' he said—or something to that effect."

"He couldn't help looking back at Heart Island, however, from Wellesley House."

"No, but probably his thoughts were more practical—what to do with it? He could afford to keep it for a while—and who would want it, anyway? Despite his provision of a resident caretaker, however, the place was almost immediately vandalized. It has always been irresistible to visitors, many of whom carried away materials. The bathrooms once had decorative wall tiles, for instance, all gone now. Many an island has one of the round granite stones intended for the colonnades that were to flank the Arch of Triumph. Hand carved woodwork was especially appealing. Everything was up for grabs. Locally, they hoped he would finish the Castle, and even believed that he would sooner or later."

"Did he try to dispose of the property?"

"He considered movements by others to have the federal government acquire Heart Island as a summer White House, but nothing came of the plans as the First World War approached."

"Do you suppose he thought his children might want the place?"

"No, I think that their contrary intentions must have been perfectly clear to him. Had they wanted it, the Castle wouldn't have been left vacant, unfinished, and vandalized for thirteen years."

"What a waste!"

"Boldt was astute as an investor, but this had been no business venture. As a writer observed, regarding other ambitious houses, even before Boldt Castle was contemplated:

"Such a dwelling is not capital. That is to say, it produces nothing. . . . It may be very foolish for the owner of capital, or of that which might become capital, . . . to spend it on fancy farms, palatial dwellings, or things of that sort. . . . I think that a man, however rich he may be, is very foolish to build a dwelling-house, which must be sold either by his children or his grandchildren, for the reason that none of them can afford to live in it. . . ."

"So the children paid the price for their parents' ambition?"

"You might look at it that way—but the children didn't make the money, so really had little claim on it. Surely George Boldt knew that a house wasn't an investment, particularly a monumental house. There's an old real estate adage: 'it never pays to own the best house on the street.' Boldt Castle was surely what George Boldt wanted it to be: the finest house on the River. Sure enough, it became a white elephant. A quarter-million dollars, the fractional appraised value placed on abandoned Heart Island when the estate was probated, was still a lot of money in 1916. But liquidation of the Boldt property at the Thousand Islands recouped very little for the Boldt children."

"So there may be something to the notion that he saw it as a monument, left incomplete, to memorialize his wife."

"Something, perhaps. But none of us ever is so single-minded. Usually we have mixed minds and conflicting intentions. Probably Boldt felt somewhat irresponsible to leave his children with the unresolved dilemma of what to do with the colossal white elephant. The whole Thousand Islands estate was an enormous burden, not merely financially. It required responsible attention. Boldt learned that he couldn't

Gazebo and Alster Tower as they appeared in the 1940s

delegate too much authority. In a very painful episode, he had to charge his estate superintendent with theft, taking him to court in a very messy public spectacle. Boldt knew his kids didn't want this sort of problem. I expect that genuine parental concern may have been more in his mind when abandoning the castle than any notion of a sentimental gesture about love lost."

"I still wonder if the kids didn't regret, in a way, that the place hadn't been completed, to live in, enjoy, for a while."

"Enjoy? They probably sensed that life there would be oppressive, and costly to boot."

"But think of the pleasure—the thrill—it would give your friends and guests. Surely that must have been an aspect of the Boldts' intentions."

"Yes—but do you really want to thrill your true friends, or more to impress strangers, particularly those you wish were friends, and maybe to get back at those who had snubbed you? Remember, the Boldts were socially marginal. The Stotesburys, who built another colossal house, Whitemarsh Hall near Philadelphia, similarly weren't members of the club—literally. Edward Stotesbury was refused membership in the elite Philadelphia Club (where Louise's father was steward and George his assistant). When Stotesbury, after intriguing the Philadelphia establishment with reports of his grand estate with Versailles-like gardens, which everyone was dying to see, finally got an invitation to the town's most exclusive ball (at Boldt's Bellevue-Stratford) he thereafter displayed the little invitation in an illuminated glass case in the entry foyer of Whitemarsh Hall.

"I recall visiting Waddesdon Manor, the Rothschild place in England. They were Jewish, of course, also marginal socially. Their chateau, similar in its French style to our Castle, sat aloof atop a hill. One approached on one of five parallel avenues. Passing through the symmetrical façade into an oval rotunda, one then stepped from marble onto thick carpeting of a long gallery, paneled in old wood, lined with jewel-like miniature oil paintings in gilded frames. It was exquisite. Anticipation mounted as we proceeded ritually down the hall to be received in a drawing room. Everyone was silent, or if they spoke, muted their voice in reverent tones. Is this the way to receive friends?"

"Do you suppose that Louise would have felt remote—alienated somehow–from others, even her old friends, once enshrined in her Castle?"

"She may have sensed this herself, as the monstrous pile was rising. "

"Perhaps she suddenly realized it was to be a colossal "Doll's House.'"

"This isn't a single-issue Ibsen play, my friend—or the movie, 'Citizen Kane.' History isn't so dramatically simple a thematic argument. The two people were real, complex people, so don't get carried away on a single track. Although there may be something to the notion that George wanted to put Louise on a pedestal, consider these references." He produced some clippings. 'Mrs. Boldt was wrapped up in her husband's River possessions and their elaborate improvements.' And here's another quotation: 'It was the dream of Mrs. Boldt to have a palace that would surpass all others.' Note that they said *Mrs.* Boldt—and not 'a place' but 'a palace.'

"But of course George made the project his own. One writer said, 'He had elaborate plans. . . . He proposed to build a great house. . . . There he would go, not for two or three days, but for two or three months. This was the dream of his old age.' He never got beyond the two-or-three-day stage. His visits to the River were occasional and brief, but another writer tells us that the running of Wellesley Island Farms was 'his one real diversion. . . . He preferred to live more simply at Wellesley House (if fifty-six rooms is simple) to be closer to the farm. Maybe he recognized that the huge Castle would be unlivable."

"Watch it. That take on the Castle is contrary to the common fantasy of visitors, 'How wonderful to live here!'"

"Is that what they say, or is it, 'What a strange place to live'?"

"What they really say most often is, "What a shame they never finished it!" But what if they had? What would it be today? As Clive Aslet observed, 'Some of the country houses built between 1890 and 1939 were patently ill-equipped for survival.' Surely it would have been gratifying had Louise Boldt enjoyed her dream house with her husband for the decade before he died. But would the Boldt children have cared, or been able, to continue their parents' fantastic way of life? Harvey Firestone, having two houses 'much larger than I need,' reflected, 'I don't know why I do it—the houses are only a burden.' He concluded that an owner of a huge establishment would be better off living in a hotel than running a country house that resembled one. After the First World War, Clover and George, Junior, unable to maintain the mammoth establishment, probably would have found no buyers for a second-hand castle. The period of grandiose country houses passed quickly. After the first years of the twentieth century, until World War I, the economy no longer accelerated, but began to decelerate. Even if Boldt Castle had been completed, during the decades of the Depression and World War II vandals no doubt would have gutted the mammoth structure anyway. Only slightly later it would have become the same empty shell known to generations of visitors—except there might be

no visitors. It could have been demolished as a hazard to the curious public—like Emery Castle opposite Clayton. There they found in the cornerstone a poignant testimonial by Charles Emery, stating his intention to build a family seat that would be home for generations to come. His son didn't even bother to open the Castle, but occasionally camped out in the caretaker's residence.

"Paradoxically, it was George Boldt's decision to abandon the Castle that saved it, for the legendary romance of Heart Island has intrigued millions of visitors, providing for its maintenance and restoration. Had Boldt finished building his Castle, its life would have been finished. Today it lives in the imagination of the public."

That wise and promising note seemed a good point for my departure—not just from this session, but indefinitely, for the summer was gone. That's the negative compensation for enchantingly disengaged resorts; the illusion is ephemeral, becoming merely a memory.

Of course, I thanked Pete profusely—still arguing that he should appear as co-author of my book—and he generously volunteered to read a draft. Before shoving off from his dock I asked one last question: how did he think the Authority would react to a different sort of Boldt story?

"Once they get over the usual human displeasure with being confronted with something different," he replied, "they ought to realize that your book will provide much greater exposure for Boldt Castle. I find people down in the City have never even heard of it. We're pretty provincial up here—or rather they are down there.

Vince Dee had vision, however. He really didn't think that the Bridge Authority should continue, in the long haul, to operate the historic property."

"No? That's a surprise. Because they weren't into the historic museum business?"

"More importantly, because he didn't think that most members of the Authority would be qualified by their particular experiences to make policy about a historic and architectural landmark. Vince told me that he really thought some sort of a new organization, with a different sort of board of trustees, should take over at some point. But Vince was always attuned to what was pragmatically possible, and there was no opening to suggest an alternative to Authority management. The operation quickly proved too successful."

"Well, I suppose sudden, overwhelming success is the Boldt story in a nutshell." With that I started my motor. We shouted our good-byes over the roar, as Pete, waving, receded on his dock.

48. A cool morning reminded one that September was waning. A breeze off the lake, channeled through Clayton's broad Riverside Drive, billowed the curtains of Meg's office. She had removed that window air conditioner, thank God.

   "So the dowager of Hopewell Hall received you?"

"She and Alec were very cordial, and very helpful."

"You've had better luck than I, or most other people. She's known to be practically a recluse. What did you think of the place? I've never seen it."

"Lovely—flowers everywhere."

"That's Boldt-like."

"But not very historic in character. The house has been professionally 'decorated,' I suspect, by Dorothy Draper, or someone of that era. The furnishing looks more like Florida 'Fifties than Gilded Age on Canadian border."

"She winters down there, of course—has a house at Delray Beach. Perhaps up here is her 'camp,' where the cast-off furniture goes. Lots of cottages here have Salvation Army décor."

"Nothing seedy about it, though. Beautifully maintained."

"Oh? I suppose—but they lopped off the big tower, took off all the roof dormers, and demolished their tall yacht house. Even folks on what's left of 'Millionaire's Row' don't have unlimited means to keep these places going. Get anything new from her—other than that same silly stuff printed in her precious little book?"

The Arch of Triumph

Round stones in foreground were intended for the unbuilt
colonnades. A bridge within the arch would be raised to allow passage of arriving boats into the protected lagoon.

"Yes. You remember we talked about the Arch of Triumph, which may mean
something more than we suspect—perhaps even intended to be an eternal memorial,
built so solid as to last forever."

"It will. I can hear Mrs. Baird now, giving you that 'Love is Forever' line."

"I wonder if there was a funerary aspect lurking there, somehow."

"In 1900? Louise Boldt didn't die for several years."

"But they say her health was deteriorating in those last years."

"Oh, why a classical arch of triumph? There are more obvious, less tenuous reasons
for that form—not merely the most obvious, the Chicago World's Fair precedent,
but the sort of monumental arches built at the time in many American cities, often
as temporary features of celebrations, especially in that era of new American imperi-
alism." Meg went to a file, looking for pictures.

"The Boldts must have known the Washington Square arch in lower Manhattan. That precedent appeared even before the Chicago Fair. At the beginning of Fifth Avenue, when the Boldts came to New York to plan and construct the Waldorf further up the avenue, the classical Arch of Triumph was being rebuilt in masonry. Construction of that local monument in fact concurred with the building of Boldt's Waldorf Hotel." She passed some photos.

"Even closer in time to the Heart Island monument was another New York City precedent, the glorious, gorgeous Dewey Arch. This celebratory fantasy was erected exactly at the time that the Boldts' Heart Island Arch was conceived. And there's an even more intimate connection. Ten blocks south of the Waldorf at Madison Square the Dewey Arch celebrated the triumphant return of Admiral Dewey, hero of the Spanish-American war. Dewey marched under his Arch with the American forces on September 30, 1899, on his way to join Mrs. Dewey at the Waldorf-Astoria Hotel. There he 'beg[ged] relief from attention,' delegating George Boldt as his liaison with the press.

"The Dewey arch was a reincarnation of the Chicago Worlds Fair, a fragment of that splendid White City reborn amidst New York's somber brownstone. The image of imperial Rome, fantasy though it was, conveyed more than historical allusion to a long-enduring world power of the past; it recalled the fair's optimistic, utopian vision of the future. Like most of the ephemeral Colombian Exposition, the Dewey arch was simulated of wood and plaster. Funds weren't raised sufficient to recast it in permanent materials; at the end of the year it was carted off to the dump.

"So the Boldts probably saw those triumphal arches. But why did they want one? Pete was strong on the symbolism."

"Of course. It's hard for us today to get back into the mindset of people a century ago. They took seriously many things we would scoff at today, considering them hokey—like symbolism and the lofty rhetoric of public ceremonies. Did Pete give you the Chicago Fair quotation?"

"Not that one, as I recall."

She pulled out a Xeroxed page. "This was a quatrain prepared by President Eliot of Harvard for dedication of the fair's triumphal arch."

To the pioneers of civil and religious liberty.

But bolder they who first off-cast
Their moorings from the habitable past
And ventured chartless on the sea
Of storm-engendering liberty.

"The bit about 'bolder' may have clicked with the Boldts, since the name means 'bold.' And 'storm-engendered' would resonate, recalling the trauma of the Waldorf's disastrous opening. And of course, Boldt had 'cast off the moorings of the . . . past and ventured chartless on the sea.'

"To make the reference more layered, Boldt had come to the River suffering from a nervous breakdown, due to the disastrous opening of the Waldorf as a severe economic depression worsened. During the summer of 1894 George Pullman retreated to his Castle Rest, escaping the violent riots of the notorious Pullman Strike at his Chicago works, as the President sent the U.S Army to Pullman, Illinois, while reporters swarmed around Pullman Island. During that appalling time the splendid wood and plaster Arch of Triumph and its great colonnades, surviving from the previous year's Worlds Fair, burned. Recollection of that mistakenly optimistic symbol six years later, now constructed in Boldt's monumental granite must have been especially significant.

"More to the point about the triumphal symbol, however, was the widely appreciated emergence of the United States as world power, now to be taken seriously. We had just become a colonial empire, remember. John Jacob Astor, who owned the Astoria portion of the hotel and who visited the Boldts at Heart Island, had figured prominently in the Spanish-American war, where we won Puerto Rico and the Philippines. Then we stole Hawaii—blatant aggression. But Americans (some, at any rate) were proud that the new century promised world greatness for the nation. Imperial grandeur was in the air.

"What was the mindset of the Boldts when they undertook the Castle campaign? A couple of quotations convey the national mood of 1899:

> It may be that history will mark 1899 as the year in which the United States
> . . . realized for the first time its might, commercial and political power. . . .
> Every barn in Kansas and Nebraska has a new coat of paint.

"Here are a few more quotes: 'It seems improbable that any other great nation has ever experienced such sweeping gains in the average income of the inhabitants.' The turn of the century was 'the consumer's millennium.' As the twentieth century opened, people sensed 'a largeness of vision, a buoyancy of spirit, an abounding hopefulness, a superb self-confidence. . . .' As they saw it, 'the world seems agreed that the United States is likely to achieve, if indeed she has not already achieved, an economic supremacy. The vortex of the cyclone is near New York. No such activity prevails elsewhere; nowhere are undertakings so gigantic, nowhere is administration so perfect; nowhere are such masses of capital centralized in single hands.' Remember that Boldt had been in despair, on the verge of ruin, only a few years before, then listen to this: 'There is not a man here who does not feel 400% bigger in 1900 than he did in 1896.' In short, there was enormous optimism in the air, and the Thousand Islands, like the rest of the nation, were awash in money."

"That surely was an aspect of it . . . ."

"I wouldn't push the Love-Forever theory too far, my friend. Remember, too, that 1900 was the peak of the great Bull Market, when euphoria was running high. Boldt may have been merely celebrating making his tenth million, or something like that. The triumph of capitalism. That's what the Arch of Triumph is about, that's what Boldt Castle celebrates."

"You're a cynic at heart, aren't you."

Meg smiled appreciatively. "Maybe just wary and weary of sentimental nonsense. Boldt Castle is a rather arrogant display by a proud man."

"But he had reason to proud of his accomplishment," I argued.

"You're right. Interpretation of Boldt Castle should stress how American this sort of accomplishment was—and this is especially relevant because Boldt arrived as a poor immigrant."

"Poor? Pete said George's father was a fairly important man on their island—or at least probably well connected to the big man on the island."

"Well, surely the family wasn't rich, if not destitute. And one couldn't be very up-wardly mobile on Rügen, as the island was largely an agricultural economy, largely the fief of its landed proprietor. There was room for only one noble family's castle on that island. Boldt had to come to America to build his own castle."

"You're saying then that the Arch of Triumph represents more than egotistical bra-vado of an individual achiever."

"Yes, it meant much more. It represented ascendancy of the New World, of a new world order."

"Realization of the American Dream. The Arch is so different from everything else on the island. What do you make of the differences in style?"

"Good observation. You're right. Although built within a few years of each other, the projects were quite different. Apparently the Boldts didn't envision a unified, final form for their estate—at least in terms of visual style. They were more process-oriented, delighting in the doing. Probably they understood a symbolic program that integrated the whole. The Alster Tower stands cheek-by-jowl next to the Arch of Triumph, but the forms have nothing to do with one another stylistically. Probably they had meaning to the Boldts that were related, however. There's a sort of dialogue going on there, between them. Probably the Tower speaks of Boldts recollection of the Old World, whereas the Arch tells us of his triumph in the New World."

"Wouldn't the visual disjunction disturb an architect?"

"We don't know that Bill Hewitt had anything to do with the Alster Tower—nor any architect, as a matter of fact. There's a fascinating story about its origin, suggesting the model was German, which seems plausible. Boldt was German, and traveled back in later years to buy German wines for his hotels. The Kaiser's brother, a guest at the Waldorf, gave him a medal that he dearly prized. The Boldts spoke German at home, you know."

"I had never imagined that, until Pete told me. I had heard the Horatio-Alger story about the youngster, coming alone to the United States when only thirteen years old, of course. Did Louise also come from Germany?"

"No, she was born in Philadelphia, but her parents came from Germany. I believe. But I wouldn't push the German connection too far, either. William Hewitt had no Germanic tendency, and the Castle, like the Powerhouse, seems more French than German. The Alster Tower, of course, is very different, and may be by another hand—but I don't think of it as being particularly Germanic, either. Surely the arch and great yacht house—both by the Hewitt firm—make no particular reference to *Mittel Europa*."

"I'm not sure whether that's disappointing or not."

"But it's gotta be good news—that nothing over there is a 'replica' of anything anywhere. At one time, Americans were insecure about their new culture, and looked to Europe for a higher culture. Once folks liked to think that Boldt Castle was an 'exact replica' of some *Schloss* on the Rhine. Now we ought to appreciate what an inventive, and good, architect Bill Hewitt was."

"Gimme some 'for-instances'."

"How much time do you have? I would have to go through the evolution of the building, which is a long and complicated story. In short, however, we have to realize that Hewitt's hands were tied, to a large extent, by the Boldts' insistence that he replicate the basic arrangement of the old frame house. He couldn't start from scratch, providing a totally new vision. He had to massage the old form—a shotgun wedding of two houses, glued together, very different in form and character.

"Although innately do-it-yourselfers, at a certain point, with a degree of reluctance, one suspects, the Boldts called upon their architect for assistance. Given a particularly difficult assignment, architect William Hewitt deserves considerable credit for bringing a degree of coherence to the resulting complex of buildings and gardens, and a measure of genuine architectural form.

"The plan of the Castle is so big, that putting a roof over the whole was a challenge—particularly as the Boldts apparently liked steep roofs, recalling northern European forms. Most observers wouldn't suspect that much of the Castle is actually covered by a flat roof. If the steep roofs had continued to rise at the angle required to make them visible from the water, they would have extended skywards so that the building would be like an inverted ice-cream cone. Instead, there are big flat surfaces up on top that you can walk out on. Quite amazing. Hewitt was clever, artful, in manipulating the form."

"Are there other aspects of the design that are particularly original—that people can actually see to appreciate?"

"The whole thing, I would say. But more particularly, the striking form of the principle elevation, facing the main channel, where the central block is crowned by that pair of very steep, pyramidal roofs, flanking the stone gable where the bronze stag stands. I know of no precedent for the odd pairing of hipped roofs in this manner. The irregular skyline and broken masses provided scale, making the large structure seem even larger. The inventive, sculptural aspect contributes greatly to the iconic, landmark quality of the building."

"You would say that this was a very creative work, then?"

"Oh, absolutely. Eccentric, even—quirky. It's quite mad, you know. Look at that great stone tower—the tallest one. It's over that big terrace area, off the dining room, which slides under the huge pile of masonry, supported on four stone piers—one of them having an outdoor fireplace with its chimney going up seven stories. What a draft! Bizarre! This arrangement of porch and tower was inherited from the old frame house, so Hewitt may not be to blame, if one finds fault with irrationality. But go down to the lowest level and look at the circular pool under the projecting curved terrace off the library. The huge masonry wall of the central block I mentioned comes down right over the center of the pool, so that great steel beams are required to carry the enormous weight. Nutty. Again, I suspect that the Boldts had their hands in these decisions, and as cost was no object, common sense became irrelevant.

"I've heard even crazier things—that they intended to have running water flowing over the rotunda's glass dome, for instance, in order to cast shimmering light below. Charming idea, but a technical nightmare. We architects always have trouble with leaking skylights, without deliberately running water over them!

"There were other delightful conceits, such as buying the chimes from the Wanamaker department store in Philadelphia, removed from there (as I recall) because they were too loud to be tolerated in the city. They rang every quarter hour in the Power House tower, reverberating throughout the village of Alexandria Bay, and tunes could be played from a keyboard in the Castle. No doubt patrons of the grand hotels there had mixed reactions, especially when trying to take a siesta. And then, they say, Boldt intended to have a set of organ pipes also installed in the Power House tower, to entertain the folks on the River, when he played the console in the ballroom. Boldt was self-taught at the keyboard, you know. But he appreciated good music, and had a good ear, so he probably would have brought a capable organist to perform."

"Back to the question of the importance of Boldt Castle—or all of Heart Island and

Unfinished pool beneath the library terrace

the nearby Yacht House . . . . It's one thing to say the place is odd, interesting, even unique. But can we say that it deserves recognition for inherent value as architecture, a work of art?"

Meg laughed. "You aren't an architect, or an artist, are you? Laymen have this simple notion that somehow there's the acid test for what is art and what is not. Artists know that public recognition doesn't necessarily relate to qualities they recognize and appreciate in the work of others, to say nothing of their own work."

"Are you being evasive?"

"No. Honest.

"But I need an assessment of the importance—the value—of Boldt Castle."

"You want a one-liner, eh?"

"You said that Boldt Castle deserved to be designated a National Historic Landmark?'

"Yes."

"Suppose you were asked to prepare a nomination. What would be your argument?"

"I'd ask Pete to convey the historic context, to interpret the meaning of the place that it had for the builders in their time. That would be important, since a landmark ought to mean something if it's to be valued."

"Would you argue that George Boldt was nationally important historically?"

"I'd argue that George and Louise Boldt were both significant, for their joint contribution to the concept of the grand hotel as urban social center and urbane way of life."

"I can understand that Louise's role might not have been adequately appreciated at the time, but what about George Boldt's?"

"No question about that. The documentation would by encyclopedic: newspapers and magazines were full of it. When he died all the department stores and shops on Fifth Avenue closed at 11 AM for his funeral. Can you imagine that today? All traffic stopped on the Avenue for an hour, due to the crowds outside the Waldorf-Astoria and St. Thomas' Church, lining the Avenue between. There was a simple family service that began in the library of Boldt's ninth-floor apartment. Motorcycle and mounted police then led the way to St. Thomas' Church. The Chief Inspector of Police said, 'George Boldt's body should go up the same street the President's body would go.' A large procession of hotelmen marched together. At the church, the police had to clear the crowd for "all the great names of the city" to enter, joining bellhops, chambermaids, waiters, chefs in the great Gothic interior—two thousand mourners—while some more socially prominent figures had to stand in the street. The children had requested no flowers, but the church was banked with more than a hundred large floral sprays."

"Appropriate—for Boldt."

"Yes, wasn't it? The honorary pall bearers who followed the casket down the aisle were a Who's Who—the likes of George Baker, Elbert Gary, and Charles Schwab—financial and industrial titans of the time—and socially prominent men such as Stuyvesant Fish and George Gould. Commodore Bourne (of Dark Island Castle) was a pallbearer, as was Thomas Gillespie (of Basswood Island), and the president of Cornell University. J.P Morgan, Nicholas Biddle, and Vincent Astor were among the mourners—and, interestingly enough, Nikola Tesla. President Wilson sent a telegram, as did John Cardinal Farley of New York. Condolences came as well from the Mayor of New York and Sir Thomas Lipton, the world-famous yachtsman. I suppose most people today wouldn't recognize many of the names so well known a century ago. *Sic transit* . . . but the works remain—the Waldorf-Astoria, Bellevue-Stratford—both still great civic institutions—and, of course, the landmark buildings of the Thousand Islands."

"And how do they compare, nationally, with other historical landmarks?

"Are you asking about them as historical artifacts, representing the period, or about the quality of the architecture? I'm not a professional critic, or an educator, you know. I've already said that Hewitt was clever—brilliant—in meeting the challenges and making something of a difficult assignment."

"But that doesn't necessarily make the product excellent as architecture, does it?"

"Excellent? You do want a one-liner—a one-worder, in fact. The truth is that standards of excellence vary, not merely with fashion, from time to time, but among critics with different values writing at the same time. One can't be very objective about values or quality. Critics, however, do try to base their appraisal on something, so often resort to ideology—talking about th*e Zeitgeist*—expression of the times—or 'honesty,' or some such philosophical stance. Artists don't worry so much about this literary, left-brained stuff." She smiled. "But you're a writer."

"Yes, and I need to be persuaded that this place is worth designation as a National Historic Landmark. Now convince me that it has merit, as architecture."

"I'll try. As I see it, simply put, all of these works—the Castle, Alster Tower, Power House and Yacht House—are very plastic (sculptural, that is), which is to say they've been intentionally modeled to compose masses artfully, modeled by sun and shadow. The complex forms provide a rich experience for the viewer who moves around the buildings, seeing them from different angles. The island location of the structures facilitates appreciation of the sculptural aspect of the forms."

"Would you place the sculptural quality foremost?"

"I hadn't thought of that, but as that was what first occurred to me when you asked, it might follow that formal composition of the masses is the most important quality."

"How would these works compare with other buildings as sculptural compositions?"

"Lord, now you want me to survey world architecture for comparison? Give me a break."

"Just the United States will suffice, thank you."

"Off hand, thinking of other great country houses of the era, none come to mind that's comparable. Biltmore is in the same idiom, but Hunt was never really into the picturesque, asymmetrical mode. That place is far more staid, less lively. The Breakers was more his métier—symmetrically formal and rationally organized. Next, Oheka, by Delano and Aldrich, although likewise executed in this French Renaissance style, was far more restrained and classical in its symmetrical composition. Same for Harbor Hill, the Mackay place by Stanford White. The folks who built those places might find Boldt Castle bizarre, but others find its imaginative fantasy more compelling than academic correctness or 'good taste.'"

"You're implying that the Boldt project wasn't in 'good taste'?"

"That's a concept that doesn't mean much to artists. Do they care, or did George Boldt? Nietzsche said, 'So long as you go on being praised, you must believe that you are not yet on your own course, but on some one else's.' But Heart Island wasn't dismissed as irrelevant. Remember that a substantial article about Heart Island was published in a national architectural journal, and subsequently has been featured in many books and more recently in media presentations." Meg paused reflectively. "But, I suppose, mostly it's the enormity of the thing. Bigness isn't necessarily betterness, but there's a sort of heroic quality to this colossal endeavor. As an architect, one appreciates the fundamental value of solidity—a quality in its own right, assuring durability and permanence. Boldt Castle was built to last, which is why it survived not merely neglect for so long, but vandalism as well. It's almost indestructible. Granite bedrock was blasted to provide level foundations, from which massive granite walls rise. Interior bearing walls and non-bearing partitions are of clay tile—likewise stable and fireproof. Floor structure employs steel I-beams with tile vault infill, a concrete fill on top to provide a level surface, and the complex roofs are framed with steel and clad in fireproof tile roofing. You see, it's not just that Boldt Castle is big. There were lots of big frame houses built at the time, but by comparison they were flimsy and ephemeral. Many on these islands burned, and others were demolished as they deteriorated and became difficult to maintain. But Boldt Castle is indestructible. It's a monument for the ages."

"In a word, then, you feel confident that the Boldt works qualify as important architecture?"

"In a word, yes."

"Would the Castle have been more important, more valuable as architecture, had it been completed?"

"Oh, oh. I see where you're headed. You want to know if we can 'improve' the place by finishing it, don't you? I suppose the hidden question is whether the Authority is doing the right thing."

"I suspect you agree with Courtney that the historic reality should have been left to tell the story, without dressing it up to make it more attractive."

"Of course—but it's a dilemma, whether to let the place fall into ruin, losing it for future generations, or to make it pay its way, so as to survive. I suppose it comes down to that. As an architect, I can be critical of how they've done some things, but you must realize the extent of what they have done. I think I mentioned, when we talked before, the prodigious roof replacement project—30,000 square feet, with all those hips, valleys, and built-in gutters to be flashed in copper. A new skylight was needed over the rotunda dome. The terrace over the long service tunnel was leaking, so a membrane was placed under a new walking surface. Same for the terrace over the swimming pool. The roofs over the verandahs had totally disappeared, and they were reconstructed. The verandah floor surfaces lacked paving. All that exterior masonry required repointing after a century, and much of the terra cotta detail, such as all the balustrade atop the verandahs, had to be recast."

"I'm getting the idea."

"Oh, no. I'm just starting. The Castle alone has some 300 windows and doors, now being replaced. And we haven't even gotten to the interior—or to the other buildings. The Alster Tower and Power House, both large masonry structures, required pretty much the same treatment, as did the Hennery. Even the Arch of Triumph needed repointing, and a stone gazebo required virtual reconstruction."

"O.K., you've convinced me. Quite a job."

"I'll say, but remember there was the huge Yacht House as well—an enormous project in itself, since it required work on the foundation cribbing initially. Every bit of exterior wood surface had to be replaced or restored. And then there was the site work . . . ."

"Stop!"

"But you need to mention all this, in fairness, if you're going to be critical about what the Authority has done. It's easy to find fault, especially when so much work has been done. Think of all the docks and seawalls, all the hard-surface walks (whether we like them or not, but remember a quarter million people walking on them every summer). Then, of course, there are the decorative floral displays. . . ."

Dining Room with temporary decor

"All right, I appreciate how much has gone into bringing the place back."

"Now let me tell you about the interior."

"Oh, I've been there, please . . . Briefly, how many rooms have they 'restored'?"

"Well, if you put 'restored' in quotes, they've done the reception room quite well, the original entry vestibule is also done, the Rotunda is underway. As the Rotunda runs up through several stories, with galleries running around all sides, that's quite a project. The billiard and dining rooms were sort of cleaned up, but let's hope the temporary décor won't be there long. At the present time, the Authority is thinking about the other major rooms on the main level—the ballroom and library, as well as the Boldt family suite on the second floor. The elevator may be made operative to serve the handicapped."

"All this work has tired me out."

"Yes, but that still leaves a lot of empty rooms. Once you get beyond the first impression on entering, the place become drearier and drearier the farther you go. It's a long way to go."

"To 'finish it'?"

Meg grimaced with mock annoyance. "You know how I feel about that by now. But it's a quandary, what to do. Once they started making a part of the place look 'finished,' even to moving in carpets, furniture, and potted plants, the contrast makes the rest seem even more unattractive. They haven't found the right *gestalt*—the convincing character to integrate the experience."

"Visitors don't complain as much as they used to, do they?"

"I'm sure that's what the Authority would point out. And it's true. Most folks think that new staircase is just grand. I've had people tell me they go back every summer just to see what new improvements will appear. But casual visitors only know what they see in a few minutes; and they only respond to what's presented to them. They don't have the choice of how the place is presented, or the sense of history that would inform such a choice."

"You're saying that most people don't question whether what's being done, like the staircase and skylight, is authentic."

"Of course not. They're gullible. So long as it's a good show, they leave satisfied, and that satisfies the Authority, apparently. If these 'improvements' have to be done, at least I hope they're done in the appropriate historical and architectural character. But the notion of 'finishing' the Castle is inherently flawed. We couldn't do it right, even if we wanted to, because we can't know how. We don't have the necessary architects' drawings. And would we really like it better, if we did have all the drawings to complete the place as it would have been? The Boldts taste might not be our own. You should see historic photographs of some interiors by Louise Boldt at the original Waldorf. Granted, they were done a decade earlier, but the character isn't to our taste—at least mine."

"Why?"

"Oh, too fussy, overwrought—too many layers of fine lace and heavy draperies, too many gewgaws and gimcracks. But it was still the Victorian mode, of course. Probably the Castle interiors would have been different, done ten years later. Taste had changed enormously."

If the Bridge Authority were not to 'finish' the interiors, I asked Meg, would she, as an architect, be able to provide visitors with some sketches of what it might have looked like?

"I've already done some. Here." She showed me two drawings of the Castle exterior, showing landscape developments that were never completed. "The grounds appear as I envision them, based on the architects' site plans. And here is an interior view of the Rotunda, seen from the ballroom. I don't know for a fact that there

Marble staircase of the Bellevue-Stratford. The main staircase of the Castle might have had such a metal railing.

would have been a bronze stair hand railing, as I've suggested, but it would be more appropriate with the marble staircase than the massive wooden job there now."

"Pete thought it looked Victorian. Your version is different—what style is that?"

"The railing model is French, which seems to have been Hewitt's preferred style. In fact, we see him using this sort of metal railing on the beautiful stairs at the Bellevue-Stratford, designed for Boldt at the same time as the Castle. It's the sort of thing that was being done at the time in other large American houses, such as the Breakers and Rosecliff at Newport, at Oheka on Long Island's North Shore, or at Nemours, near Wilmington. And if they're going to get a chandelier to hang from the center of the dome, as suggested by the escutcheon there, they ought to look at the hanging fixtures in the hall of the Breakers."

"The space seems less cramped, with the lighter metal railing."

"Of course. I can't imagine the designer wanting to fill the volume with such massive construction, with all those appended lighting fixtures. Less is more."

"Agreed, in this instance, surely. Did the Bridge Authority see these sketches?"

"No, it wouldn't be appropriate professionally to intrude, where another architect is engaged. And I'm not altogether confidant that this is the way it would have been. There have been several accounts of old-time visitors, who recalled seeing marble on the staircase. One person remembered a black-and-white marble floor, as we find in many great halls of country houses. We know more surely that there would have been dark wood on the walls, as it was crated in the lower levels and a few pieces probably remain, although much was sacrificed to tourists over the years, when brought up and left unattended in the Rotunda."

"You wouldn't try to 'finish' the interior—or install the stained glass in the dome overhead?"

"Of course not. I can't see them getting it right."

49.   Meg again mentioned her concern over inventing a fictitious new stained glass dome to cover the rotunda, where none had ever existed or even been designed. With anticipation—not pleasant—I opened a box to find a rolled print. In lovely color, it reproduced Julie Sloan's design for the dome. This wasn't the giant Tiffany lampshade that we feared, vibrant and varicolored, chock-full of luscious fruit and flowers. The design wasn't Victorian in character at all. She got it right! Quite simple and classical, it looked like 1904. Tasteful—elegant, in fact—it might restore some

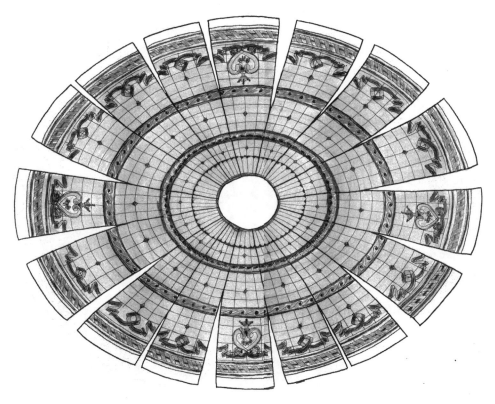

Julie Sloan's recent design for the stained glass dome of the Boldt Castle Rotunda

The unfinished dome
and skylight, 1940s

of the appropriate period character to the interior. Even critical Meg agreed. "If they had to invent something, this seems reasonable. They should learn, if they haven't yet, that the Victorian era didn't extend into the early twentieth century."

Meg referred me to books about other important country houses being built about the same time as Boldt Castle. An important contemporary review was the large book by Herbert Croly and Harry Desmond, *Stately Homes in America*, published in 1903. That was the year that Edith Wharton's bitter and biting novel about life in these great houses, *The House of Mirth*, appeared. Edith Wharton and Ogden Codman had written *The Decoration of Houses* in 1897, before the Castle was built. Louise, who was interested in decorating, probably knew this book, or the work of Codman, who was the rising star of interior design at the time. He did some Vanderbilt interiors at 'The Breakers.' Wharton's own tasteful house, "The Mount," was being built at Lenox, in the Berkshires as the Castle was rising. It's now newly restored, according to Meg—a knockout. In fact, even earlier the Astoria addition (where Louise this time wasn't an interior designer), which was completed before the Castle was built, had décor that was 'somewhat lighter and more floral in tone' than the original Waldorf. In the new hotel, they said, 'simplicity and classic taste is taking the place of mere gorgeous underplanned decoration.'

"The Castle would have been finished and decorated in the decade when another avant garde decorator, Elsie De Wolfe, was painting woodwork a fresh ivory white—as we see the interiors of Wellesley

Incomplete stained-glass dome,
viewed from fifth-story corridor

House. Meg suggested that the Heart Island management ought to visit other important houses of the period, to see how to get things right. They, or their interior design consultant, ought to go to Newport, which has so many splendid interiors of this period—at least if the Authority intends to pursue this fiction of 'finishing' the Castle. She mentioned that some of these houses not only retain original furnishings and décor but also have the new technical gadgetry of the period so dear to Boldt's heart.

"Such as?"

"Oh, at one there was a plant for making a huge quantity of ice from ammonia and salt water. Of course, at Heart Island they might cut cooling ice from the River, to be stored in icehouses, but probably they would have produced a more sanitary form of ice for human consumption. There weren't yet modern, electric refrigerators that use Freon. At the time iceboxes were still in use and they required large quantities of ice, in large blocks, to be transported to the Castle. That's one reason for the elaborate service passage under the Italian Garden terrace. Not only ice, but also large quantities of baggage and supplies had to be delivered inconspicuously from the service dock to the Castle. Coal, even."

"Coal?"

"Yes. Not merely for cookstoves and ovens, or for hot water heaters, but for the steam boiler. The Castle was to be heated, you know."

"Everyone thinks of it as merely to a summer place."

"It could be occupied year 'round, although ice on the River would make access difficult in deep winter. Knowing Boldt, however, he might have had an icebreaker, to keep a channel open. More probably, however, the Boldts would have gone to fairer climes then, but they might have enjoyed Christmas at Heart Island."

"I never thought of such a thing."

"George Boldt came to the River in the fall to hunt. He had a duck blind over on the Lake of the Isles. Autumn is the also Muskie season, you know—the colder and rainier, the better the fishing. Probably the Castle would have been occupied long after the tourist season. George Boldt often came out of season, because of his interest in the year-round farm operation and his many building projects here. While the railroad connected the River with the City, access was easier than now, in any season."

"I wondered about all the space at the lowest level. Other than the indoor swimming pool, it seemed useless. But I suppose there would have been much equipment and supplies."

"Imagine the quantity of laundry. As at their hotels, linen would be changed daily—seventy to a hundred cloth napkins alone every day. There would be large mangles to press sheets and table cloths. I know of no evidence for an outdoor drying yard, so many lines might have been strung in the basement areas, unless Boldt had some mechanical drying apparatus. He was famous as a wizard at logistics—running a hotel was then, as now, a career of crisis management. To maintain the reputation of the Waldorf, Boldt had to anticipate every possible thing that could go wrong. No doubt the Castle, like his grand hotels, would have been prepared for malfunction with all sorts of alarms and back-up equipment. It wouldn't do to be entertaining dignitaries and have a lady's jewels stolen or suddenly to be without hot water or electrical lights. So there would have been rooms full of machinery at the lower level—but also root cellars for food supplies, and of course the large wine cellar, connected by a stairway directly to the butler's pantry. There would also be recreational and lounge spaces adjoining the pool, as evidenced by the fireplace in one room. The regimen might have been similar to Nemours, where after dinner, when the ladies adjourned to the drawing room, the men shed their jackets and went down to the basement to enjoy an elaborate complex of recreational facilities."

"Such as . . ?"

"Oh, bowling alleys, billiard and pool tables, shuffleboard, simulated horseback riding machine—even early movies."

"Or at Boldt Castle they might take a dip in the pool."

"I doubt it, after dinner. They had to return in those vests and starched shirts to rejoin the ladies upstairs, remember."

"Today's visitors to Heart Island need more of this sort of information—a sense of what life would have been like there."

"Are you practicing your pitch to publishers?"

Our laugh together seemed the right note for another farewell. Meg would stay here for most of the winter, which she said was far preferable to closing up a summer home, leaving a place one loved for a long duration. "Did that as a kid," she recalled. "Hated this back-to-school time of year. No more!"

Boldt Castle, watercolor by Michael Ringer

50. "I suppose you object to those floodlights," I commented to Courtney. He had reserved the same table for a final dinner together, with the same view that I had first seen of Boldt Castle. Nice touch. Courtney would stay on at Heron Island until Columbus Day, as he always did, but I had to return to the City in the morning. Our play was unfinished, but as suspected, finishing or producing it really didn't seem a pressing concern for Courtney. He glanced out at Heart Island.

"Oh, I guess the lights do little harm. Electric lighting is reversible—just turn the switch and it's off. And the Castle surely is a landmark to be highlighted. To my taste, the floodlights are garish, but my taste isn't everyone's taste. And, for better or worse, we still have Boldt Castle—and the other buildings—in much better condition than ever, with their future secure. They're minting money over there, pouring it all back into improvement—which is, of course, part of the problem. But Vince Dee would be pleased, and rightly proud, to see what he had started, now carried so far." Perhaps his favorite Scotch mellowed Courtney's expected criticism.

"Oh? I supposed you thought they had carried the improvement business too far. But maybe the presence of the place is too powerful to be changed—maybe it has too much of a life of its own. Boldt Castle has this compelling story to tell, one that everyone wants to hear—I hope."

"You think your book will tell that story—a new and different story—now?"

"Well, I've talked to lots of people. I've thought a lot about what might have been. It seemed I was coming close, but still couldn't quite get it, somehow—or I got several different things, maybe all true—like that clock with the four faces in the Waldorf lobby, telling different times, depending on how you look at it. Then a gut intuition surfaced. Maybe I finally had it. The notion came to me when thinking about building that great stone arch, so utterly useless. Meg put me on to it, showing me the similar triumphal arch that the Kaiser's widow built at her home, dedicated to her dead husband. The Arch of Triumph was a monument to something, a testament intended to last forever—what? There it was: the granite keystone of the arch, carved with—you got it: the heart." Courtney raised an eyebrow incredulously.

"'Love is Forever'—wasn't that the motto favored by Clover in her silly little book?" He smiled at my chagrined retreat.

"Yes. Sentimental, corny. But you know what? Maybe she was right. But there was more. Heart Island meant more than a Valentine: it was intended not merely to celebrate love between the living, but dedicated to love that would survive after one of them would be gone." Courtney's mocking attitude became serious.

"You think they both knew she was dying?" His sudden interest surprised me.

"Consider this: according to one report—the one that seemed so well informed about her health problems, the one that mentioned her physician by name—Louise began to evidence her illness symptoms 'four or five years' before she died. When would that have been? 1899 or 1900. When did they erect the Arch and launch the Castle campaign? You got it."

"The Last Hurrah."

"Here's how it might have been: Louise's health was failing. They both suspected, feared what was inevitably ahead. George sensed they might have only a few more years together. What would all his millions be for, after she would be gone? The frantic compulsion to spend whatever it took, the obsessive quality of the campaign, and its instant abandonment. That explains it." Courtney's smile was gone now.

"So it really is 'Love is Forever,' eh?" He began toying with a spoon.

"That explains how the Castle began, but not how it ended. There still lurks that darker aspect: the overdose. I've been looking at newspapers during January of 1904, during that brief thirty days that Louise was in her new New York City town house, before the telegram arrived at Heart Island. There's one piece, written only four days before she died, headlined: 'Collapse . . . Bringing Ruin and Loss to Thousands. . . .' And another said, 'Disaster and Ruin.' It reported unfinished houses abandoned in Manhattan, boarded up and for sale. George's new Bellevue-

Stratford Hotel was not yet complete—he had millions in it, as another depression seemed to be setting in—just like 1893, when George had his first nervous breakdown. And here they were pouring more millions of dollars into her dream Castle. Perhaps she knew then that she would never live to see it completed." Courtney leaned forward, catching the drift, as I slowly formulated my thoughts. "She may have suspected the truth all along, probably more than George. He was so busy with pressing business, she probably spared him concerns for her health, hiding as much as she could. . . . The rising castle, the whole vision of a courtly way of life—compelling, yes, but it must have seemed unreal, like those dreams we have when we know we're dreaming, but still the dream controls us. Why was she possessed by it?"

Courtney guessed. "Compensation, of course—for what she didn't have."

"Love?" My question was rhetorical. "No, that's too much the supposition of the local gossips. George and Louise loved each other."

"So what was it that Louise missed, when she seemed to have everything—including love?" I suspected that Courtney knew the answer to his question, but was leading me.

"What her husband had," I answered. "Fulfillment. George was engrossed in his projects; she was alone, surrounded by servants who did everything for her. The children were grown, leaving the nest. George was consumed with business, making millions upon millions more. Once the hotels were well established, George became the self-described 'capitalist' who was engrossed with finance, playing the markets for high stakes. Louise, meanwhile, had these building projects, but she couldn't keep building forever. She wasn't raised to be an indolent queen in her Castle. She had been a working wife, engaged in a genuine partnership. No more. George had surpassed her, had moved on into the major leagues. Even though he still loved her, she had now become a trophy, like this monstrous house—a jeweled doll in this colossal doll's house." Courtney reverted to his skeptical mode.

"Are you sure he was just playing the markets—not playing around?"

"Oh, there were no other women. Totally out of character for Boldt." Courtney seemed unconvinced by my confident tone.

"But why the colossal house—a trophy, you say? A pastime to keep her occupied?"

"Surely there was more to it—a new way of life, a new horizon—the 'American Dream.' American dreaming was Boldt's business. Henry James recognized that, and Willa Cather, writing about the Waldorf. She sensed the danger lurking in the glamorous fascination of the Waldorf-Astoria." Courtney scowled.

"Oh, it was just a fine hotel. It didn't cause Paul's problem."

"The point is, Courtney, that at the very end, when Paul's money has run out and he's dying, Cather didn't have him wistfully recall a vision of bubbling champagne at the Waldorf, did she?"

"I don't remember."

"No, there was another vision: 'the blue of the Adriatic water, the yellow of the Algerian sands'."

"Strange. How could the boy have known those places, if he only left Pittsburgh for New York recently?"

"He couldn't. That's the point. He might have seen them, had he lived. He missed seeing what was real because of his attraction to the artificial. Cather was telling us that Paul was 'lookin' for love in all the wrong places'. He might have walked out of his gritty Pittsburgh slum into the wooded Pennsylvania mountains, instead of stealing in order to reach Fifth Avenue. What Paul really needed was right there. It wasn't lack of money, as he supposed, that prevented him from finding his way out."

"So what's the connection?"

"There's a line from an old song: 'The best things in life are free.' Consider this: the Boldts owned unspoiled Harbor Island—wild and natural like your place, Courtney—there it was, right next to Heart Island. Why did they need to transform Heart Island into something unnatural? The unnatural was what Boldt had to offer. Not natural wonder but urbane artifice. He was a purveyor of privilege. George and Louise bought into privilege themselves. The immigrant boy and the tavern-keeper's daughter. That's the American Tragedy part."

Beyond the glass, across the water, the great, hulking pile loomed, mute and mysterious as it had been for a century. "Maybe that's part of the magic—the unnatural, bizarre quality—the inscrutability about the why of it all—that really fascinates people."

Courtney didn't turn to follow my gaze but commented, "I suppose the exotic strangeness is both alluring but slightly alienating—that's the magic. But the simple story line, of a great love and unbounded happiness suddenly terminated by the cruel hand of fate—you know, that may be more accessible than your psychological probing about the ambiguities of human relationships. Will the audience be with you if you can't answer the questions you raise?" Courtney was the composer who

appreciated the space between the notes. He savored the pause, awaiting my response.

 "But the conventional story of the unfulfilled dream, of love lost, of abandonment
 of the great project by the broken-hearted builder —that's all too simple, just too
pat, too worn a cliché. The underground stories persist because people demand
more." Courtney's knowing smile returned.

 "—Which you'll provide. I take it then that you're not content with the 'Love
is Forever' theme of Clover's little book?"

"Heart Island is about love. She's right there. Yes, I do think it would be wrong to

George C. Boldt in his Waldorf-Astoria office, with a photograph of a granddaughter

view the Castle merely as extravagant compensation for love."

Courtney smiled. "You're not the cynic I supposed."

"No, there was love between them. I'll buy that. But sometimes love is not enough. One can't live on love alone. Only juvenile lovers suppose that. What else is required? Success? Success may not suffice, if by 'success' we mean castles and yachts. From Louise's point of view—and this is really her story, isn't it?—grandeur may have been merely isolating. The tavern-keeper's daughter enshrined in a vast palace—would she have relished the awed respect of visitors, to be received regally under that lofty, stained-glass dome? Is that what she wanted?"

Courtney had a ready answer: "George may have wanted it for her."

"Of course. And now we're getting to the crux of the tragedy."

"The 'tragic flaw'?" I was surprised by his erudite question, and by the intent expression on his tanned and weathered face. I hadn't suspected the outdoorsman-musician to be so literate.

"You're talking about classical tragedy. . . ." I ventured. "I suppose what the Greeks called 'the tragic flaw' comes down to the hero's character, and human mistake."

"If I remember," Courtney asserted, "the Greeks called it *hubris*—that's the quality of confident daring that we admire in our heroes. It was, however, a quality of personal ambition that annoyed the gods." Courtney seemed transported to his old Princeton seminar. I could play that game.

"Yes, the tragedy is classic, isn't it?" It was my turn to smile with self-satisfaction, to think that my book's story would be "classic."

"Ah, but you just said that this was Louise's story, didn't you?" Courtney peered at me, his Cheshire Cat grin indicating that he had me pinned. "Whose tragedy is this?" I really had no ready answer, so he bore in. "Is it Louise's tragedy, simply because she died? Is that all we mean by a 'tragedy'? Everyone dies. Surely the tragedy is not merely that a preposterously ambitious house was never completed."

"No. It was not so much a tragedy for Louise, who died and so escaped, but more for George, who had to live on for thirteen more years."

"There you have it, my friend. You thought your story was about Louise and her plight, but now you know that your tragedy is about George. He's your classic tragic hero."

"You're right," I agreed. "The classic hero doesn't recognize his tragic flaw, but does what he must, which destroys him."

"Yes, and destroys others, perhaps?" Courtney looked at me quizzically, wondering if I got his implication.

"'Others'? You mean Louise, don't you? But I suppose he never suspected."

"Self-actualizing types—our heroes—never do, do they? They're too self-absorbed in their heroic mission to be very aware of other people."

"Do you think he understood, too late, and felt guilty after she died?"

"That might explain why he was so 'devastated,' as they said, and never recovered. The true tragic hero is horrified to realize what he has done and how he has harmed others. But George Boldt still had his work—his consolation."

"They tried to rein him in," I recalled, "but no one—physician, family, friends—could stop him. He needed his work, even more, after he was left alone. He need it to distract him."

"So there you have the lost story of Boldt Castle, eh? More than the Love Story."

"You're right—not a romance, but a tragedy. But what we really want to know isn't merely what made George tick, but how Louise felt, isn't it? . . . What did she do, or mean to do, when she took those pills?"

Courtney was suddenly reflective, as if trying—or perhaps wondering if he wanted—to recapture something. "That may not be the right question, since it suggests that what happened was intentional, or willed."

"You think it was merely an accident?" I had no more than said it than I realized that Courtney was a widower. He didn't look at me, but gazed at the ceiling, speaking with difficulty:

"Between pure chance accident and an act of will there may be something else. Louise was ill—perhaps not merely physically ill. Isn't it ironic that it was Mrs. Astor's treatment for neurasthenia—and her confinement at the little Bellevue Hotel—that launched the Boldts' stunning ascendancy? Louise Boldt had been there, with Mary Astor, in that bed room—the one with the 'Yellow Wall-Paper.' I wonder, when George became rich and famous himself, if Louise's own bedroom, in that new town house he gave her, didn't have the same yellow wallpaper. When one suffers from severe depression, the will is not a factor, since action of the will requires a rationality that is lost." He stroked the tablecloth reflectively. "So what was Louise Boldt thinking, you ask?"

Courtney gazed out again, searching for something across the water, in the dark, pinnacled pile of Boldt Castle. I waited until he confided, "Have you ever been through a great personal crisis? I have. We seem fairly certain—less uncertain, that is—about the attitudes of others regarding the situation. We know, or suspect, their attitudes and motivations better than we understand our own genuine feelings and honest intentions. Everything seems unreal, insubstantial—as if the earth underfoot had melted and we were awash in the currents. It should be that 'no man (or woman) is an island,' but in a crisis one is indeed an island, alone. That's the worst part . . . The heart is an island."

"So you suppose that Louise was alone when she died—alone in that splendid new town house he gave her."

"Probably."

"Where was George?" My question was unnecessary. I anticipated his inevitable answer:

"Working, of course. Where else? George Boldt couldn't change, even if he wanted to, even if he never forgave himself—and if his children never forgave him either. He had this tragic destiny. You see, he was a hero."

Heart Island looked like the spectacular Michael Ringer painting of it, floodlit but outlined against the last glow of twilight. With a twitch of a wry smile, Courtney added, "You know, George Boldt himself, when asked why he didn't refute popular stories about him, replied, 'What's the use? . . . When people get an idea firmly fixed in their heads it is futile to attempt to correct them'."

Courtney squinted to scrutinize the distant Castle. "See that light, way up in an upper window?" He paused for dramatic effect. "Local folks say that when that glow appears, as it sometimes does, unexpectedly, on dark nights—more noticeable before they began the nightly illumination—that's the ghost of Louise Boldt."

*   *   *

Louise Boldt and her Castle

NOTES

Despite a conversational style that may suggest fiction, this account is factual regarding the Boldts and their Castle. Discussion of sources follows. The narrative presents authentic historical information mostly in the form of dialogue, much of it between imaginary characters. Some conversations report actual interchanges, however—meetings with Clover Boldt and Alec Baird, meetings with Clifford Dobbins, Bud and Eleanor Forrest, Jean Hammond, Andrew McNally, and Alden Merrick. The author's familiarity with the recent development of the Boldt property derives from his many years' association with the late Vincent J. Dee, Chairman of the Thousand Islands Bridge Authority, while engaged in interpretive projects such as the initial media presentation at Boldt Castle. Together with designer Robert Charron, they developed a proposal for a Visitors' Information Center for the Thousand Islands that included varied media presentations that would convey the regional history. Sponsored by New York State Senator (now U.S. Congressman) John McHue, the project was granted substantial funding by the New York legislature, but funds were not approved by Governor Mario Cuomo. Some of the material from that enterprise has been used here.

The four major conversationalists—Courtney, Peter, and Meg, and the narrator—are merely roles played by the author (whose wife says he is always talking to himself anyway). The device of multiple voices hopefully has enlivened what otherwise might have been a less varied exposition of factual material. The narrative suggests that research was done in a single summer. In truth, the "Search of the Lost Story" has spanned many decades, but the narrative strategy has compressed the time span. Clover Boldt Baird died in 1993, for instance, whereas the stained glass dome was being fabricated at the time of the writing, 2000. The presentations relate other actual activities of the author—collaborating with composer and lyricist Franklin Courtney Ellis on a musical comedy, its action set in the Thousand Islands of 1905, as well as drafting the manuscript of a more complete Boldt biography. The three fictitious Islanders—Courtney, Pete, and Meg—are composites, devised to focus different aspects of the subject but are not intended as portraits of particular individuals. I hope my friends may forgive me if they recognize a few familiarities.

In order to include many illustrations while keeping the size of the book reasonable, footnotes and other features of scholarly studies have been eliminated from the publication. A draft copy contains 874 notes and citations, which consume many pages of small type. Questions about the source of particular information may be answered by reference to the fuller manuscript, available at the MacSherry Library, Alexandria Bay, New York.

Contributors

Visual quality of the book derives from contributions of many persons and organizations. The author was particularly pleased by generous contributions of works by the painters John A. Morrow and Michael Ringer. More of their art appears on their web sites (www.jmorrow.com and www.michaelringer.com). The North Country photographer Daniel Boyce provided many images, including the cover photograph. More of his photography may be viewed at his web site (www.northernphotography.com). In addition to the author, other photographers, most of who shared several images, are:

Patrick Bink	Lorraine Herreros	Cindy Spurbeck
Brown Brothers	Harley J. McKee	Diane Szlucha
Robert Charron	Ray Knapp	Jason Valentine
Jean De Vaughan	Shane Sanford, TIBA	Christine Wands

Dudley and Kathy Danielson provided the photograph of the Hart House (www.harthouseinn.com). Julie Stone shared her design drawing for the stained glass dome (www.jlsloan.com). Sculptor Earl Rumsey Durand recalled his restoration work at Boldt Castle (http://members.tripod.com/~durand_e/index.html). Architect Rick Tague discussed his several projects at Heart Island and the Yacht House. Rick has been partner-in-charge of restoration work by the architects, Bernier, Carr & Associates (www.berniercarr.com). The author is indebted to those whose comments appear in the narrative and grateful to many others, especially Michelle McFadden, my editor Marielle Risse, and Shane Sanford, who is Boldt Castle Operations Manager, Jim Elidrisi, senior Bellman at the Waldorf-Astoria, as well as to my copy editor Leonard Senecal, and finally my wife, Judith Wellman.

Documentary Sources

The Boldts and Boldt Castle

Many items from the old Waldorf-Astoria are retained in the archives of the New York Public Library. They contain no personal papers of George C. Boldt, however. The Cornell University archives hold a few of his letters to Cornell President Andrew D. White. The Cornell archives also retain some records of George C. Boldt, Jr.. The library of the Statler School of Hotel Management at Cornell University holds the papers of Oscar Tschirky, including many scrapbooks of relevant clippings. That library has many other trade publications that contain Waldorf-Astoria information. The New York Historical Society has Abner Bartlett's copybook, which is extremely fragile and largely illegible. As mentioned in the text, Mr. and Mrs. William Forrest have copies of photographs from George Boldt's personal album. Hazel McMane Simpson, Town of Alexandria Historian, compiled extensive files that she shared, together with personal recollections. Lawrence Roy also shared personal memories. Conversations with Mr. and Mrs. Alec Baird, Vincent J. Dee, Clifford Dobbins, Jean Hammond, Andrew McNally, and Alden Merrick have been mentioned. Rebecca Hopfinger, curator, and Phoebe Tritton, librarian of the Antique Boat Museum have provided information. The Waldorf-Astoria Hotel contributed photographs. Probably many others who have assisted the author over his many decades of Thousand Islands research ought to be thanked here, but it is difficult to sort out the particular Boldt contributions from others related to the larger regional history.

As a world-famous institution, the Waldorf-Astoria has been the subject of published material for more than a century, so a complete bibliography would be long indeed. Far less has been published about the Boldts and Boldt Castle. Although clearly hagiographic in his reverence of George Boldt, the personal memoirs of Oscar Tschirky (see Schriftgiesser, Karl, below) provide more material about George and Louise Boldt than any other single work. A list follows of other sources that were particularly helpful in preparation of this work or have been quoted, but by far most information was derived from the methodical scanning of newspapers and other periodicals of the period.

Baird, Clover Boldt, with Julie Benbow Malear, *The Love Story of Boldt Castle*. 1978.

> As mentioned in the text, the granddaughter of George and Louise Boldt was a lifelong summer resident of Hopewell Hall not far from Boldt Castle. This booklet, largely the product of a journalist acquaintance, is a sentimental tribute, not reliable in its particulars.

Crockett, A. S., "George C. Boldt's Life a Continuous Romance: Reminiscences of Waldorf-Astoria's Proprietor, Who Rose from the Kitchen to be the Most Famous Hotel Man in the World." *New York Times Magazine*, 10 December 1916.

Johnson, James L., Sr., *The Powerhouse, Heart Island, Alexandria Bay, N. Y.: A Historic Structures Report*. Unpublished undergraduate thesis, School of Architecture, Syracuse University.

Kelley, Fred C., "How a Great Hotel Man Handles the Human Race." *American Magazine*, vol. 82, Dec. 1916.

Lincoln, Nanette, *Heart Island, Its Castle and Towers*, Alexandria Bay, Heart Island Operating Company, n.d.

> This familiar publication, still well known although long out of print, was commissioned by the Heart Island Operating Company as a guide for visitors. When this author long ago inquired about authorship of the guidebook, the publisher identi-

fied Ms. Lincoln, giving the date of publication as 1923. The date may have been incorrect, as in that year another guide to Heart Island appeared, written by Frances MacLean Ward, mentioned below. Apparently her booklet was published privately, however, rather than by the Heart Island Operating Company. Accordingly, it is possible that both works first appeared in 1923. A copy of the Lincoln booklet at Queen's University Archives, Kingston, identifies Edward J. Noble, owner of Heart Island, as its author, but more properly he may be identified as the publisher.

Lucas, Roger, *George C. Boldt: Research Review*. Cheektowaga, N. Y.: Research Review Publications 1983.

As mentioned in the text, Roger Lucas has compiled Boldt material from various sources into booklets. This, the first of his series, presented his initial findings in a newspaper format. Like subsequent volumes, this was largely a compilation of direct quotations with reproductions of period photographs.

_____ *Boldt Castle, Heart Island*, Cheektowaga, N. Y.: Research Review Publications, 1992.

This was largely a new edition of Lucas's *Research Review*, recast in booklet format.

_____ *Boldt's Boats*, Cheektowaga, N. Y.: Research Review Publications, 1993.

This booklet is companion to *Boldt Castle, Heart Island*, mentioned above

McCarney, Hal, *Chess With Violence: Rum-running in the 1000 Islands*. Gananoque, Ontario: McCarney, 1992.

This fictitious adventure is illustrated with excellent drawings of Heart Island by Bud Brown.

McDonough, Dennis, *Little Abner & His Ark: Abner Bartlett's Role in Constructing the Largest Hotel in the World, The Waldorf-Astoria Hotel*. Bruce Campbell Adamson Books.

Schriftgiesser, Karl, *Oscar of the Waldorf*, New York, Dutton, 1943.

In these memoirs, Oscar Tschirky, who was close to George Boldt for many years, provides valuable observations about the man and his professional practice.

Sherwood, Bruce T., *Historical Documentation . . .*

Unpublished report prepared for nomination of the Boldt Yacht House to the National Register of Historic Places.

Tatman, Sandra L. and Roger W. Moss, *Biographical Dictionary of Philadelphia Architects, 1700-1930*. Boston: G. K. Hall and Company, 1985.

"The Originator of Hotel Magnificence." *Hampton Magazine*, vol. 25, September 1910.

Thompson, Shawn, *River Rats: The People of the Thousand Islands*, Burnstown, Ontario, General Store, 1989.

This volume reports an interview with Clover Boldt Baird. Two other books by Thompson that focus less on Boldt Castle but provide excellent information about the region are: *Soul of the River* and *The River Rat's Guide to the Thousand Islands*.

Ward, Frances MacLean, A *Story of Heart Island and Its Castle on the St. Lawrence,* 1923.

> Of the same genre as Miss Lincoln's work, it similarly contains some moving prose as well as a few interesting facts about the early public showing of Heart Island. As the little booklet apparently was largely supplanted by Miss Lincoln's much re-printed work, it is less familiar, never becoming quite such a classic piece of Thousand Islands memorabilia.

Willey, Day Allen, "A Thousand Islands Estate," *Architectural Record,*

Vol. 25, February, 1909, pp. 125-130.

> This substantial, illustrated article was written for a professional journal five years after work stopped at Heart Island. As George Boldt was still alive to confirm the facts, this is a basic source of information.

Web Sites

[Flack, Lois Boyce], "Boldt Castle—Gift of Love."
   http://www.geocities.com/Heartland/Meadows/3702/boldt1.html
   This large site contains building plans for Boldt Castle.

"Boldt Castle." http://www.boldtcastle.com

"Thousand Islands Bridge Authority." http://www.tibridge.com/boldtcastle.htm

"Shadowlands Haunted Places." http://www.snopes2.com/info/search/search.htm

"'Paul's Case: A Study in Temperament,' WillaCather, 1906."
   http://www.shsu.edu/~eng_wpf/authors/Cather/Pauls-Case.htm
   The complete text of the short story.

"The Yellow Wall-Paper Site" http://www.cwrl.utexas.edu/~daniel/amlit/Wall-Paper/Wall-Paper.html
   The complete text of the short story, plus the author's comments and other commentary.

"Thousand Islands Club Restaurant," http://www.1000-islands.net/TI-Club/

"1905 APBA Gold Cup," http://www.lesliefield.com/races/1905_apba_gold_cup.htm

"American Architects' Biographies," http://www.sah.org/aame/bioh.html

"Antique Boat Museum," http://www.abm.org

[Dark Island Castle]" Jorstadt Castle,"
   http://www.dupontcastle.com/castles/jorstadt.htm

[Dark Island Castle]" Jorstadt Castle," http://www.gold-mountain.com/pm.html

[Dark Island Castle]" Jorstadt Castle, Album,"
   http://www.who2c.com/jorstadtcastle/index.htm

[Dark Island Castle] " Welcome to Jorstadt Castle,"
   http://www.merlespearls.com/islands/Jorstadt/

[Dark Island Castle] "Pictures of the Famous Thousand Islands,"
   http://www.ganboatlines.com/pictures.htm

[Dark Island Castle] "The World of Private Islands," http://www.vladi-private-islands.de/sales_islands/sites/3b_dark.html

The Boldt Hotels

Boldt, George C., *The Waldorf.* New York: 1893.

Boldt, George C., *The Waldorf-Astoria.* New York: Editions de lux, New York, American Lithographic Co., c.1903.

Crockett, A. S., *Old Waldorf Bar Days; with the Cognomina and Composition of Four Hundred and Ninety-one Appealing Appetizers and Salutary Potations Long Known, Admired and Served at the Famous big Brass Rail; also, a Glossary for the Use of Antiquarians and Students of American Mores.* Illustrations by Leighton Budd. New York, Aventine Press, 1931.

_____, *The old Waldorf-Astoria Bar Book; with Amendments Due to Repeal of the XVIIIth.* New York, Dodd, Mead and company, 1934.

_____, *The old Waldorf-Astoria Bar Book; with Amendments Due to Repeal of the XVIIIth; Giving the Correct Recipes for Five Hundred Cocktails and Mixed Drinks Known and Served at the World's Most Famous Brass Rail before Prohibition, Together with More than One Hundred Established . . . .* New York, A. S. Crockett, 1935.

_____, *Peacocks on Parade: A Narrative of a Unique Period in American Social History and Its Most Colorful Figures.* New York: Sears, 1931.

Crowninshield, Frank, *The Unofficial Palace of New York: A Tribute to the Waldorf Astoria.* New York: Huxley House, 1939.

Dearing, Albin Pasteur, *The Elegant Inn: The Fabulous Story of the Original Waldorf-Astoria. 1893 – 1929.* Secaucus, NJ: Lyle Stuart Inc., 1986.

Famous Guests of the Waldorf-Astoria. New York: Hotel Waldorf-Astoria, 1962.

Farrell, Frank, *The Greatest of Them All.* New York: K.S. Ginger Co., 1982.

Gates, John D. *The Astor Family.* New York: Doubleday, 1981.

Fortune Magazine, Oct 1931 Vol. IV no 4, 1931.

Hungerford, Edward, *The Story of the Waldorf-Astoria.* New York: G. P. Putnam's Sons, 1925.

Lent, Henry Bolles, *The Waldorf-Astoria; a Brief Chronicle of a Unique Institution Now Entering its Fifth Decade.* New York: Waldorf-Astoria Hotel, 1934.

Lucas, Roger, *The Bellevue-Stratford Hotel.* Cheektowaga, N. Y.: Research Review Publications,1994. This booklet likewise is companion to *Boldt Castle, Heart Island,* mentioned above.

McCarthy; James Remington, *Peacock Alley: The Romance of the Waldorf-Astoria.* New York: Harper & Brothers, 1931.

Morehouse, Ward, III, *The Waldorf-Astoria: America's Gilded Dream.* New York: M. Evans & Co., 1991. Although this work largely repeats material made familiar by a series of earlier histories of the famous hotel, the author adds some information derived from his personal acquaintance with the River and old-timers associated with the Boldts.

Smith, Horace, *Crooks of the Waldorf, Being the Story of Joe Smith, Master Detective.* New York: Macaulay, 1929.

Stokes, I. M. Phelps, *The Iconography of Manhattan Island, 1488-1909.* New York: Robert H. Dodd, 1926.

Sutton, Horace, *Confessions of a Grand Hotel: The Waldorf-Astoria*, New York, Henry Holt & Co., 1951.

Teitelman, Edward, *Architecture in Philadelphia: A Guide* Cambridge, Mass.: M. I. T. Press, 1974.

Truax, Carol, *Father Was a Gourmet: an Epic of Good Eating at the Turn of the Century.* New York: Doubleday, 1965.

The Waldorf-Astoria Manuals. Stamford, Conn., Dahl Pub. Co., 1947-49.

Web Sites:

"Bellevue-Stratford Hotel,"
      http://www.multiline.com.au/~mg/Legionnaires_Disease_Bellvue_Stratford_
      Hotel.htm
"Boldt Action, Urban Legends Reference Pages,"
      http://www.snopes2.com/info/search/search.htm
"Hotel Profile: Waldorf-Astoria"
      http://www.hospitalityonline.com/profiles/202582/
"National Trust for Historic Preservation," [Park Hyatt at the Bellevue]
      http://historichotels.nationaltrust.org/pennsylvania4.htm
"National Trust for Historic Preservation," [Waldorf-Astoria]
      http://www.nthp.org/main/hotels/newyork12.htm

Country Houses

American Country Houses of Today. New York : The Architectural Book Publishing Company, serial, volumes c. 1911 and subsequent years.

Aslet, Clive, *The Last Country Houses.* New Haven: Yale University Press, 1982.

_____ *The American Country House.* New Haven: Yale University Press, 1990.

Bacon, Mardges, *Ernest Flagg: Beaux-Arts Architect and Urban Reformer*, Cambridge, Mass., MIT Press, 1986. Flagg was architect of The Towers, Dark Island.

Batterberry, Michael and Ariane. *On the Town in New York, from 1776 to the Present.* New York: Charles Scribners' Sons, 1973.

Bedford, Steven M. "Country and City: Some Formal Comparisons." The Country House Tradition in America." *The Long Island Country House, 1870–1939.* Southampton, N.Y.: Parrish Art Museum, 1988.

Bryan, John M., *Biltmore Estate: The Most Distinguished Private Place*. New York: Rizzoli, 1994.

Carley, Rachel, *A Guide to Biltmore Estate*. Ashville, N.C.: Biltmore Co., 1994.

Cavalier, Julian, *American Castles*. New York: A. S. Barnes and Company, 1973. Flagg was architect of The Towers, the Dark Island property of Frederick Bourne.

Croly, Herbert, "The Residence of the Late F. W. Woolworth, Esq.", *The Architectural Record*, Vol. XLVIII, No. 3, March, 1920.

Desmond, Harry W. and Herbert Croly, *Stately Homes in America, from Colonial Times to the Present Day*. New York: D. Appleton and Company, 1903.

Deutsche Burgen und Feste Schlösser aus Alen Ländern Deutscher Zunge, Konigstein: Langewiesche, n.d.

Fitch, James Marston *American Building, 1: The Historical Forces That Shaped It*. Boston: Houghton Mifflin, 1975.

Fletcher, Sir Banister, *A History of Architecture on the Comparative Method for Students, Craftsmen & Amateurs*. London: B. T. Batsford, 1896, 1897, 1898, (etc.), 1928.

Folsom, Merrill, *Great American Mansions*. New York: Hastings House, 1936.

Franklin, Jill, *The Gentleman's Country House and its plan 1835-1914*. London: Routledge & Kegan, 1981.

Giedion, Siegfried, *Mechanization Takes Command: A Contribution to Anonymous History*. New York Oxford, 1948.

Girouard, Mark, *The Victorian Country House*. Oxford, England: Clarendon Press, 1971, and New Haven, Yale University Press, 1978 (1985 printing).

_____ *Life in the English Country House: a Social and Architectural History*, New Haven, Yale University Press, 1978.

Handlin, David P., *American Architecture*. London: Thames & Hudson, 1985.

_____ *The American Home: Architecture and Society, 1815 – 1915*. Boston: Little, Brown, 1979.

Hewitt, Mark Alan, *Architect and the American Country House*, 1890-1940. New Haven : Yale University Press, c1990.

Howe, Samuel, *American Country House of Today III*. New York : Architectural Book Publishing Company, 1915.

Kennedy, Robert Woods, *The House and the Art of Its Design*. New York: Reinhold, 1953.

Lynes, Russell, *The Domesticated Americans*. New York: Harper & Row, 1957.

_____ *The Taste-Makers*. New York: Harper, 1949.

MacKay, Robert B. et al, eds. *Long Island Country Houses and Their Architects, 1860–1940*. New York: W.W. Norton, 1996.

Maher, James T., *The Twilight of Splendor: Chronicles of the Age of American Palaces.* Boston: Little, Brown, 1975. A model study of three historic country houses.

Meigs, Arthur Ingersoll. *An American Covntry Hovse.* New York City: The Architectural Book Publishing Company, Inc., 1925.

Metcalf, Pauline C., ed., *Ogden Codman and the Decoration of Houses.* Boston: Boston Athenaeum : D.R. Godine, 1988.

Moss, Roger W., *The American Country House.* New York: H. Holt, c. 1990.

Muthesius, Hermann, *Das Englische Haus: Entwicklung, Bedingungen, Anlage, Aufbau, Einrichtung und Innenraum.* Berlin, 1904-5, also E. Wasmuth, 1908-1911, translated as *The English House,* edited by Dennis Sharp. New York: Rizzoli,1979.

Newton, Norman T., *Design on the Land; the Development of Landscape Architecture.* Cambridge, Mass., Belknap Press of Harvard University Press, 1971.

Parrish Art Museum. *The Long Island Country House, 1870-1930.* Southampton, N.Y.: Parrish Art Museum, 1988.

Platt, Frederick, *America's Gilded Age: Its Architecture and Decoration.* New York: A. S. Barnes, 1976.

Piaerson, Mary Louise and Ann Rockerfeller Roberts, *The Rockefeller Family Home: Kykuit.* New York: Abbeville, 1998. A beautiful and thorough model study.

Preservation Society of Newport County, *A Guidebook to Newport Mansions.* Newport, R. I.: The Preservation Society of Newport County, 1984.

Sawyer, Joseph Dillaway, *How to Make a Country Place.* New York: Orange, Judd, 1914.

Sievers, Johannes, *Die Arbeiten von K. F. Schinkel für Prinz Wilhelm Späteren König von Preussen.* Berlin: Deutscher Kunstverlag, MCMLV.

Smith, McKelden, ed., *The Great Estates Region of the Hudson River Valley.* Historic Hudson Valley Press., 1998.

Thorndike, Joseph J., Jr., *The Magnificent Builders and Their Dream Houses.* New York: American Heritage, c. 1978.

Thronton, Tamara Plakins, *Cultivating Gentlemen: The Meaning of Country Life among the Boston Elite,* 1785-1860. New Haven: Yale University Press, 1989.

Vivian, H. Hussey, Baron Swansea, *Notes of a Tour in America.* London: E. Stanford, 1878.

Wagner-Rieger, Renate and Walter Krause Eds., *Historismus und Schlossbau.* München. 1975.

Wharton, Edith, and Ogden Cogman, Jr.. *The Decoration of Houses.* New York: Scribner, 1902. Reprint: New York: Norton, 1978.

Weincek, Henry and Donna M. Lucey, *National Geographic Guide to America's Great Houses: More Than 150 Outstanding Mansions Open to the Public.* Washington, DC: National Geographic Society, 1999.

Wilson, Richard Guy. "Picturesque Ambiguities: The Country House Tradition in America." *The Long Island Country House, 1870–1939*. Southampton, N.Y.: Parrish Art Museum, 1988.

Web Sites: (Sites for Thousand Islands subjects were mentioned, pages 285-6).

"The Astors' Beechwood,"
        http://www.astors-beechwood.com/BeechwoodTheatre.html
"Biltmore Estate," http://www.biltmore.com/
"Castle Hill, The Trustees of Reservations." http://www.thetrustees.org/
"Edith Wharton Restoration-The Mount," http://www.edithwharton.org/
"Hearst Castle," http://www.hearstcastle.org/
 "Kykuit, The Rockefeller Estate" http://www.nthp.org/main/sites/kykuit.htm,
        http://www.hudsonvalley.org/, http://www.acorn-online.com/100kykuit.htm
[McCormick's] "Villa Turicum," http://cti.itc.virginia.edu/~rmr/docs/17.01.03-later.html
"Newport Mansions," http://www.newportmansions.org/
"Oheka Castle," http://www.oheka.com/
"Vanderbilt Mansion . . .," http://www.nps.gov/vama/vamahome.html
"Whitehall: . . . Flagler Museum," http://www.flagler.org/whitehall.html
"Whitemarsh Hall" http://www.serianni.com/wh.htm, a model web site by Gerry
        Serianni site that recreates a vanished country house.

An early post-card view of Heart Island. The photograph probably was taken during George Boldt's last years, since great steam yachts largely disappeared from the River during World War I when the U.S. Navy commissioned many. Thereafter internal combustion engines generally supplanted coal-burning steam engines and large crews no longer were retained to operate such large vessels.

Appendix A

A Composite Portrait of George C. Boldt

"He was, I would say, a character. A hard-working man, nice man, crazy about children." So recalled Grant Peacock, who was only a youngster on nearby Belle Isle when Boldt was alive, but his observation about Boldt's way with children probably is authoritative for that reason. It is corroborated by recollections of others. Some other characterizations, often more flowery, in the idiom of the time, were better informed by close adult acquaintance:

"So overwhelmingly great was Boldt's personality, . . . the innate lovableness of the man endeared him to every one with whom he came in contact. . . . Immensely popular, . . . he was the most charming and gentle of men, a lovable, simple person,. . . earnest and true, . . . [with a] personality that kept old friends, and made new ones. . . . You could not keep him from making friends. . . . [He] does not allow his wonderful energy to obscure his affability. He nearly always smiles. . . . On the floor, he was never too busy to stop . . . for . . . intimate talk. His affection knew no bounds. . . . Of all the men I have ever known, [he] had to the most marked degree the power of making and holding friends.

"Gentle, mild-mannered, unassuming, . . . modest in his demeanor, . . . [his] human quality [conveyed] the enthusiasms of the perpetual boy that he was at heart. . . . Optimistic, [with his] restless mind [and] fast-flying imagination, . . . he was never happier than when working out some curious mechanical detail...[and] he always could see every reason for doing a thing that popped in his head.

"At all times a most temperamental man . . . [he was inclined to be] quick-tempered. . . . Offtimes his subtle emotions were touched . . . and he was moved to tears. . . . [A] passionate lover of flowers and beauty, . . . closely attuned to the beautiful in music, color and form, . . . [he was] a dreamer, . . .a visionary [with] prophetic judgement. . . . If ever a man had vision, it was George Boldt . . . but [he was] also a man of action.

"An untiring worker himself, he expected all of us to work as long and just as hard. . . . [With the] energy of a dynamo, . . . he was a stickler for detail . . . on the job twenty-four hours a day, . . . from nine in the morning until two the next, [seeing his] wife and children for only fleeting minutes. . . . Literally he slept on the job, when he slept at all.

But he "was not at all the high-pressure executive. For all his quiet charm, he was a rigorous executive [with] remarkable organizational skill, daring and imagination, . . . conducting the multitudinous details of his business with personal zest. . . . [His] keen, observant mind . . . [made him] a shrewd judge of men and of conditions [and] enabled him to select the best of assistants. . . . He was his own school of big business, [attaining] power and prestige such as no hotel-keeper had ever enjoyed.

"The fact that he is probably the largest salaried man in this country, if not the world, and that he has made a vast deal of money outside of hotels, has changed him little. He is only a trifle busier and more reserved.

"Canny beyond his generation in the knowledge of the powers of publicity, . . . he understood the value of social prestige. . . . A real past master in the art of publicity, . . . a master propagandist and public relations expert, . . . he knew just what would get people talking. . . . In his way, [he was] a psychologist, . . . a remarkable student of human nature. . . . He liked people [and] had sentiment without being senti-mental. . . . A true diplomat, . . . refined, . . . his charm of manner [and] never fail-ing politeness [were] suave and dignified. . . . [In twenty-five years,] I never had one word of unpleasantness with him. . . . Strong himself, he was quick to forgive weak-ness in others. . . . Always on the side of the weak and the wronged, [he] was never happier than when he was helpful to aid of some human. [Because of his elite con-nections, some accused him of being a snob, but he was] in himself the very essence of democracy, showing his friendliness and his help to struggling and oppressed folk of every sort. . . . . Always accessible, . . . he was kindly and friendly to all.

"A many-sided man, . . . a man of exceptionally varied and multiform activities, . . . he could turn his hand to anything. . . . He could have been successful as engineer, lawyer, artist, architect or musician. . . . An inveterate reader, . . . thoughtful, . . . [with] . . . taste, . . . reason and philosophy, . . . he was a patron and student of the arts, . . . good judge of saddle horses . . . and an old time sportsman."

"Mr. Boldt is a lover of the different games and is willing to . . . work for the pleas-ure of the many island residents and visitors . . . and it can be truthfully said that there has never been a man that has done as much for Alexandria Bay and the St. Lawrence River as the above-named gentleman."

"The Waldorf-Astoria [was] the creation of the heart and soul of George Boldt—uniformly recognized as a one-man institution. He did like to call himself a perfectionist, [and although he] was something of a genius . . . his never failing ami-ability, genial and lovable qualities, . . . his great heart, . . . the laughter of his own harmonic soul [made him] the man we all loved . . . 'the Chief'."

George C. Boldt

"... He would 'shake his head slowly, wink a
liquid blue eye very slowly, and remark ....'"

Boldt Castle on Heart Island
seen from the Boldt Yacht House

Lynewood Hall
Country House of P.A.B. Widener, near Philadelphia, Horace Trumbauer, architect

Appendix B

Some Great American Country Houses of the Gilded Age

Important country houses had been built in America since colonial times. European "stately homes" were precedents, imposing seats of landed families whose agrarian estates were foundations of family fortunes. During the nineteenth century, as new wealth derived from industry and commerce, an emerging urban class created rural establishments as alternatives to primary residences in town. Generally these country houses were not regarded as primary residences but were occupied irregularly, often only during a particular season of the year.

The summer cottage was a species similar to, but distinctive from, the traditional country house. The cottage was intended to be an occasional abode, not a primary family seat on a rural domain. Proper country houses, as distinct from mere cottages, required land to provide an "estate." The distinction became blurred in the late nineteenth century however, when "cottages," as they still called them, at some colonies such as Newport, R.I. became monumental. Although grandiose, most of the huge houses were improbably located on relatively small village lots.

Some prominent Newport houses are even without water frontage, such as The Elms, Kingscote, and Chateau-Sur-Mer.

Brick country houses had been common on rural estates throughout the nineteenth century, while colonies of wooden cottages developed at seaside and mountain resorts. During the 1890s, however, the wooden summer cottage became monumentalized in stone. At Newport in 1892 a masonry château, Ochre Court, replaced Robert Goelet's large frame house. At the Thousand Islands, Charles Emery supplanted his wooden cottage with a sandstone "castle" the following year, the same year that Cornelius Vanderbilt commissioned design of the Breakers at Newport. Boldt Castle followed at the turn of the century. Unlike the Newport cottagers, however, both Emery and Boldt, like George Vanderbilt at Biltmore, acquired land and established farms, recalling the historic domains of landed families.

The ambitious size and mode of construction made Boldt Castle not merely distinctive at the Thousand Islands, but placed it in a class with the greatest American country houses. As mentioned in the narrative, Biltmore and Oheka were two of the larger country houses both, like Boldt Castle, designed in French chateau mode. Two grand houses of neoclassical style, both designed by Horace Trumbauer and built near Philadelphia, were Lynewood Hall, residence of P.A.B. Widener, and Whitemarsh Hall, one of the several homes of Edward Stotesbury. Lynewood Hall with 110 rooms was one of the largest houses in America. Whitemarsh Hall was said to contain 147 (or 145) rooms, although it appears somewhat smaller than nearby Lynewood Hall, suggesting how different definitions of "rooms" may yield varying numbers. Boldt Castle does not seem to be quite so large as the Widener palace but might be comparable to Whitemarsh Hall. Regardless of exact ranking, all of these houses were clearly in a distinctive class, having more than a hundred rooms.

William Randolph Hearst's San Simeon in California, with about a hundred rooms in its main building, is comparable in size to Boldt Castle. San Simeon has thirty-eight bedrooms and thirty-one bathrooms in the main house. Both estates supplemented the central building with smaller structures for additional guests, servants and services. San Simeon designed by the architect Julia Morgan, now a museum house, has been the subject of several books.

Shadowbrook, the Anson Phelps Stokes country house at Lennox in the Berskshires, was likewise in the class, having more than a hundred rooms. Shadowbrook subsequently was acquired by Andrew Carnegie, who died there. It became a Jesuit seminary. Indian Neck Hall, Frederick Bourne's Long Island country house (now La Salle Center at Oakdale) also was in this hundred-room class. Ernest Flagg was architect of this regal residence as well as "The Towers," Dark Island Castle.

The Breakers

"Cottage" of Cornelius Vanderbilt II, Newport, R.I., Richard Morris Hunt, architect

The Breakers, the Newport "cottage" designed by Richard Morris Hunt for Cornelius Vanderbilt II, is not so large by room count, having less than a hundred rooms, but they are grand indeed. The Preservation Society of Newport County gives seventy as the number but another source (Handlin) gives the number as only fifty-two. Still another writer (Amory) notes that while there were seventy rooms, thirty three of them were assigned to servants, leaving thirty-seven. The Breakers is a museum house operated by the Preservation Society of Newport County.

For comparison, by the author's count, Boldt Castle might have had about sixty *finished* rooms, excluding corridors, bathrooms, and closets, which may be comparable to Handlin's count of fifty-two rooms in the Breakers. Many chambers in the basement of Boldt Castle were to be unfinished, as were some attic spaces, probably accounting for the varying, higher room counts.

The Vanderbilts' Marble House at Newport is tiny by comparison but is sumptuous, probably one of the costliest residences per square foot ever built in America—again suggesting that mere size does not suffice to rank importance. Like the Breakers, Marble House is open to the public.

Whitehall, at Palm Beach, and the Frederick W. Vanderbilt house on the Hudson, as well as the Harold F. McCormick residence at Lake Forest, near Chicago were important country houses elsewhere. Whitehall, designed by Carrère and Hastings, was built for Henry M. Flagler in 1901-2. With fifty-five rooms it is relatively small, but like Marble House, the character is grand. Whitehall is now the Flagler Museum. The Frederick W. Vanderbilt house, designed by McKim, Mead, and White, was constructed in 1896-8. It likewise is smaller, with about fifty rooms, but they are sumptuous. The expense of decorating and furnishing the house was more than double its construction cost. The National Parks Service operates the Frederick Vanderbilt House, which retains its period décor, as a public historic site. The McCormick house, "Villa Turicum," was designed by Charles A Platt on an estate developed between 1903 and 1918. These are but representative, well-known examples by some important American architects of the time. Others less well known were equally grand, such as the Glen Cove, Long Island palace of Frank Woolworth, designed by C. P. H. Gilbert in an Italianate style similar to the Vanderbilt house on the Hudson.

One of the last of the grand country houses, built just before the Great Depression, is Castle Hill, the splendid Crane estate at Ipswich, Mass. The Great House is said to have a mere fifty-nine rooms, whereas Boldt Castle has seventy-two spaces that similarly might be designated "rooms." Castle Hill is distinguished less for its size than for its fine architecture, superb natural setting, and spectacular landscape design. The Great House, considered by some to be the masterwork of the architect David Adler, is a museum operated by the Trustees of Reservations.

The definitive study of the American Country House is yet to be written. Attractive books have represented examples selected from across the nation, often built over a span of two or more centuries. These works, like this article, have provided mere samplings. A more thorough survey, *Long Island Country Houses*, although geographically restricted, provides an exemplary model of thoroughness. Ambitious in its inclusive scope, the inventory comprehensively views country houses of many sizes and characters, providing a profile of what was being built during a particular period, albeit by an elite class of exurbanites in a single region. The approach of another exemplary model is quite different, focusing more intently on a few selected case studies: Maher's *Twilight of Splendor*. The author was particularly concerned with why and how these buildings were built. This is one of the few studies to consider contractors and craftspeople in relation to architects and clients. These two volumes may serve as substantial bookends for a shelf of varied publications about American country houses. As mentioned in the narrative, a major work of the period, Desmond and Croly's *Stately Homes in America* is basic.

Two short essays by Bedford and Wilson in another book, *The Long Island Country House*, serve as an overview of the country-house phenomenon. The major resource however is period literature, professional periodicals such as the *Architectural Record* and more popular magazines, and series of volumes such as *The American Country House of Today*, as well monographs devoted to particular architects.

Indian Neck Hall

Country House of Frederick K. Bourne, Oakdale, Long Island, Ernest Flagg, architect

The same architect who designed The Towers at Dark Island for Commodore Bourne designed his principal country house on Long Island's largest estate, now known as La Salle Center. Bourne's Dark Island Castle in contrast was a mere "shooting box" for occasional use, principally in the fall.

Appendix C

Landmark Houses of the Thousand Islands Open to the Public

The grand summer cottage, as distinct from the major country house, is well represented by a residence now open to the public at the Thousand Islands, Casa Blanca. The wood frame house of twenty-six rooms was the summer home of Cuban sugar baron Luis Marx on Cherry Island near Alexandria Bay. The interiors have not been redecorated since 1893 and retain much original furnishing. Groups of ten or more may visit Casa Blanca by appointment.

http://www.roundthebend.com/thousand/thouhist.html
http://www.1000islands.com/alexbay/battract.htm

Another regional house about this size, substantially constructed of stone, is splendid Fulford Place at Brockville, Ontario. Whereas Casa Blanca may be characterized as "Victorian," Fulford Place (1899-1901) is virtually "Edwardian" in character. Fulford Place likewise retains original family furnishings and is open to the public.

http://www.heritagefdn.on.ca/Heritage/built-fulford.htm
http://www.slip-passport.org/fp.htm

Dark Island Castle, as mentioned in the narrative, is an important landmark structure of the region designed by Ernest Flagg for Frederick Bourne. Originally called "The Towers" and by a recent owner "Jorstadt Castle," it likewise retains much original furnishing and decor and may be visited on occasion. Several web sites were mentioned in the Notes (Documentary Sources, The Boldts and Boldt Castle).

An earlier nineteenth-century villa, appropriately restored and open to the pu b-lic is Bellevue House in Kingston. At one time the home of Sir John A. Macdonald, Canada's first Prime Minister, the refurnished property with period garden is main-tained as a National Historic Site by Parks Canada.

(http://www.parcscanada.gc.ca/parks/ontario/bellevue_house/Bellevue_house_e.htm) Many other important houses of the Thousand Islands may not regularly allow public viewing of interiors but present exteriors of landmark quality. The Pratt house on Niagara Island, near Gananoque, Ontario, is a "modernistic" concrete structure of the 1930s' Art Deco style. The Vincent LeRay House at Cape Vincent is an early nineteenth century stone villa built by the son of the French landowner. Across the river, the city of Kingston, in addition to Bellevue House mentioned, retains a rich architectural heritage, as does the city of Brockville and villages on both shores of the St. Lawrence. Thousand Island Park on Wellesley Island is a community with charming nineteenth-century character. Its historic district, listed on the National Register of Historic Places, warrants a visit, as do villages of Alexan-dria Bay and Clayton in the United States and Gananoque in Canada, together with smaller hamlets on both shores.

Abandoned Boldt Castle as it appeared in January, 1904 after death of Louise Boldt, when her husband's telegram arrived to terminate work at Heart Island

Index